THE COURT ROLLS OF THE MANOR OF WAKEFIELD

VOLUME I

THE
WAKEFIELD COURT ROLLS SERIES
OF THE YORKSHIRE
ARCHAEOLOGICAL SOCIETY

Volume 1

THE COURT ROLLS OF THE MANOR OF WAKEFIELD

from October 1639 to September 1640

Edited and Calendared by
C. M. Fraser
and
Kenneth Emsley

Claremont
Clarendon Road
Leeds LS2 9NZ

ISBN 0 902122 23 1

Filmset in Great Britain by
Northumberland Press Ltd, Gateshead, Tyne and Wear
and printed by
Fletcher and Son Ltd, Norwich

TABLE OF CONTENTS

GENERAL EDITOR'S PREFACE

The aim of the new Wakefield Court Rolls Series is to contrive the work of publishing this very important and rich body of source material which was begun at the beginning of this century. Volumes 29, 36, 57, 78 and 109 of the Yorkshire Archaeological Society's Record Series contained the rolls for the period 1274–1331, with the exception of those for 1311, 1326 and 1329. The present plan is not to proceed in chronological order but, as this volume testifies, to give priority to rolls of particular interest and of varying date. It is, however, intended to include among the early volumes the rolls for 1311, 1326, 1329 and those for the early 1330s.

The Wakefield court rolls were given to the Yorkshire Archaeological Society by the earl of Yarborough in 1943. Some 670 rolls survive, making up a fragmentary series from 1274 to 1326 and an almost uninterrupted run from thence until the latest record in 1925. The courts whose activities they record were the court baron which was held at Wakefield every three weeks throughout the year, and the court leet or tourn, which was held twice yearly in Wakefield, Halifax, Brighouse or Rastrick and Kirkburton. The competence of the two courts was by no means clearly differentiated, but, in general terms, the court baron dealt with land transactions and tenurial matters, while criminal cases and breaches of commercial regulations were reserved for the tourn. A glance at the contents of this volume is sufficient to demonstrate the value of the Wakefield court rolls both as a source for local history and for legal, social and economic history in general. But their real importance lies in the near-unique way in which they portray the activities of a strictly localised society over a very long and continuous period of time. In doing this they illustrate the changes in that society, in particular its transformation from one type of rural agricultural society to another, between the medieval and early modern periods (herein lies the especial relevance of the present volume, in contrast to those already published), and, at a later date, the partial transformation of this agricultural society into an industrial one. Let us hope, therefore, that this resumption of the publication of these documents by the Society will be sustained and intensified and eventually brought to completion with the printing of the entire series.

RICHARD VAUGHAN

THE WAKEFIELD COURT ROLLS SERIES

A Publishing section of the Yorkshire Archaeological Society

INTRODUCTION

The origins of the complex of lands looking to Wakefield as their administrative centre are discussed elsewhere.[1] Their relations to the centre and each other changed over the centuries. Between 1554 and 1629 it was deemed to form part of the royal duchy of Lancaster. The present volume, which represents the contents of the pair of rolls for the twelve months starting at Michaelmas 1639, was selected both to illustrate the business of the manor courts on the eve of the Civil War and to enable a comparison to be made with the business of the West Riding Quarter Sessions, within whose jurisdiction Wakefield lay. A volume of Quarter Sessions proceedings between 1611 and 1642 has already been printed by the Yorkshire Archaeological Society (Record Series 54, 1915).

The Court Baron

The manor of Wakefield was subdivided into twelve graveships, namely Wakefield, Stanley, Alverthorpe, Thornes, Sandal, Ossett, Horbury, Sowerby, Holme, Hipperholme, Rastrick and Scammonden. The areas varied greatly in size, there being four for the western half of the manor and eight for the eastern half. The officer responsible for execution of administrative orders in the graveship was known as the grieve or grave. He was selected annually on the basis of tenure of specific lands, and the office was held in rotation.[2] The name of the new grave was presented at the Michaelmas Great Court by four sworn men of the graveship,[3] when the grave or his deputy took his oath of service. The formality of these presentations in 1639 is emphasised by the nomination of 'the heirs of Francis Roper' as grave of Stanley, and of Agnes Lawe, widow, and Joshua Brooke, gentleman, jointly as grave of Rastrick. In both cases a deputy was accepted by the court.[4]

By 1639 the main business of the court baron of Wakefield was

[1] J. W. Walker, *Wakefield, Its History and People* (Wakefield, 1934) passim. M. E. Francois, 'The Social and Economic Development of Halifax 1558–1640' *Proceedings* of Leeds Philosophical and Literary Society, Literary and Historical Section, XI viii (1966) pp. 217–80.

[2] J. Charlesworth (ed), *Wakefield Manor Book, 1709*, Y[orkshire] A[rchaeological] S[ociety] Record Series 101, 1939, pp. 53–54.

[3] The expression 'sworn men' is used here interchangeably with 'jurors'.

[4] Below, pp. 3–4.

the registration of land transfers, with the occasional intervention by the lord of the manor when land was forfeited for breach of custom, such as irregular leasing or failure by heirs to claim copyholds. (At a later date all such registered transfers were numbered, to enable an index to be compiled for easy reference by the steward of the court.[5]) Whereas in earlier times the business of the court baron had also included breaches of the assizes of bread and ale, brawling and trespass, as well as debt, the proportion of each roll devoted to the conveyance of copyhold land steadily increased from the middle of the sixteenth century. Cases of debt were not enrolled after 1630, although judging from the record the defaulting parties had ceased to attend these proceedings many years previously.

The court baron for the whole manor was held at Wakefield every three weeks on a Friday, with free weeks at Christmas and Easter, giving seventeen courts in the year, of which the first after Michaelmas and Easter were called 'great courts'. All the free tenants of the manor, from Sir William Savile and Sir Arthur Pilkington baronets downwards, were expected to attend these 'great courts' to perform their traditional suit of court. The suitor might appear in person or send a representative. If he had a valid excuse for absence he essoined. Each circumstance was noted by the clerk of the court against the suitor's name. In some cases the free tenant was under age, or dead. Where he simply defaulted, the clerk noted the fine incurred. These fines varied from session to session but were calculated on status, from baronet down to yeoman holding lands worth less than £10 a year. Free tenants might also be required to attend the lesser courts as jurors, although this seems rarely to have happened. The jurors of the courts baron seem usually to have been of humbler status. Their duty was to testify as to the customs of the manor and as to whether any land transfers were in violation of these customs.

By 1709, when the Wakefield Manor Book was compiled, the customs of the manor seem to have dwindled to the tariff for calculation of entry fines on the transfer of occupancy. This was based on a decree of 19 July 1611 made in the duchy court, reinforced by another from the court of Exchequer, which enabled copyhold tenants to compound with the lord of the manor (then the king as duke of Lancaster). In return for payment of a lump sum equivalent to the ground or lord's rent for thirty-five years the tenant and his

[5] These Docket Books are preserved by the YAS at Claremont, Leeds. They survive in a double series. The paper version comprises one ledger for 1603–1707, with conveyances listed by the year and written in one hand, except for 1645. The vellum version is in two parts, 1603 to 1651 and 1651 to 1707. The latter is written in one hand from 1603 to 1678, with a second hand copying from 1678 to 1703 and a third from 1704 to 1707. These indexes are in Latin. The succeeding Docket Book for 1708 to 1759 is in English.

successors in the land would pay an entry fine equivalent to three years' ground rent, leases being calculated at the rate of a year and a half's ground rent and annuities at the rate of a penny in the shilling.[6] The name of the compounder was then attached to subsequent records of transfers of the copyhold affected, for ease in verification.[7]

The custom of the manor meant considerably more in 1639. At the court baron held on 24 July 1640 an indenture of transfer was found unacceptable by the jurors because the parties had failed both to pay the lord his entry fine and also to obtain the approval of the court.[8] In another case, on 1 April 1639, the formalities were observed of surrendering the land into the lord's hand 'with a straw' by an approved 'tenant of the lord and sworn', but the previous permission of the court had been overlooked.[9] On 12 September 1639 Mary Milnes quitclaimed with a straw her rights in a close of land and meadow in Scholes, but the jurors on 22 November found that she had only a life interest therein.[10] In another case none of the kin had applied for the copyhold within the customary period of three great courts next after the death.[11] Wives had to be examined out of court by the steward or his deputy to make sure that they were willing parties to land-transfers where they had a joint interest with their husbands.[12] Whenever these conditions were not observed the court jury would lodge an objection and an order would issue in the name of the high steward to the appropriate grave or his deputy to seize the specified tenement situated within his graveship. (Every transfer is identified in the margin of the court roll by its graveship.)There are traces of attempts being made to exploit the custom of the manor to provide a loophole for conversion of copyhold into freehold (see below pages xiv–xv).

The Manor of Wakefield had passed from the Crown in 1629 to Henry Rich, first earl of Holland, who transferred it to Sir Gervase Clifton shortly afterwards. The circumstances of Clifton's acquisition are slightly obscure. The earl's sister had been Clifton's first wife, but she had died in 1613 and the statement in the Wakefield Manor Book that the manor was her marriage portion is obviously inaccurate.[13] Sir Gervase was a substantial landowner in Nottinghamshire and created a baronet in 1611. In 1614 he was elected to represent his county in parliament, where he served, except for short

[6] *Wakefield Manor Book*, p. 17.

[7] Examples may be found below on pp. 8–9 and 66.

[8] Below, p. 52.

[9] Below, pp. 31, 35–36.

[10] Below, pp. 11–12.

[11] Below, p. 23.

[12] Below, pp. 9, 14, 17, 24, 25, 26, 27, 28, 32, 38, 40, 43, 47, 49, 50, 53, 57, 64, etc.

[13] *Wakefield Manor Book*, p. 3; *Dictionary of National Biography* XVI, 1008; Burke, *Landed Gentry* 17th edition, 1952, p. 467.

intervals, until 1629 and again from 1661 to 1665. He sat for the borough of Nottingham in 1626 and for East Retford between 1640 and 1644. He attended on Charles I at Newark and Oxford during the Civil War, and was fined £7,650 by Parliament. He died in 1666, having been married no less than seven times. His wives, apart from Lady Penelope Rich, included daughters of the earls of Cumberland and of Huntington, and the widow of a London alderman.[14]

The president of the great court at Wakefield was usually the high steward, namely in 1639 Thomas, baron Pontefract, viscount Savile – later created earl of Sussex in 1644. He had been granted the office of high steward for life in 1619 while the manor of Wakefield was still part of the royal duchy of Lancaster. Thomas was the third but eldest surviving son of John, first baron Pontefract. He entered the Inner Temple in 1610 and hence might have qualified as the 'able Lawier' who 'sits Judge at the Moot hall in Wakefield every Court Day in all Copyhold Causes whatever whether by Common Law or Equity'.[15] His interests, however, were political. His father had joined issue with Thomas Wentworth for leadership of the Yorkshire gentry, and consolidated his position by obtaining the interest of the duke of Buckingham. In 1624 the Saviles, father and son, secured both seats as parliamentary representatives for Yorkshire, so driving Wentworth into opposition to the Crown. In 1627 Thomas Savile was returned as member for York, but was unseated on petition the following year. On his father's death in 1630 Thomas succeeded to the title as viscount Savile.

The influence of Savile waxed and waned in inverse relation to the fortunes of Thomas Wentworth, now first earl of Strafford. In 1638 Savile was committed to the Fleet prison, London, in the course of an investigation before Star Chamber. With the fall of the earl in 1640 Savile was appointed successively by Charles I as a privy councillor, as lord president of the Council of the North, as lord lieutenant of Yorkshire, and eventually as lord treasurer of the king's household. In 1642, however, he was seized by the duke of Newcastle on suspicion that he was plotting to abduct Queen Henrietta Maria as she made her way to York from the coast, and he was imprisoned in Newark castle for six months. (His explanation of his behaviour was so convincing that he was released and received both the royal pardon and an apology from the duke.) In 1644 Savile was back in prison on a charge of high treason, but released on condition he lived in exile in France. Before he left England he fell under suspicion of Parliament that he was conspiring with the Scots and was sent to the Tower of London. Having revealed the names of fellow conspirators he was allowed

[14] Burke, 467.
[15] *Wakefield Manor Book*, p. 35.

to retire to his home at Howley Hall near Batley, where he died in 1658. He has been described as a shifty intriguer who betrayed both king and parliament for his own ends, and as being 'of an ambitious and restless nature, of parts and wit enough, but in his disposition and inclination so false that he could never be believed or depended upon'. He was 'a bold talker'.[16] He may have relished his high stewardship as an opportunity to use influence, but not always been at liberty to attend sessions of the great court.

More often the court's president was the deputy or sub-steward. This office was held in 1639 by John Midgley, younger son of William Midgley, yeoman, of Headley Hall in Bradford-dale. Both John and his elder brother William were trained in the law to act as conveyancers. William Midgley junior died in July 1600 and was buried in Bradford parish church. William Midgley senior died the following year, when John succeeded to the estate at Headley. He enlarged the Hall and was joined in his legal practice by his son John in 1615. John the younger had entered at Lincoln's Inn in February 1611; but in his father's practice he took his turn writing the court rolls for the manors where John the elder was deputy steward, such as Bradford in the honor of Pontefract, the sub-manor of Halifax, and Wakefield. John Midgley senior was able in the way of business to acquire lands from impecunious neighbouring gentlemen including the Vavassours, the Sherburnes, and even George Savile of Thornhill. In 1638 he bought the right of the manor of Thornton from John Watmough. He did in December 1642, seven months after his son, John the younger.[17]

Land Law and the Wakefield Court Baron

The court baron at Wakefield was concerned almost exclusively with land transfers. Its only other business was consideration of applications for inheritances and guardianships, authorising forfeiture of copyhold for breach of manorial custom and approving their re-allocation, and the occasional boundary dispute. These conveyances shed light on the working of English land law relating to copyhold in the early seventeenth century.

The transfer consisted of two stages, the indenture of agreement, and the formal presentation of the transaction within the lord's court. For the sake of simplicity it has been assumed in this introduction that this business was confined to the court baron held at Wakefield. In fact, this business was also transacted on a very limited scale at the courts leet held at Halifax, Brighouse and Kirkburton within

[16] *Dictionary of National Biography* XVII, 863–866.

[17] W. E. Preston, 'Headley in Bradford-dale' *The Bradford Antiquary* New Series, VI, 1940, pp. 95–107.

the manor. These latter courts will be considered in more detail in the subsequent section.

The transfers or conveyances represent sales, mortgages, and family arrangements including entails, endowments and family trusts. There are also varieties of leases, ranging from three years to three lives. The brutal fact of purchase price is rarely revealed, this belonging to the indenture part of the transfer which only became incorporated in the record if the transaction was quoshed by the court (cf. pp. 53–55). A deferred sale, however, is recorded where Michael Bentley of Siddal Hall, his son and grandson, agreed on 3 July 1640 to surrender a holding in Northowram in favour of Elias Mawde of Warley, clothier, who was to pay £105 to them in the south porch of Halifax parish church on 2 February 1641 (p. 49).

The conveyance which is really a security against a loan is represented by the surrender by Francis Sprigonell of Painthorp of his inheritance to Francis Nevile of Chevet against repayment of £150 at Chevet Hall at Whitsun 1651 (p. 57). Similarly Jeremy Grenewood. clothier, surrendered his land in Warley to Henry Murgatroid to cover a debt of £30 owed by them jointly to Luke Crowther senior of Ovenden representing a true payment of £16 2s. 4d. due on 26 January 1641, plus legal expenses (p. 142). A more complicated arrangement is illustrated by the conveyance between Abraham Stansfield of Warley, clothier, and Richard Tattershall with his son John. Stansfield was required to pay £2 7s. 6d. for three successive years, a lump sum of £12 7s. 6d. on 24 November 1643, a further annual payment of £1 11s. 8d. for three years, a lump sum of £11 11s. 8d. on 24 November 1647, a further annual payment of 15s. 10d. for three years, and a final lump sum of £10 15s. 10d. on 24 November 1651. This represented a total of £49 1s. to be paid over twelve years before the tenements in Warley would be restored (p. 11). On several occasions the place of repayment was the south porch of the parish church, presumably for maximum publicity.[18]

The word 'mortgage' is actually used once. Here Oliver Robert and Mary Charlesworth surrendered lands in Wooldale to the use of Godfrey Crosland of Booth House, conditional on their repayment to him of £60 in annual instalments of £10. They waived any residual rights of redemption, which reinforces the opinion that by 1625 'the Chancery has come to give relief against forfeiture of the land [by defaulting mortgagors] as a matter of course'.[19]

Copyholders in the manor of Wakefield were not above attempting to use the court machinery to bring about a change in tenure. Copy-

[18] Cf. repayment at Holmfirth Chapel is specified on page 32, and at Halifax on pages 49 and 141.

[19] Below, p. 43; A. W. B. Simpson, *An Introduction to the History of the Land Law*, Oxford, 1961, p. 227.

hold land carried various legal restrictions as to free alienation, and several copyholders including Francis Leake of Thornecliffe, and Henry Northend of Quarlers in Northowram among others, entered into an indenture 'to give a voluntary cause of seisour ... to reduce the same into a perfect estate in Fee simple ... that the same may be regranted from the Lord ...' The forfeiture duly took place, but there is no suggestion in the registered regrant to the original parties that any change in tenure had been effected.[20]

Some transfers were for a specified purpose or trust. Jonas Bordall of Skircoat, clothier, and Mary his wife pledged their house in Sowerby to Michael Lomme, clothier, to indemnify him against payment of £140 to John Lomme. The latter had agreed to act as surety in a bond of £120 made to the archbishop of York and his commissary for the education of James and Susan Holroid, Mary's children by a former husband, and for the payment of their filial portions (pp. 26–27). The difference of £20 in the bonds was to cover any legal expenses incurred by John Lomme. Samuel Wade of Midgley surrendered two tenements in favour of his sister Anne for six years after the date of his death, for satisfaction of all debts owed to her or to any others. After this term they would revert to his second son Richard. Should Samuel later change his mind, it was provided that the agreement would be revocable by his offer of 6d. to certain persons named in the presence of two or more witnesses (p. 21). John Scatcherd surrendered four closes in Stanley to enable trustees to apply the proceeds of the sale to the liquidation of his debts, any residue to be paid to his four children in equal portions when they attained the age of twenty-one. Meanwhile the interest on this residue would be paid to the father (pp. 22–23).

These latter trusts merge with transfers for the benefit of the conveyors' family. Sometimes it was to provide for a widow, younger child, brother or dependent kinswoman (pp. 18–19, 24, 52–53, 61, 153–154). Thomas Oldfield surrendered part of a croft in Warley to the use of John Cotes of Halifax, badger, who would pay Susan Oldfield, Thomas's wife, an annuity of 15s. for her life-time (p. 89). William Walker of Midgley provided for his bastard son, who had preference over the legitimate daughter (p. 90). Reluctance to allow land to pass out of the male line is a noticeable feature of a number of reversionary transfers (pp. 18, 19, 60–61). Once we have the winding-up of a family trust. Michael Slater of Hipperholme had in 1610 settled lands on his heir, his intended bride and their male offspring. The trustees were both dead by 1639, as were Michael himself, his son, and the only grandson. The son of the senior trustee surrendered the trust land in court to Sara Richardson as daughter and next heir of Michael Slater senior (pp. 60–61).

[20] Below, pp. 52–55, cf. pp. 34–35, 66–67.

Court proceedure was similar in the case of a lease of copyhold land. Once again the registered holder appeared through an approved party – a 'lord's tenant and sworn' – and surrendered his interest in the land, but this time for a limited period and the use extended only to the executors of the beneficiary and not to his heirs. Sometimes it was stated explicitly that no subletting was allowable, in whole or in part (pp. 27–28, 50, 88). The difference between the ground (lord's) rent and an economic rent is pointed in the twenty-one-year lease made by John Allott of Bentley to William Rowley of Butterley, the sitting tenant. The lord's rent was 19s. 6¼d. Rowley was to pay £10 in equal portions annually to the lessor at Whitsun and Martinmas, and provide a team of three shearers to work for one day at harvest, a gallon of honey at Michaelmas, and two capons and fourteen cockerels at Midsummer 'if required' (p. 50). John Booth of Hayslack and Isabel his wife made a twenty-one-year lease of their house to William Marsh on condition that he maintained it in good repair (p. 108). Henry Wilson of Soyland, clothier, leased a cottage to Simon Sharrocke for life at a rent of 1d. payable at Christmas (pp. 141–142). It may have been a less charitable act than it appeared, because there was a stipulation that Sharrocke 'repair or build' the cottage at his own expense and make it habitable. Should the rent fall in arrears by twenty days the lease would become void. Joshua Castell of Cartworth and Elizabeth his wife leased a sheepcote with common pasture in Cartworth to John Nicholls, Agnes his wife, and Mary Cartwright for a hundred years, 'should they live so long' (p. 163). This represents a curious hybrid according to land law.[21]

The Court Leet

The jurisdiction of the courts leet within the manor of Wakefield stemmed from the ancient franchise of return of writs and the custom of concurrent jurisdiction with the shire court.[22] Unlike the court baron the court leet was held in the name of the king. Also it was held only twice a year, at the centres of Wakefield on the Saturday after the Michaelmas and Easter great courts, Halifax on the following Monday, Brighouse in Hipperholme on the Tuesday and Kirkburton on the Wednesday. For the convenience of interested parties some conveyances were registered at these latter three centres after the proper business of the court, which was the regulation of community affairs at a local level. It saved the need for a journey to the three-weekly court baron, held solely at Wakefield. Out of a total of forty-five transfers of land within the graveship of Sowerby, while

[21] R. E. Megarry & H. W. R. Wade, *The Law of Real Property*, London, 1957, p. 569.

[22] *Wakefield Manor Book*, p. 16.

twenty-four were handled at Wakefield, nineteen were dealt with at Halifax and two at Brighouse. Out of forty-four transfers within the graveship of Holme, twenty-seven were handled at Wakefield, one was dealt with at Halifax and sixteen at Kirkburton. (Curiously the townships of Emley and Flockton looked to Wakefield for their court leet but were within the graveship of Holme for land transactions under the jurisdiction of the court baron.)

The courts leet, presided over by the high steward at Wakefield and by the deputy steward at the other three, fined the inhabitants of the townships within their jurisdiction for assault and bloodshed and for breaches of local bye-laws. Each township by its four sworn men presented at the Michaelmas court its new constable, although deputies were sometimes substituted by agreement. Since the borough of Wakefield consisted of the townships of Northgate, Kirkgate and Westgate, it had the services of three constables. Halifax had two constables, whose area of responsibility was undefined. At the Brighouse court leet on 15 October 1639 it was presented that Thomas Flather had been 'elected Constable this day for Rastricke being a man of good estate, that either he or a sufficient debiti (i.e. deputy) by him to be provided shall repaire before some of his majesties Justice of peace befor the end of six daies next cominge and there take his corporall oathe to performe the said office of a Constable for this yeare next following upon pain of £10.' It is odd to find Flather being presented that same session by his predecessor as a fold-breaker.[23]

This solitary reference to oath-taking by the township constable, an officer of the court leet, before a justice of the peace invites speculation as to the degree the jurisdiction of the court leet overlapped with that of the quarter sessions. James Harward and Robert Thomas are both referred to as 'constable of Wadsworth' in the records of the West Riding quarter sessions and of the Halifax court leet between 1638 and 1641.[24] The names of the three constables of Wakefield presented at the Wakefield court leet of 12 October 1639 are identical with those constables claiming expenses from the justices in quarter sessions at Wakefield on 8 October 1640 for conducting to York two Scotsmen arrested in the town as spies and sent on the authority of Mr Conyers Darcy, a justice, before the Council of the North.[25] The township selected its constable, who then served under both systems.

Continuing this examination of references to constables, we find

[23] Below, pp. 99, 101.

[24] Below, p. 87; YAS MS, Wakefield Court Roll for 1640/1, m 13; *West Riding Sessions Records 1611–1642, II* (ed J. Lister) YAS, Record Series LIV, 1915, pp. 263, 312, 351.

[25] Below, pp. 68–69; *West Riding Sessions Records II*, 238–239.

among the presentments from Soothill in October 1639 the complaint that both William Speight and Anthony Fearnley had refused to serve as constable. Each was fined 40s.[26] Some deputies served for two years under successive constables.[27] James Fearnley, selected as constable for Dewsbury at October 1639, was fined 5s. at the same court leet for divulging what was said among the jurors at the previous court.[28]

In some townships the incoming constable was introduced by the outgoing constable and only two sworn men. The clue may be in the township's style of 'Flockton Half' or 'Cumberworth Half', i.e. the township was split and only half owed suit to the Wakefield (or Kirkburton) court leet.[29] Other places sending only two sworn men with the constable were Walton, Bretton, West Ardsley and Eccleshill within the area of the court leet of Wakefield, Clifton and Hartshead in the area of the Brighouse court leet, and Holme within Kirkburton. Another variant, of two sworn men but no constable, occurred in the Kirkburton jurisdiction at Scholes, Austonley and Upper Thong. Four sworn men, without a constable, presented that all was well in the townships of Wooldale, Cartworth and Hepworth.[30]

As for the procedure of the township juries, we learn that Thomas Dun, a 'sworn man' for Horbury, was fined 10s. at the court leet held at Wakefield on 11 April 1640 for refusal to take his oath.[31] At Criggleston, Ovenden and Erringden there was a rota system for the sworn men, although it is not clear how it worked. Possibly the election was 'staggered', with two coming in at Michaelmas and two at Easter, each pair serving for twelve months in all.[32] At the Halifax court leet on 13 April 1640 the constable of Ovenden was fined 10s. for failure to appear with the bill of presentments.[33] At the same court the Erringden sworn men mentioned that 'the high Wayes and all other things belonging to our office was viewed by vs the last weeke'.[34]

Bye-laws and the Courts Leet

Whereas the courts baron were concerned with property and inheritance the courts leet regulated law and order at township (i.e. hamlet) level. Assaults and bloodshed attracted fines of 3s. 4d. and

[26] Below, p. 70.
[27] Below, pp. 69, 107.
[28] Below, pp. 71, 85.
[29] Below, pp. 72, 84, 109, 112–113.
[30] Below, pp. 72, 100, 109–110.
[31] Below, p. 122.
[32] Below, pp. 127, 146, 150.
[33] Below, pp. 136, 146.
[34] Below, p. 150.

10s. respectively. The two constables of Halifax presented no less than thirty-one cases on 14 October 1639 and twenty-five on 13 April 1640.[35] Sometimes the brawler was charged by the township sworn men and sometimes by the victim of the assault or a witness.[36] Various constables and their sworn men made the return that stocks, whipstocks, archery butts and pinfold were all in good repair.[37] The remainder of the business involved fines for repeated infraction of 'pains' for omissions ranging from maintenance of highways to prevention of pigs roaming unyoked and unringed, and mastiffs running unmuzzled, infected horses being turned onto the common land, fences round the winter and spring corn being broken, and crossing land without the owner's agreement.

The basis for business in the court leet was the list of 'pains', from the Latin *pena*, a penalty or fine, because flouting the bye-law would be grounds for a subsequent fine. These lists or 'bills', with named offenders, were presented to the court by the constable and sworn men of each township for examination by the court jury. The latter performed the function of the grand jury at the quarter sessions to the extent of scrutinising the list and endorsing it with the signatures of the foreman of the jury and a panel ranging from one to the whole body of jurors.[38] Sometimes a member of the jury made a separate and personal complaint against some offender. John Crossland of Halifax, 'beeing one of the [court leet] Jury dothe present Miles Croysdale and his wife . . . for A noyance done vnto him vnder his parler widow 3s 4d', this being added to the bill from Halifax township.[39] At the same session Thomas Hoult as a private individual presented Henry Horsfald for diverting a watercourse and John Boye for letting his maid contaminate the water. He was examined on oath by the court leet panel, who were satisfied thereby as to the truth of his charges. The following April he submitted another private bill, accusing four women of 'defiling the water'.[40] (Occasionally bye-laws were promulgated at the court baron. By an interesting coincidence the jury at Wakefield on 11 October 1639 laid pains relating to Scammonden, the only township within the manor of Wakefield that was outside the court leet system.[41])

These bye-laws offer a valuable source of information about life in 1639 because they are not yet stereotyped, repeated unaltered from year to year. A comparison between the pains for 1639/40 and those for 1640/41 show variations in wording and order of offences. The

[35] Below, pp. 86, 135, 143–144.
[36] Below, pp. 158–159, 173–174.
[37] Below, pp. 93, 94, 95, 96, 98, 145, 146, 149.
[38] Cf. below, pp. 73, 74, 75, 83, 84, 93, 104, 118.
[39] Below, p. 93.
[40] Below, pp. 92, 145.
[41] Below, pp. 5–6.

names of offenders change even if some offences, such as failure to ring and yoke swine, scour ditches, switch hedges, hang gates, repair pavements and remove muck heaps are obviously hardy perennials. One offence which occurs regularly in the Kirkburton jurisdiction is cutting and carrying green or dry wood without consent of the owner of the land – but this was unknown in the other jurisdictions.

It should be emphasised that the township bills were not enrolled as such in the formal record of the court leet. While the sworn men for Cartworth and Hepworth at the Kirkburton court leet of 16 October 1639 were blandly recorded as saying that all was well, the Cartworth bill included warnings 'that no person goe over the grounds of James and Jane Charlsworth at Hilhouse with horseloads of Coales or other Caryages without their licence but as a bridle-stythe in payne of euery default 3s 4d: and that John Charlsworth doe scoure the dich betwixt the spoute and ould Coale pitt in the laneside above his house that the water or filth do not annoy the hy way and that he doe it before the first day of November next in paine of 10s'.[42] At Hepworth the sworn men proposed 'that John Tyas doe keepe his Masty dogge musled in the day time in payne of 20s'.[43] Items in the bill were only enrolled if they resulted in a fine being imposed by the court. In other words the 'pain' was a formal notice of township disapprobation, which if disregarded would lead six months later to the imposition of the threatened penalty or fine. Occasionally the township jury expressly stated that the offender 'pained' had since seen the error of his ways (pp. 98, 146).

It is not clear whether the township recommended the amount of the fine. Sometimes the sum was filled in in a different ink. Sometimes the original amount was cancelled and a smaller fine inserted.[44]

Another omission from the engrossed roll is any suggestion that a presented offender might deny the charge. In fact some did 'traverse' their presentment, as the bill shows in its margin.[45] The item was not enrolled presumably because no fine had ensued. The significance of some offences is not immediately apparent, but may be revealed in a subsequent court entry. The bills for Kirkgate, Westgate and Northgate in Wakefield suggest a very real problem arising from unpaved streets and obstructions in the road ranging from muck to timber. The following year, at the Wakefield court leet on 17 October 1640, George Beckitt and Widow Hardwick were ordered under pain of 6s. 8d. to 'remoue such goods as come from T..bridge

[42] Below, pp. 108, 116–119.
[43] Below, p. 118.
[44] Cf. below, pp. 132, 144–145, 156, 166–167, 169–171.
[45] Below, pp. 76, 95, 146, 148, 159.

oute of the streete into theire warehouse, and soe sufficiently repayre and mend the said street befor the warehouse nowe rutted vpp with waynes, before may day next'.[46]

The West Riding Quarter Sessions and the Courts Leet

Because of the apparent overlap of jurisdiction it seems desirable to note where the courts leet were meddling with quarter sessions business.

Both were highway authorities. As shown above, the township jurors were constantly presenting offences relating to roads and sometimes to bridges. The townships of Eccleshill, Hipperholme and Northowram even gave the names of their overseers of highways, while Rastrick named its overseers 'for Commondayes Work'.[47] At Holme, Cartworth and Upper Thong it was specified that every householder within the township must provide a workman to mend the highway 'as there shal bee warning giuen by the Collector' under pain of a fine of 3s. 4d.[48]

Equally, supervision of alehouses was a quarter sessions responsibility, yet at Kirkgate in Wakefield and at Criggleston it was pained 'that noe Alehousekeeper doe keepe any mans servants drinkeing in their houses after Eight of the Clock in the night'. Also 'that euery Alehouse keeper doe brew good and wholesome drink and Bake good breade'.[49] At the Wakefield court leet of 12 October 1639 there were presentments of offenders in Westgate and Northgate, Wakefield, for defects in the quality or weight of their butter and bread.[50] Another cause for concern was the vagabond, and householders were responsible for all under their roof. The sworn men of Horbury threatened a monthly fine of 10s, 'that no man in our towne do kepe any Inmates Contrarie to the statute', and the Hepworth jury ordered William Bever to 'remove John Shirt forth of his house before the end of one month' in pain of 39s. a month.[51] (There is no evidence that the court leet was limited to imposing fines of less than £2. The Brighouse jurors recommended fines of up to £10 for offenders against highway maintenance.[52]) As for the game-laws, the Kirkburton panel on 16 October 1639 presented two men for tracing in the snow and killing hares.[53]

We have already examined the fact that township constables

[46] YAS MS, Wakefield Court Roll for 1640/1, file for October Wakefield court leet, document [E].

[47] Below, pp. 134, 156, 157.

[48] Below, pp. 169, 171, 173.

[49] Below, pp. 73, 128.

[50] Below, pp. 68, 69, 76.

[51] Below, pp. 80, 174; cf. *West Riding Sessions Records II*, 165.

[52] Below, pp. 102, 103, 106.

[53] Below, pp. 107, 110.

appeared before both bodies. Assessments for collection of various rates seem to have been authorised only by the justices in quarter sessions.[54] Finally, the court leet like the quarter sessions might be used as a court of reference. An apology for slanderous words was filed at the end of the record of the Wakefield court leet for 11 April 1640. This had been read in court, following a suit by the aggrieved party.[55]

Format of the Wakefield Court Rolls

Possibly at all times but certainly during the seventeenth century the clerk to these Wakefield courts drew up a draft record of proceedings to which he added at the end of each session of court baron or court leet a file of documents including cancelled indentures, verdicts of juries, warrants and bills of presentment. From this paper draft the clerk copied his engrossed roll on parchment. In the engrossed version the courts follow in sequence on the membrane. In the draft each court forms a separate section. In both cases the rolls are sewn, Exchequer fashion, by the head. Both sets of rolls are in reasonably good condition, although the paper roll is getting brittle at the margins.

The language of the draft and engrossed rolls is law Latin. The language of the indentures and bills is English, with the occasional caption or odd word in Latin. The struggle of clerk, constable and sworn men to express themselves coherently in Latin is amusingly revealed in such barbarisms as the constable's return for Fixby in April 1640:— 'As for presentments we haue none – omney beney'.[56] In many places the clerk had difficulty in expressing in Latin the niceties of field names, outbuildings or customary expressions, and gave an English translation alongside. A little close is glossed as a 'pingle', a yard as a 'backside', a cowhouse as an 'amistall', *vnum brocum mellis* as 'one gallon of honey'.[57] The most common macaronic expression is 'vxor' for wife, as in: 'we present Richard Denton and vxor forbisher for thare part of the Pinfolde being not sufficientlie made, either of them 12d'. On another occasion: 'Item we paine vxor Hughe Romsdon, Edward Northing of the knightroyd and his mother, Georg whitlay, Marmaduck Baull to mak a suficient horsway euery one against their owne ground ...'[58] Parenthetical round brackets were used rather than grammar to separate elements of property, as for example, Richard Brigge late of Quickstavers

[54] *West Riding Sessions Records II*, 93, 239, 258, 260–261, 309; but cf. below, pp. 107, 115, where the ex-constables of Shepley and Holmefirth were penalised for failure to present their accounts.

[55] Below, p. 134.

[56] Below, p. 156.

[57] Cf. below, pp. 19, 25, 32, 33, 50, 108, 163, 165.

[58] Below, pp. 84, 156.

and Martha now his wife surrendered certain tofts including le Spowtefeild (previously divided into two parts), le Milnefeild (previously divided into two parts and now into four parts), les Birkes (previously in two parts), ... and le Moorehey (previously in four parts and now in five).[59]

The subsidiary documents filed at the end of each court often bear signatures. This is particularly the case with township bills of presentments which have the signatures, or more often the marks, of the constable and sworn men as well as the endorsements of the panel of court leet jurors. These provide a rough indication of local literacy. It should be noted that 'marks' are usually in the form of initials or the initial of the Christian name, sometimes a private squiggle, but rarely the conventional cross. One senses the pride of the man who could sign his name, even if with difficulty.

Editorial Method

Because there are two rolls available, a decision had to be made as to the authoritative version. The basic text as printed here derives from the engrossed roll, which was the final version and the better written. Since, however, it is a copy of the draft, the latter has been scrutinised for variations and where the engrossed version seems manifestly a misreading the draft version has been followed, the emendation being printed within square brackets. It may be a single letter of a name that has been omitted, or part of an acreage. No attention is normally paid to deletions in the draft version. Where they occur elsewhere, particularly in the subsidiary documents, every effort has been made to decipher the original entry, as indicating a change of mind. Such deleted words are printed within asterisks. One example of such a deletion occurs among the bye-laws: '*that every person doe pull the yeate close after them at Booth-House on pain of 5s*'.[60] This is one of the set of bye-laws presented at the Wakefield great court on 11 October 1639 instead of at the court leet on the following day.

Because the roll is written in Latin it has been decided to present this abridged edition in translation. Every item is noted, but the legal terminology compressed to the limits of comprehension and the detailed list of appurtenant rights in the conveyances drastically curtailed. In contrast the subsidiary documents, where in English, are printed in their original form, with the eccentric spelling and capital letters. To prevent doubt, the word 'Latin' precedes a filed document when it is printed in calendared form. Numerals have been generally altered to Arabic form, they being indiscriminately Roman and Arabic even on the same sheet in the original.

[59] Below, pp. 38–40.
[60] Below, p. 6.

WAPENTAKE OF MORLEY
Wadsworth
Heptonstall
Stansfield
Langfield
Erringden
Midgley
Ovenden
Shelf
Northowram
Warley
Halifax
1
Hipperholme
Brighous
2
Sowerby
Skircoat
Morland
12
Rastrick
Barkisland
Stainland
Fixby
Quarmby
Rishworth
3
WAPENTAKE
Austonley
Cartworth
Wooldale
Upperthong
11
Holme
Scholes

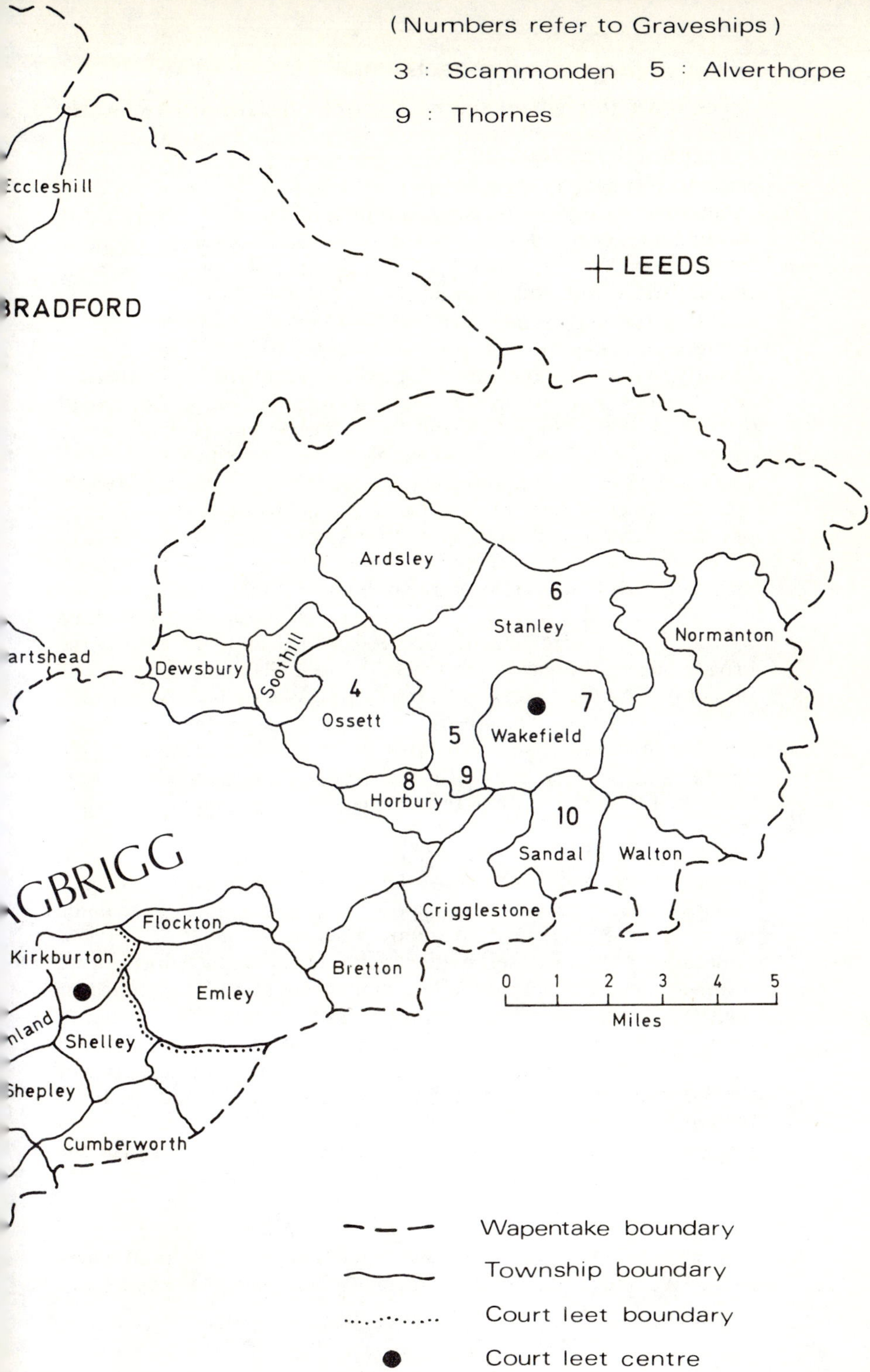

(Numbers refer to Graveships)
3 : Scammonden
5 : Alverthorpe
9 : Thornes
Eccleshill
LEEDS
BRADFORD
Ardsley
6
Stanley
Normanton
artshead
Dewsbury
Soothill
4
Ossett
7
Wakefield
5
8
9
Horbury
10
Sandal
Walton
AGBRIGG
Flockton
Crigglestone
Kirkburton
Bretton
Emley
nland
Shelley
Shepley
Cumberworth
0 1 2 3 4 5
Miles
Wapentake boundary
Township boundary
Court leet boundary
Court leet centre

The order throughout the book is the official court record, in abridged English, followed by its file of subsidiary documents, derived from the draft roll. Each court starts a fresh page. As the original rolls have no numbering of membranes or files, a notional number has been given to the membranes of the engrossed roll and a notional letter to the subsidiary documents. Because these identification marks do not appear on the actual rolls, they have been printed here within square brackets.

Within the files, some townships used several slips of paper to record their presentments, and it seemed desirable to emphasise the unity by giving the set the same letter but providing a further numerical identification. For example, at Halifax court leet on 13 April 1640 the names of the constables and sworn men occupy two sheets of paper [A^1], [A^2]. The list of the names of the court jury follow [B]. The third sheet [C] contains the name of the foreman with the succeeding names of jurors bracketed in groups without any apparent practical purpose such as subcommittees responsible for the scrutiny of particular townships. This is followed by three sheets of presentments of assault at Halifax, corresponding with the opening section of the engrossed roll [D^1], [D^2], [D^3]. The fifth item is represented by the Halifax infringements of bye-laws [E] and the sixth is the private bill of Thomas Hoult of Halifax [F]. These are followed by the returns for Skircoat [G], Sowerby [H], Warley [I], Ovenden [J], and Wadsworth [K]. The returns for Midgley occupy two sheets [L^1], [L^2]. Then come Rishworth with Norland [M], Stansfield [N], Heptonstall [O], Langfield [P] and finally Erringden [Q]. A new page then emphasises that the business of the Halifax court leet is terminated.

All signatures have been noted, but in paragraph form instead of the columnar arrangement usual in the original document. The initials or marks have been transposed from the middle of the name to its end, and placed within square brackets.

Because it seemed self-evident, the editors omitted the note on many documents to the effect that they had been examined or registered. Other marginal comment has been retained, printed in italics at once to differentiate it from the normal text and to add emphasis. Particularly in the court baron sections the purpose of the marginal note was essentially to catch the eye and facilitate reference to lands in specific graveships. (The amount of the entry fine was also repeated in the margin from the main record for the same reason, but has been omitted in this edition as it figures sufficiently prominently at the end of each item.) Interlinear comment is printed in italics immediately after the appropriate word.

The spelling of place names has been copied exactly, even where as at 'Wakefeld' the modern form differs from the seventeenth century usage. This decision was taken because of the large number of field names involved, which would have been difficult if not impossible to identify in their modern form. The modern form of settlement names, however, is used in the court headings and in the index, for convenience of reference. Christian names have been given their contemporary spelling where indicated. 'Jacob' normally is the latinised form of James, but in the two cases where it has not been declined in a conveyance it has been regarded as the Biblical name, matching the numerous 'Abrahams' (pp. 58, 89).

Calculation of the commencement of the new year in 1639 was still from 25 March. For dates between 1 January and 24 March the year has been rendered here as 1639/40 where '1639' is the reading of the roll. Where the year is calculated from the king's accession the editors have supplied the date by modern reckoning, for example '2 February 15 Charles' is 2 February 1640, but '2 February 1639' would be printed as 2 February 1639/40. Both refer to the same day.

Conclusion

It is hoped that the foregoing explanation will enable the reader to utilise the court roll for 1639/40 printed here, explore its information about land tenure and manorial custom in the manor of Wakefield, and enter into the lives of its inhabitants. Among other insights the roll offers are descriptions of smallholders' houses and farmbuildings. Widow Firth lived in a tenemented house in Rastrick in a 'kitchen now made into a dwellinghouse, with an upper room and a stable adjoining the barn', and her holding consisted of 'a parcel of land 6½ yards by 5 yards to the north of the house, part of a fold, and 3 closes in Rastrick estimated at 6 acres'.[61] Another conveyance dealt with a house set between two closes, two barns and a little 'backside' adjoining, all near a fulling mill whose accessway for repairs was carefully preserved.[62] There was a third conveyance concerned with the division among five co-heiresses of 'le Auncient old house' at Blackhill in Northowram. The outbuildings included a barn and a threshing floor called 'le Overbarne' of seventeen yards in length. In addition there was a fold, crofts of arable, meadow and pasture, and rights of common, estimated in all at ten acres.[63] Such references should be examined in the light of recent work on vernacular architecture in the Halifax area.[64]

[61] Below, pp. 27–28, 153.

[62] Below, pp. 42–43.

[63] Below, pp. 19, 64.

[64] Cf. E. Mercer, *English Vernacular Houses* Royal Commission on Historical Monuments, 1975, pp. 14–16, 21–22, 32, 45–48, 51, 111, 127, 221–224, 225, quoting F. Atkinson and R. W. McDowall, 'Aisled Houses in the Halifax area', *Antiquaries Journal*, XLVII, 1967, pp. 77–94, and C. F. Stell, 'Pennine Houses: an Introduction', *Folk Life*, III, 1965.

One use of the rolls for considering local literacy and language has been already noted. The field names as recorded in the conveyances provide a picture not only of natural features, such as the 'close in Sandale called Foulewells' (p. 13), another called 'Rye Pighell' (p. 19), and a messuage called 'le Horsehead' (p. 25). They also indicate the formation of place names from recent tenants. Among the lands which owed the service of grave we find 'Nocketts', 'Clarkesons' (p. 3) and 'le Bairstowe land' (p. 4), a close called 'Robinson Close' abutting 'Flanshawe Lane' (p. 7), an acre in Horbury west field called 'Jenkinbanks' (p. 18), and finally the little close 'sometime Fleemings' which had been compounded for by John Fleeminge (p. 61).

The overall impression left by the roll is a tight community bound by strict conventions. Land must be exchanged and allocated openly. Anti-social behaviour, be it brawling or obstructing the highway, is deplored. Yet a new individual assertion can be seen in the bye-laws against the cutting and carting of other men's wood without permission, and of taking short cuts across enclosed land. The form of the disrespect for the old customs may have been the infringement of other men's private rights or it may have been the appropriation of common woodland and pasture. In either case the courts of the manor of Wakefield were attempting to preserve a way of life with as much in common with the Middle Ages as with the eighteenth century.

N.B. It is only fair to the Northumberland Press to assure readers that the following pages are as near to the original texts as is possible. Let the results be a sombre warning to all advocates of free spelling.

THE COURT ROLLS OF THE MANOR OF WAKEFIELD

[membrane 1]

WAKEFIELD: the Great Court Baron of Gervase Clifton, knight and baronet, lord of the Manor of Wakefield, held there on 11 October, 15 Charles [1639]

William Savile bt, Arthur Pilkington bt, John Savile kt *appeared*, Thomas Middleton kt *appeared by attorney*, John Savile esq *under age*, Thomas Beaumont esq, Thomas Watterson esq *appeared by attorney*, Mathew Wentworth esq, John Armitage esq *appeared by attorney*, Henry Grice esq *appeared*, Thomas Thornhill esq *essoined*, John Farrer esq, William Savile esq *under age*, William Ramsden esq *dead*, Ashton Stansfeild esq, Edward Lowden gen *appeared by attorney*, Cotton Horne gen, Ralph Arthington gen *appeared*, Edward Goodwyn gen *appeared by attorney*, heirs of John Hanson, John Nayler of Clifton *appeared by attorney*, Henry Barraby *appeared*, Thomas Pymont *appeared*, John Wibsey *appeared*, Richard Pearson *essoined*, Richard Liversedge *appeared*, Thomas Crosland, Thomas Walker *appeared*, William Dodgson *appeared*, Richard Archer *essoined*, Robert Priestley *appeared*, Michael Foxcrofte *appeared*, Nathaniel Chadwicke, Jonas Bynns gen *appeared*, John Sprigonell, James Foxcrofte, John Drake *essoined*, Thomas Burnley, Robert Brigge, Robert Mitchell, Edward Boardman *essoined*, Robert Johnson of Dirtcarre, Richard Oxley of the same *appeared*, Francis Stocks, Gervase Norton of Kettlethorpe *appeared*, Gervase Norton of Newmilnedamme, Thomas Wright of Milnethorpe *essoined*, Brice Norton and Richard Johnson of Paynethorpe *appeared*, for their lands and free tenements owe suit of court every three weeks by ancient custom and make fine for release until the next great court, viz. Michaelmas, unless their presence is necessary meantime.

Inquisition taken for the lord of the manor on the oath of Thomas Roberts yeoman, John Boyne, Thomas Savile gen, William Robinson, Robert Johnson, Edward Johnson, John Batty, William Cartmell, Thomas Garnett, Thomas Nettleton, George Lee, Richard Roberts, Robert Awdisley, John Linley, James Hinchcliffe, George Wilson, William Mallinson, Isaac Bates and Richard Bothomley, jurors, who presented that William Savile bt *6s. 8d*, Arthur Pilkington bt *6s. 8d*, Thomas Beaumont esq *2s.*, Mathew Wentworth esq *2s.*, John Farrer esq *2s.*, Ashton Stansfeild esq *2s.*, Cotton Horne gen

2s., the heirs of John Hanson *12d.*, Thomas Crosland *12d.*, Nathaniel Chadwick *12d.*, James Foxcrofte *12d.*, Thomas Burnley *12d.*, Robert Brigge *12d.*, Robert Mitchell *12d.*, Robert Johnson of Dirtcarre *12d.*, Gervase Norton of Newmilnedamme *12d.* and Brice Norton yeoman *12d.* owe suit but neither appeared nor essoined.

They testified that John Allott of Bentley had died since the last court: John Allott was his son and next heir: they were ignorant of the disposition of his lands.

that Henry Savile late of Horbury, gen, had died since the last court: John Saville was his next heir.

that James Hall of Sladley Lane in the graveship of Stanley was dead: his heir was unknown.

that Thomas Earnshawe of Holme was dead: his heir was unknown.

that Richard Grice, gen, was dead: his heir was unknown.

that William Jenkinson was dead: his heir was unknown.

that George Fournes was dead: his heir was unknown.

Sandall (*1*) Thomas Beaumont of Whitley Hall, Gregory Armitage of Shitlington and Henry Grice of Milnthorpe in the township of Sandall Magna, Yorks, esquires, by Thomas Pollard, lord's tenant and sworn, surrendered into the lord's hands two closes in Sandall called les Twowooll greaves, now occupied by the same Henry Grice and John Bedforth, lying beside the lands of Thomas Roades of Flocton, yeoman, to the north and south and including a highway between the closes, owing a lord's rent of 16d, and certain fine, with all ways, waters, common pasture and easements appurtenant: to the use of the same Thomas Roades, his heirs, etc for ever, by custom of the manor. Agreed: entry fine of 4s.

Ossett (*2*) John Stocks by Thomas Haldisworth, gen, lord's tenant and sworn, surrendered a close called Netherstockwellatch in Earlesheaton in the graveship of Ossett, owing a lord's rent of 8d and certain fine: to the use of Richard Stocks for ever. Agreed: entry fine of 2s.

Holme (*3*) John Bynnes of Bankend, clerk, and Mary his wife, she having agreed after personal questioning by the steward, by Francis Mathewman, lord's tenant and sworn, surrendered the messuage called Mawkinhouse and 26 acres in Cartworth in the graveship of Holme, occupied by John Moorehouse and Gilbert Cartwright, owing a lord's rent of 10s 10d and certain fine, together with a close called 'Brearylee' of about two acres in Cartworth in the same graveship, owing a lord's rent of 8d. and certain fine: to the use of John Dokeson of Glossoppe, yeoman, for ever. Agreed: entry fine of 34s 7½d. *Compounded for by John Bynns and Elizabeth his wife* [mem 1d]

Holme (*4*) Godfrey Cuttell by Francis Mathewman, lord's tenant and sworn, surrendered the reversion after the death of the said Godfrey Cuttell of a close called Stound close in Wooledale in the graveship of Holme, now occupied by the same Godfrey Cuttell, owing a lord's rent of 4d. and no certain fine: to the use of John Cuttell junior. Agreed: entry fine of — *Fine not compounded.*

WAKEFELD: John Sunderland, Robert Howley, Thomas Thompson and William Thompson, jurors, present that for his lands in Wakefeld, lately of Edward Copley, James Pearson of Hunsworth has been elected grave of Wakefeld for this year. Being sworn, he appoints as representative John Briggs, who is received and sworn.

STANLEY: William Hanson, Richard Birkehead, Richard Kent and John Sugden, jurors, present for the lands in le Woodside sometime Nocketts the heirs of Francis Roper as grave for this year. They have the aid of John Roper for the lands in le Woodside sometime of Alverd Haldisworth, the aid of John Wade for land in the same sometime of John Roper and sometime of Alverd Haldisworth, the aid of Widow Jenkinson for Clarkeson's land and of Anne Roper. Being sworn they appoint John Roper as representative, who is received and sworn.

ALVERTHORPE: Thomas Cotes, Robert Clarke, Middleton Goslinge and Christopher Haldisworth, jurors, present that for the lands lately of Robert Burgh the heirs of Christopher Naylor, late of Flansawe gen deceased, have been elected grave. Christopher Naylor of Wakefeld, son and heir, is sworn and appoints Arthur Edmondson as representative, who is received and sworn.

THORNES: Francis Stocks, Joseph Waterhouse, Edward Watkinson and Robert Burrowe, jurors, present that Arthur Pilkington bt is elected grave for lands called Snapethorpe.

SANDALL: Richard Johnson, George Hutchinson, Robert Coward and Thomas Pollard, jurors, present that for a messuage and lands in Hollingthorpe, lately of Richard Bilcliffe and now occupied by Robert Cooke, Thomas Horsfall is elected grave. He should have aid from the occupier of the land lately of John Addy.

Sowerby: John Grenewood, Isaac Nayler, Francis Preistley and George Fairebanke, jurors, present that for a messuage called Luddingdendeane Roid, sometime of – Holgate, Michael Foxcrofte is elected grave. He should have the aid of Isaac Haldisworth for 2 messuages and a cottage called Shepheardhouse, and the aid of the heirs of Samuel Haldisworth and that of John Midgley for nine messuages and cottages called Wainstalls and Colledge, and of the heirs of George Holgate for a cottage called Westroid. Being sworn he appoints James Foxcrofte, his son, who being received and sworn appoints as representative William Midlebrooke, who is received and sworn.

HOLME: John Hirst, Henry Jackson, Godfrey Morton and Thomas

Ellis, jurors, present that for a messuage called Hullocke with lands appurtenant in the graveship of Holme, Oliver Roberts is elected grave. He should have the aid of James Roberte and Roger Robucke for 9 acres lately appurtenant to the messuage, and of John Moorehouse for 17 acres in Wooledale, and of William Dokeson and of Anthony Wilson for 4 acres in Wooldale. Because Oliver Roberts is a minor Henry Jackson, his guardian, is received and sworn.
HIPPERHOLME: Jonas Haldisworth, Michael Bentley, Robert Hargreaves and John Bentley, jurors, present that for the lands sometime of Robert Burgh and of the heirs of Joseph Drake of Lee, Joseph Fournes is elected grave. He should have the aid of the heirs of Francis Tayler late of York City and of the heirs of James Stancliffe for le Skowte Land and of the heirs of John Bairstowe for le Bairstowe Land. He appoints John Lomme as representative, who is received and sworn.
RAISTRICKE: Richard Ramsden, Arthur Hanson, Thomas Hanson and Edmund Fox, jurors, present that for the lands late of John Hanson late of Overwoodhouse, deceased, Agnes Lawe widow and Joshua Brooke gen are elected grave. They appoint as representative John Fox, who is received and sworn.
SCAMONDEN: Richard Bothomley, James Dyson, Thomas Denton and James Walker, jurors, present that for two messuages called Heyfeild within Scamonden, Thomas Crosley is elected grave. Being sworn he appoints Joseph Wilson as representative, who is received and sworn.

[A] Panel for the great court at Wakefeld, 11 October 15 Charles [1639]
[B[1]] At the Court houlden at Wakefeild eleventh day of October in the 15th yeare his highnes Raigne Ano domini 1639 as followeth

In primis The Juorye doe present all knights and barronets which have not appeared at this Court vpon the call .vj.s. .viij.d.

Item we present all gentlemen for the same default euery one .ij. s.

Item we present every yeoman which hould land vpon this manour aboue the value of tenne pounds per annum for default making .xij. d.

Item every one which houlds lands at an vnder value .vj. d.

[signed]	Thomas Roberts		John Boyne
	Thomas Savil		
	John Battye		George Lee
	Robert Audsley	Isack Bates	Robert Johnson
	Thomas Nettleton		John Linley
	William Malinson		George Willson
	William Robinson		
	James Hinchlif		Richard Bothomley [B]

[B2] The Juory doe fynd that

John Allott of Bentley is dead and John Allot we suppose to be his heire

Item mr Henry Sayvile of Horbury is dead and John S[ ]

Item James Hall of Stadley land within the graveship of Stanley is dead: two daughters we take to be his heir[es]

Item Thomas Earnshaw of Holme is dead, his heir[ ]

Item mr Richard Gryce *of Sandall* is dead. Thomas Gryce is supposed to be his heire

Item William Jenkinson is dead: we know not his heire

Item George Fournes is dead: we know not his heire

[signed] Thomas Roberts Isacke Bates Thomas Savile

[C] Item The Juory doe lay in payne that Richard Beckett of *Stanley* Wrenthorpe doe scoure one ditch lying betwixt the grounds of the said Beckett and Thomas Sayvile and make his fence belonging to the same sufficient betwixt this and Candlmas day next in payne of .x. s.

Item the Juory doe lay in payne that James Greene of Yateholme shall forbeare to sleate or dryue other mens goods vpon the wast, for every default making .iij. s. .iiij. d.

Item we lay in payne that John Batemanson of Thornes shall make his fence sufficient betwixt his orchard and croft and the croft of Thomas Garnett betwixt this and next court in payne of .iij. s. .iiij. d.

Item we lay in payne that the Inhabitants of Horbury John Armitage and Robert Bargh shall not make any vsuall way over a shutt of ground called wheatley where of right there is noe way in payne of euery default seene or taken .iij. s. .iiij. d.

Item we lay in payne that all such inhabitants within the towne or hamblett of Scamaden shall make their out fence of all grounds as are on the north parte of the same betwixt this and next Court in payne of person making default .iij. s. .iiij. d.

[signed] Thomas Roberts John Boyne Thomas Savil
John Battye

[D] At the great Court holden at Wakefeild the xjth day of October in the xvth yeare of the raigne of our soueraigne Lord Charles by the grace of god king of England etc. Annoque domini 1639

Paynes layd by the Jury as foloweth vizt.

Inprimis wee lay in payne that no person nor persons goe over the grounds in the ocupation of Godfray Crosland called Netherfeild and Wellcrofte at Boothouse nor any other his grounds out of the right accustomed wayes in payne of every default .xij. d. *.x. s*

Item we lay in payne that Luke Firth shall make his fence sufficient and so keepe it at all times betwixt his grounds and the ouerfeild and wellcroft in the ocupacion of Godfray Crosland, *and the bottom* in payne of .xij. d *.x. s*

Item that the said Luke Firth nor his family shall throw downe the walls or fence of one close of Nicholas Charlsworths called bothom nor go over the same without his licence where there is noe vsuall way in paine of euery defalt *.x.s* .iij. s. .iiij. d

Item we lay in payne that Luke Firth and Richard Firth doe make their seuerall fences well and sufficiently betwixt their grounds and the grounds in the ocupacion of Thomas Charlsworth both at Boothouse and Bothoms, and so keepe them well and sufficiently made, and that they doe it before the 2[d] day of February next *xxth day of this instant October in payne of* .vj[s]. viij[d].

Item we lay in payne that euery person doe pull the yates close after them, and not leave them open in any of the grounds of Thomas Charlsworth at Boothouse in payne of euery person that maketh default for euery default .v. s.

[signed] Thomas Roberts John Boyne Thomas Savil
John Battye

[mem 1 dorse]

WAKEFIELD: the Court Baron of Gervase Clifton held on 1 November 15 Charles [1639]

Inquisition on the oaths of Isaac Haldisworth, Robert Burgh, Richard Spurr, Francis Gill, William Thornes, Thomas Metcalf, John Wade, John Swifte, Paul Ramsden, Thomas Milner, Thomas Leake and Robert Coward, who testify that John Milnes, son of John Milnes, late of Holmefirth Chappell, deceased, was copyholder of a parcel of 9¼ yards by 6¼ yards and a new house by Holmefirth Chappell and a close called Childynge, estimated at an acre, in Wooldale in the graveship of Holme, lately held by John Milnes the father, deceased, or his assigns, owing a lord's rent of 4d and certain fine as of eighteen years previously. Since no one had claimed the holding within the space of three great courts after the death of John Milnes the son the estate should revert to the lord of the manor, and an order was given to the grave of Holme to take possession.

Wakefeld (*5*) William Savile of Thornhill bt by Charles Jackson of Wakefeld, gen, lord's tenant and sworn, surrendered 3 messuages or cottages called le Chauntreyhouses at the lower end of Kirkgate near the mill-pond of Wakefeld in the graveship of Wakefeld with all houses, structures, orchards, gardens, tofts, crofts, etc occupied by Nicholas Fraunce, John Musgrave, Effamia Musgrave, Anne Clarke, widow, and Anne Whitesides or their assigns, owing a lord's rent of 10½d and certain fine: to the use of Gervase Nevile of Wakefeld, gen, his heirs and assigns. Agreed: entry fine of – .

Aluerthorpe (*6*) John Whittam of Earby in Craven by Henry Taylor of Silcoates, lord's tenant and sworn, surrendered the third part of a close to the north of the messuage of Christopher Smith in Flanshaw called le Netherynge, with the third of another close called Robinson Close abutting the vennel called Flanshawe Lane [mem 2] in Flanshawe in the graveship of Alverthorpe, now occupied by Christopher Smith or his assigns owing a lord's rent of ½d and certain fine: to the use of Christopher Smith, his heirs etc. Agreed: entry fine of 1½d.

Sowerby (*7*) Testimony by Jonathan Platt, lord's tenant, that Michael Earnshawe yeoman on 19 October 15 Charles [1639] surrendered the toft called les Overbrocks and four closes of land, meadow and pasture in Sowerby, known severally as le Workhouse hill, le Little crofte under the house, le Litlemeadow and le Steeleynge, now occupied by John Gawkroger or his assigns, with three other closes called les Roids, parcels of land pertaining to a messuage in Sowerby, occupied by the same, together with all houses, buildings, barns, structures, stables, folds, gardens, ways, passages, waters, water-courses, liberties, profits etc, together with half a vennel between Soyland Milne and Sowerby commonly called Gateland Lane, all owing a lord's rent of 2s 10d and certain fine: to the use of John Gawkroger, his assigns etc from 1 May last past for 21 years, paying annually to Michael Earnshawe, his heirs etc £13 at Martinmas and Whitsun in equal portions, with right to distrain for arrears after a lapse of 40 days until full satisfaction be made, as by indenture. Agreed: entry fine of 4s 3d. *Compounded for by John Wood and Nathan Carter*

Sowerby (*8*) Appearance of Richard Fournes of Sowerby yeoman, great uncle and next heir of George Fournes deceased, son and heir of George Fournes late of Boothhouse in Blackwood below the township of Sowerby, deceased, son and heir apparent of Thomas Fournes late of Woodlane in Sowerby, deceased, brother of the aforesaid Richard Fournes, who fined £3 6s 4d as heriot for that messuage called Booth house and 9 acres associated in the graveship of Sowerby now occupied by Isabel Dobson or her assigns, with 3½ acres in Blackwood in the same, occupied by the same, and 3½ acres with buildings thereon, occupied previously by John Lomme and Margaret Lomme or their assigns and now by John Wilson or his assigns, with a cottage in Blackwood now occupied by James Crowther or his assigns, all owing a lord's rent of 5s 4d and certain fine: and also a messuage commonly called Westfeild, a barn, a garden, a croft and 4 closes called Overthwaits, containing about an acre in Warley in the same graveship, now occupied by Thomas Carre or his assigns, a house or cottage and 4 closes in Warley in the same graveship, occupied by Peter Moore or his assigns, and a parcel of land 6 yards by 1 yard with all structures thereon once lying in the lower part of the close of Thomas Oldfeild of Newland on the north of Harwoodwell in Warley and now occupied by Samuel Denton or his assigns, these lands in Warley owing a lord's rent of 3s 4d and certain fine: also a parcel of land used as a lane on the west of a close called Overthwaite, owing a lord's rent of ½d and certain fine: also two messuages commonly called Hollings and all houses, buildings, gardens etc associated, estimated at 20 acres 1 rood in Blackwood now occupied by Richard Wadisworth, John Hopkinson, Joseph Meller and the said Isabel Dobson at a lord's rent of 6s 9d and certain fine: a messuage and 9 acres 3 roods approx. in Blackwood occupied by Richard Brookesbanke, deceased, and now by Isaac Crowther or his assigns, owing a lord's rent of 3s 9d and certain fine: also a messuage commonly called Woodlane and all houses etc thereon [mem 2d]

estimated at 9 acres 3 roods in the same graveship lately occupied by Thomas Fournes deceased, and two cottages beside the same, now held severally by Daniel Culpon and Stephen Hoile or their assigns, owing a lord's rent of 3s 4d and certain fine: also 6 closes in the same graveship, now made into 7 closes, with all houses and structures containing 3 acres 1 rood and now occupied by James Fawcett or his assigns, owing a lord's rent of 13d and certain fine: also a quarter of 3½ acres of meadow with buildings between the land of William Ouldfeild deceased to the east and the land of John Crowther to the west and the north, now in two closes called Ynges in the same graveship, now occupied by Isabel Dobson or her assigns, owing a lord's rent of 3½d and certain fine. Succession after the death of George Fournes the son was granted to Richard Fournes the great uncle *The 5s 3d and 3s 3d rent was compounded for by Thomas Fournes. The halfpenny rent was compounded for by Thomas Oldfeild of Cliffhill. The 6s 9d rent was compounded for by William Wadisworth, the 3s 9d rent was compounded for by Richard Brookesbanke, the 3s 4½d rent was compounded for by George Fournes, the 13d rent was compounded for by Edmund Hileley and the 3½d rent was compounded for by James Hileley the elder*
Sowerby (9) John Ramsden of les Hightrees and Elizabeth his wife (she agreeing separately) by John Midgley gen, deputy steward, surrendered outside court the messuage called le Feildhouse and 14 acres 1½ rood associated and a parcel of land of 6 yards by ½ yard lying in a close called Rowleybank with its watercourses, ways etc in the graveship of Sowerby, now occupied by Joseph Briggs of Feildhouse or his assigns, owing a lord's rent of 5s and certain fine: to the use of the said Joseph Briggs, his heirs etc. Agreed: entry fine of 15s.

[A] Panel of jurors, 1 November 1639
[B] The jury do present and say that John Milnes sonne of John Milnes of Holmefirth Chappell deceased who late held to him and his heires by Copy of Courtroll accordinge to the custome of the Mannour of Wakefeld one parcell of land conteyninge by estimacion Niene yeards and the Fourth parte of a yeard in length and six yeards and the foueth parte of a yeard in breadth and one new house there vpon builded neare Holmefirth Chappell And also one Close of land and meadowe called Childynge conteyninge by estimacion one acre with all and singular there appertunce in Wooldale within the graveshippe of Holme and late in the tenure or occupacion of the said John Milnes the father deceased or his assignes, of the yearly rent to the lord of .iiij. d. And Compounded for, died thereof seised about .xviij. years and that no person or persons came in and prayed to be admitted to make fyne with the lord within three greate Courts

next after the death of the said John Milnes as he ought to have done by the custome of the same Mannour And therefore all his the foresaid Copyhold lands and tenements are forfeicted and ought to be seised into the lords hands.

[signed] Isaack Houldsworth/John Swift/Thomas Metcalfe/John Wad [I] Thomas Myllner/Francis Gill/Robart Bargh/Paule Ramsden/

Recorded at Court 1st November 15 Charles [1639]

[mem 2d]

WAKEFIELD: the Court Baron of Gervase Clifton held on 22 November 15 Charles [1639]

Inquisition on the oaths of Thomas Cotes, Robert Killingbecke, Stephen Bateman, John Swifte, Robert Clarke, Paul Ramsden, Thomas Milner, Thomas Wright, Francis Gill, William Gill, Robert Bradford and William Thornes.

Sowerby (*10*) Memo. that on the previous 19 November Abraham Stansfeild of Warley, clothier, for greater security of payment surrendered before John Midgley gen, deputy steward, out of court as by indenture to the use of Richard Tattersall of Hollings in Warley, yeoman, and John Tattersall his son, their heirs and assigns, that messuage and estimated 6 acres in the middle of les Withens in Warley in the graveship of Sowerby once occupied by Abraham Croyser and his assigns, then by Gilbert Sladen and Thomas Hartley and their assigns, and now by Abraham Stansfeild and, his assigns, owing a lord's rent of 2s: on condition that if Abraham Stansfeild his heirs etc satisfy Richard and John Tattersall their certain attorney etc at the home of Richard at Hollings in an annual sum of 47s 6d on 24 November for three years, the first payment being on 24 November 1640, also the sum of £12 7s 6d on 24 November 1643, and an annual sum of 31s 8d on 24 November for three years, starting on 24 November 1644, and the sum of £11 11s 8d on 24 November 1647, and an annual sum of 15s 10d on 24 November for three years, starting on 24 November 1648, and the sum of £10 15s 10d on 2[4] November 1651 [mem 3] the surrender is to be void, but in case of default of any payment to stand in full force. Agreed: entry fine —

Stanley (*11*) Allen Clarkson late of Stanley by William Hanson, lord's tenant and sworn, surrendered a selion of arable called Headland on a shot or forelong called Cromblands in le Netherfeild of Stanley in the graveship of Stanley, owing a lord's rent of 1d and certain fine: to the use of Gervase Hatfeild of Stanley gen, his heirs etc. Agreed: entry fine of 3d. *Compounded for by Robert Clarkson*

[A] Panel of jurors, Wakefeld, 22 November 1639

[B] 12 Sept 15 Charles, 1639

Memorandum that the day and yeare abouesaid Mary Mylnes

daughter of Abraham Mylnes deceased by Godfrey Cuttell and John Fisher tenants of the lord and to be sworne, hath given and surrendred upp with a strawe into the hande of the lord accordinge to the custome of the manor of Wakefield and also remised releassed and from her her heirs and assigns and from euery of them quite claymed vnto William Matson of Holmefrith his heires and assigns foreuer, all that her right title state enterest reuersion and reuersions clayme and demand whatsoeuer of the said Mary Mylnes, which she the said Mary Mylnes now hath or which she her heires or assigns or any of them hereafter may or can haue of and in one closse of land and medowe called Childynge with appurtenance in scoles in the graveshipp of Holme and now in the tenure and occupacion of the said William Matson or his assigns and is of the yearely rent domino regi of .iiij. d. and Compounded for, So verely that neither I thaforesaid Mary Mylnes nor my heires nor assigns nor any of them nor any other person or persons in my name or for me any state right title vse enterest reuersion or reuersions clayme or demand whatsoeuer in or to the said closse of land and medowe called Childynge with appurtenance or in or to any parte or parcell thereof att any tyme hereafter shall pretend clayme or challendge, but from all accions of right state title vse entrest reuersion and reuersions clayme and demand whatsoeuer therein to be had or taken to be vtterly excluded debarred and foreuer shutt out by these presents giuen and surrendred the day and yeare abouesaid.

the marke of Mary Milnes *the woman hath estate for life*
witnesse Robert Bradford *Recorded at the Court at Wakefeld, 12 June 1640*

[Latin] *Noted that the surrender was respited because the lands were seised into the lord's hands*

[mem 3]

WAKEFIELD: the Court Baron of Gervase Clifton held on 13 December 15 Charles [1639]

Hipperholme (*12*) Inquisition on the oaths of Thomas Wright, Edmund Sykes, John Scott, Peter Andrew, Jeremy Mawde, Paul Ramsden, John Walker, John Jagger, John Wade, Richard Dawson, Francis Gill and William Gill, who testify that John Deane late of Blackhillend in Northowrome, deceased, son and heir of John Deane late of the same, deceased, held 2 acres with ways etc in the graveship of Hipperholme, lately occupied by the same as parcel of the lands of the late Robert earl of Leicester. Prudence Deane and Sara Deane, his sisters of the whole blood, are his co-heirs. They pay an entry fine of 8d, viz. 4d each *Relief for lands late of earl of Leicester .viij. d.*

Holme Testimony by the grave of Holme of his seizure into the lord's hand of a parcel of land estimated at $9\frac{1}{4}$ yards by $6\frac{1}{4}$ yards and a new house thereon by Holmefirth Chappell with a close called Childynge of approximately an acre in Wooldale in the same, lately occupied by John Milnes, deceased, owing a lord's rent of 4d, following an order given in court on 1 November last. The first proclamation was made for any claims *certificate of grave: first proclamation*

Sandall (*12*) Thomas Beaumont of Whitley hall and Gregory Armitage of Nethershitlington esq by Thomas Pollard of Great Sandall, lord's tenant and sworn, surrendered 2 acres approximately of arable and pasture in graveship of Sandall lying in le Castlefeild and in Woodthorpefeild, being parcel of 8 acres in Sandall of which 3 acres were sold and surrendered to the use of Francis Nevile esq and his heirs and another 3 acres sold and surrendered to the use of William Lambert and his heirs, and a close in Sandall called Foulewells now in two closes, and part of another close called Haslawell, being customary land, owing a lord's rent of 18d. and certain fine: to the use of Henry Grice of Milnethorpe esq and his heirs etc. Agreed: entry fine of 4s 6d.

Ossett (*13*) Thomas Awdisley and John Awdisley his son, of Ossett, clothiers, by Thomas Hemingway of Earlesheaton, lord's tenant and sworn, surrendered two houses, a croft and a fold now occupied in Ossett and in the graveship of Horbury, abutting to the north the close called Godhames, being the land of Christopher Awdisley, and to the south le Townegate, occupied by Thomas Awdisley, owing

a lord's rent of ½d: to the use of James Speight of Earlesheaton, parish of Dewisbury, his heirs etc. Agreed: entry fine of 1½d *Compounded for by Thomas Awdisley*
Sowerby (*14*) Benjamin Wood, son and heir of Michael Wood, deceased, Abraham Butterworth of Sowerby, clothier, and Sara, now his wife, daughter of the said Michael, she agreeing separately, by Jonathan Ramsden, lord's tenant and sworn, surrendered a messuage called Ellenroid or Ellesholme and 6 closes leased with the same and containing approximately 6 acres in the graveship of Sowerby, lately occupied by James Procter or his assigns and now by Henry Radcliffe or his assigns, owing a lord's rent of 20d and certain fine: to the use of Michael Briggs of Warley, yeoman, his heirs etc. Agreed: entry fine of 5s. *Compounded for by Michael Wood*
Sowerby (*15*) Samuel Townend of Shawedge in Soyland, clothier, and Susan now his wife, she agreeing separately, by Nathan Hoile, lord's tenant and sworn, surrendered the reversion on the death of Thomas Townend, father of the said Samuel, of the customary messuage called Shawedge and all houses, buildings, lands etc of approximately 4 acres in Soyland in the graveship of Sowerby, occupied by the same Samuel Townend and Thomas Townend and their assigns, owing a lord's rent of 18d and certain fine (reserving an annual rent charge of 50s to the use of John Hoile, son of Isaac Hoile late of Hirsthouse, deceased, his heirs etc): to the use of John Kershawe of Soyland, yeoman, his heirs etc. Agreed: entry fine of 2s 9d. *Compounded for by Thomas Townend*
Sowerby (*16*) John Hoile of le Hirsthouse in Soyland and Susan now his wife, she agreeing separately, by Nathan Hoile, lord's tenant and sworn, surrendered an annuity of 50s from a customary messuage at le Shawedge in Soyland now occupied by Thomas Townend and Robert Crosley and their assigns, owing a lord's rent of 18d, this annuity with right of distraint being payable at Martinmas and Whitsun equally with the first payment due at Martinmas next: to the use of John Kershawe of Soyland, clothier, his heirs etc. Agreed: entry fine of 4s 2d. *Compounded for by Thomas Townend*
Sowerby (*17*) Appearance of Jonathan Bairstowe of Brownesthirst, son and heir of Michael Bairstowe late of the same, deceased, before the steward of the court to fine 26s 3½d as heriot for 2 messuages and all lands etc associated in Northowrome in the graveship of Hipperholme now occupied by Marmaduke Hall and Mary Waterhouse widow or their assigns, owing a lord's rent of 8s 7½d, and another messuage or house within a close in Warley in the graveship of Sowerby now occupied by John Jenkinson or his assigns owing a lord's rent of 2d and both held by certain fine. Jonathan Bairstowe admitted to hold by custom of the manor *Compounded for by John Bairstowe of Brownesthirst*

Sandall (*18*) George Allott of Criglestone yeoman appeared before Thomas, viscount Saville, baron Pontefract, chief steward of the manor of Wakefeld, and took that close or pasture commonly called Mold-Roid in Criglestone in the graveship of Sandall with its profits etc lately occupied by Isabella Oxley of Sandall, widow, or her assigns owing a lord's rent of – and certain fine. This was seized into the lord's hand because the said George Allott by an indenture of 18 July last past leased the same to Richard Johnson of Crofton, yeoman, for ten years without licence of the court, contrary to the custom of the manor, as shown by an enquiry presented at the court at Wakefield on 19 July. Proclamation was made publicly in three courts at Wakefield on three separate occasions, according to the custom of the manor, offering the same to any claimant willing to pay the lord of the manor the customary dues and services for it. As only George Allott made a proffer the close is granted to him by the ancient dues and services, and Allott fines —.

Alverthorpe (*19*) Richard Spurre by John Scott, lord's tenant and sworn, surrendered a parcel of land from the lord's waste estimated at a half rood on Alverthorpe greene adjoining the highway leading from a place formerly in Wakefeld Outwood called Lindale to the town of Wakefeld with the cottage built thereon in the graveship of Alverthorpe, now occupied by James Wrightman or his assigns, owing a lord's rent of ½d in new rent: to the use of the same James Wrightman. Agreed: entry fine of 6s 8d. *Fine not compounded, 6s 8d paid: New rent ½d.*

[A] Panel for 13 December 1639

[B] Wakefeild Manor

Amongest other thinges it is presented and found that John Deane late of Blackehill in Northowrom deceassed Sonne and heire of John Deane late of the same deceassed who late held to him and his heires of the Lorde of the Mannor of Wakefeilde Two acres of land with all wayes waters and easiaments to the same belonginge with appertenncy in the graveshipp of Hipperholme late in the tenure or occupacion of the said John Deane late parcell of the lands and possessions of the late right honorable Robert late Earle of Leicester is late deade, And that Prudence Deane and Sara Deane (beinge the onlie Sisters of the whole bloude vnto the said John Deane the Sonne are his Cooheires and ought to pay vnto the Lord in the name of Releife for the same .viij. d. (to witt) for either acre .iiij. d.

The Jury do present and say that John Deane sonne of John Deane is dead and that Prudence Deane and Sara Deane are his sisters and coheirs.

[signed] Thomas Wright
Paule Ramsdene   Record' ad curiam tent' apud Wakefeld

John Scott .xiij. die Decembris Anno Regni Regis
Francis Gill Caroli Anglie etc. xv°
William Gill

[C] [Latin] Warrant from Thomas viscount Savile etc to the grave of Holme and his deputy to seize into the lord's hand the parcel of land containing an estimated 9¼ yards by 6¼ yards and a new house built thereon by Holmefirth Chappell with a close called Childynge of about one acre in Wooldale in the graveship of Holme lately held by John Milnes deceased, owing a lord's rent of 4d and certain fine, to be accomplished and returned at the next court at Wakefeld.

Dated 1 November 15 Charles. [signed] J. Midgley

First proclamation

[endorsed] executed by me James Gonne grave of Holme

[signed] Thomas Savile/
Godfray Mathewman/
Anthony Batty/ Copyholders
Christofer Tucker/

[mem 3 dorse]

WAKEFIELD: the Court Baron of Gervase Clifton held on 10 January 15 Charles [1640]

Thornes: Inquisition on the oaths of Francis Mathewman, Thomas Wright, Peter Moxon, Thomas Leigh, John Wade, John Swifte, John Roberts, Francis Gill, John Hirst, Richard Dawson, Robert Barghe and John Forrest, who present that Jeremy Mawde refused to pay his entry fine for a parcel of land about half an acre by the end of the street called Kirkegate [mem 4] at Pennywalls in the graveship of Thornes, whereby the parcel is forfeit and should be seized. Order to the grave of Thornes to seize the same for the next court.

Holme: Second proclamation in court for claims to the parcel of land measuring 9¼ yards by 6¼ yards with a new house thereon by Holmefirth Chappell and a close called Childynge of about one acre in Wooldale in the graveship of Holme lately occupied by John Milnes deceased at 4d and certain fine.

Sandall (*20*) Henry Grice esq by Gervase Norton of Kettlethorpe, lord's tenant and sworn, surrendered an acre in a close called Hesle-well in Sandall and two selions arable of half an acre in one field of Sandall called Woodthorpfeild between the lands of Richard Tayler to the east and west in the graveship of Sandall, now occupied by the same Henry Grice or his assigns, owing a lord's rent of 6d and certain fine: to the use of Thomas Wightman, his heirs etc. Agreed: entry fine of 18d. *Compounded for by Elizabeth Savile widowe*

Ossett (*21*) William Rodes and Elizabeth his wife, she agreeing separately, by John Forrest, lord's tenant and sworn, surrendered a messuage and a toft with other structures in Ossett occupied by the same William Rodes and his wife or their assigns, with half an acre in le Westfeild of Ossett on a shot there called Netherfardingroid, and a rood in le Eastfeild of Ossett on a shot called Sowdell also in their occupation, owing a lord's rent of 2d and certain fine made by Robert Fairbanke: also a rood on a shot called Wheatley in the Eastfeild of Ossett and a half rood in the Northfeild of Ossett on le Towne Knowle, and a rood on le Furshutt called Overmoorecrofte in the graveship of Ossett in the occupation of the same, which latter three parcels pay a lord's rent of 2d and certain fine made by Edward Midlebrooke: also a rood in the Eastfeild of Ossett on a shot called Brodeoller between the land of the heirs of John Pickard to the east and the land of Richard Awdisley to the west in the graveship of Ossett now occupied by the same William Rodes and his wife at a lord's rent of 2d and certain fine made by John Saxton: also a close commonly called Stonyflatts in the graveship of Ossett in the occupation of the same at a lord's rent of 18d and certain fine made by John Awdisley: to the use of George Glover, his heirs etc. Agreed: entry fine of 6s 3d.

Horbury (*22*) Robert Dawson of Horbury by John Issott, lord's tenant and sworn, surrendered that messuage in which he now lives with all houses etc, 3 acres arable and a close of meadow called Towne carre ynge estimated at 1½ acres with all profits and easements, and an acre arable in le Westfeild of Horbury called Jenkinbanks in Horbury at a lord's rent of 2s and certain fine, together with 7 roods arable in the three fields of Horbury with common of cow pasture there, owing a lord's rent of 9d and no certain fine, now occupied by the said Robert Dawson or his assigns: to the use of Robert Dawson for life, with reversion to William Dawson his son and heir, with remainder to John Dey son of Thomas Dey of Darfeild and the heirs of his body, with remainder to William Dey, second son of Thomas and the heirs of his body, with remainder to Alice Dawson, daughter of the said Robert Dawson and the heirs of her body. Agreed as life tenancy to Robert Dawson with reversion to William Dawson, with an entry fine of 3s for the life term, and of – for the land not covered by agreement. William Dawson paid for reversion of the land covered by agreement 3s and for the rest – . *The 2s rent compounded for by Elizabeth Woodrove and by Roberte Dawson*

Sowerby (*23*) Richard Holgate son and heir of George Holgate late of Wheatleyroid in Sowerby by John Lomme, lord's tenant and sworn, surrendered an annuity of £14 5s from all that messuage called Wheatleyroid and 6 closes of meadow associated with the same, called separately Wheatleyroid, Calsikey, Stubynge, Brockhoiles, Netherhey and Beitefeild, situated in the graveship of Sowerby, lately occupied by the same George Holgate deceased or his assigns and now by Richard Holgate, Richard Denby and Joseph Hanson and their assigns, with that messuage and 5 acres of land, meadow and pasture usually leased with the same in the graveship of Sowerby and now occupied by Edward Stansfeild or his assigns at a lord's rent of 13s 8d and certain fine, with 2 houses or cottages in Sowerby now occupied by Andrew Pilkington and Sara Tilson or their assigns at a lord's rent of 2d and certain fine: to the use of Susan Illingworth late wife of the abovenamed George Holgate deceased and mother of the said Richard Holgate for life. This rent of £14 5s is payable at Whitsun and Martinmas or within 40 days with the right to distrain in case of default, in lieu of dower in the lands of Richard Holgate. [mem 4d] Agreed: entry fine of 23s 9d.

Hipperholme (*24*) Testified in court on the oath of John Bentley, lord's tenant, that Jonathan Bairstowe of Brownesthirst in Ovenden yeoman on 4 June last past surrendered that messuage called Knightroid and all houses, outbuildings, folds, gardens, 'backsides', lands, ways etc in Northowrome now occupied by Marmaduke Hall at a lord's rent of 5s $1\frac{1}{2}$d and certain fine: to the use of the said Marmaduke Hall from 2 February next for 21 years at an annual rent of £10 payable at Whitsun and Martinmas. Agreed: entry fine of 7s $2\frac{1}{4}$d. *Compounded for by John Bairstowe of Brownesthirst*

Hipperholme (*25*) Whereas elsewhere in court at Wakefeld on 23 April 22/57 James [1624] John Deane late of Blackhillend in Northowrome, son of Robert Deane late of Jackroid in Ovenden deceased by Michael Bentley, lord's tenant and sworn, surrendered a messuage called le Auncient old house at Blackhill in Northowrome and all houses etc with an 'overbarne' 17 yards long, half a fold lying to the north of the house door with free access through the other half for all purposes, a close called le Kilnecrofte, a parcel of land, meadow, wood and pasture in 2 closes called Sholebrode, another called Rye Pighell, another called Over Church bothome, the north half of a meadow called Crawoodynge and 3 other closes called le Over blackhillbankes adjoining lands lately of Abraham Wood on the south and the lands lately of Samuel Haldisworth to the north, with all ways etc all containing by estimation 10 acres and occupied by the said John Deane or his assigns, at a lord's rent of 2s 9d: to the use of John Deane son and heir of the said John Deane and his lawful heirs, with reversion to the male heirs of Grace, then wife of the said John Deane the father, should she be pregnant at the time of John's decease, with reversion to the heirs male of the said John Deane the father, with reversion to Isabella, Grace, Judith, Prudence and Sara Deane, daughters of the said John Deane: now, because the said John Deane had no other male issue than John, who is dead without issue, the lands should pass to the said Isabella, Grace, Judith, Prudence and Sara Deane by virtue of the surrender. Isabella married Denis Illingworth and Judith married Richard Ramsden. Accordingly Denis Illingworth and Isabella his wife, Richard Ramsden and Judith his wife, and Grace Deane crave to be admitted to fine for three parts of the total of five. Agreed: entry fine of 4s $9\frac{1}{2}$d and $\frac{3}{5}$ of 4d.

Hipperholme (*26*) Prudence Deane and Sara Deane, two sisters and co-heirs of the whole blood of John Deane junior late of Blackhill in Northowrome deceased came before the steward and fined 3s $3\frac{1}{2}$d for two parts of five shares of a messuage etc at Blackhill in Northowrome in the graveship of Hipperholme, these two parts containing by estimate 4 acres, lately occupied by the said John Deane or his assigns at a lord's rent of 13d and a third of a halfpenny and certain fine. Agreed.

[A] Panel for 10 January 1640

[B] The Jury do find that Jeremy Maude doe refuse to pay his fine assessed upon his lands, a parcell of land meadowe and pasture containing by estimacion half an acre lyinge neare the end of Kirkegate at a certayne place called Painwalls these appertenaunces in the graveship of Thornes late bought of Edward Smith and therefore the same parcell is seazable into the lords hands.

19 May Charles 13 [1637] to use of Jeremy Mawde

[signed] Francis Mathewman Thomas Wright John Wade John Swifte John Roberts John Hirst Peter Moxon Robart Bargh Francis Gill

[mem 5]

WAKEFIELD: the Court Baron of Gervase Clifton held on 31 January 15 Charles [1640]

Miles Cooke was elected to the office of pinder in the township of Ossett.

Inquisition on the oaths of Edward Smith gen, Robert Bargh, John Forrest, Brian Peace, John Wade, Francis Gill, Richard Dawson, Thomas Langfeild, Paul Ramsden, Alvered Pickard, Robert Fairbarne and George Glover.

Holme Third proclamation for claims for a parcel of land of 9¼ yards by 6¼ yards with a new house by Holmefirth Chappell and a close called Childynge of an acre in Wooldale in the graveship of Holme lately occupied by John Milnes deceased at a lord's rent of 4d and certain fine.

Sowerby (27) Testified by William Sutcliffe of Foote, lord's tenant, that Samuel Wade of Midgley in the county of York, yeoman, on the last day of October, 15 Charles [1639], surrendered 2 messuages with buildings in the graveship of Sowerby, one called Miriewall, now occupied by Abraham Longebothome or his assigns, and the other Leyend, occupied by Abraham Holme or his assigns, at a lord's rent of 2s 6d and certain fine: to the use of Anne Wade, sister of the granter, from the date of his death and for six years after, for satisfaction of all debts owed to her or to any others, with the reversion of the lands to Richard Wade, his second son, and his heirs etc on condition that if Samuel Wade offer or tender during his lifetime to Richard Hoile or the said William Sutcliffe or their heirs or for their use the sum of 6d before two or more sufficient witnesses this shall render the surrender void. Agreed: fine for entry of 3s 9d paid by Anne Wade, for the remainder, 3s 9d paid by Richard Wade.

[A] Panel for 31 January 1640

[mem 5]

WAKEFIELD: the Court Baron of Gervase Clifton held on 21 February 15 Charles [1640]

Inquisition on the oaths of Thomas Wright, Richard Brodebent, Richard Roberte, Paul Ramsden, William Cartmell, John Harrison, John Wade, Thomas Metcalfe, Richard Dawson, Robert Clarke, William Gill and Christopher Brooke.

Horbury: Testimony that Robert Kay who lately held by copy according to the custom of the manor of Wakefeld a house called a Kilnehouse with a garden of 80 feet and also a path encroached from the lord's waste in Horbury near the mill lately occupied by Robert Kay or his assigns died, and none made fine for the same within the space of three great courts after his death, wherefore it was forfeited into the lord's hand. Order to the grave of Horbury to seize the same for the next court.

Hipperholme (*28*) John Lister of Overbrea yeoman and Phebe now his wife, she agreeing separately, by John Lomme, lord's tenant and sworn, surrendered the toft and 7 closes of land, meadow and pasture in Northowrome in the graveship of Hipperholme now occupied by Robert Hebblethwaite or his assigns at a lord's rent of 2s and certain fine, also 2 closes commonly called le High Roide in Northowrom in the graveship of Hipperholme now occupied by Joseph Butterworth or his assigns at a lord's rent of 7½d and certain fine: to the use of Thomas Lister of Shibdenhall in Southowrome gen, his heirs etc. Agreed: entry fine of 7s 10½d. *The 2s rent is compounded for by Robert Hemmingway of Overbrea and Samuel Crowther, and the 7½d rent is compounded for by John Drake*

Stanley (*29*) John Scatchard by Andrew Smith, lord's tenant and sworn, surrendered 4 closes of land, meadow and pasture in Wrenthorpe and Wooldale in the graveship of Stanley commonly called le Woodside closes now occupied by Richard Sikes at a lord's rent of 2s 1d and certain fine: to the use of James Lister, clerk, John Story and Thomas Cooke, their heirs etc to the end that James Lister, John Story and Thomas Cooke etc should surrender and sell the same 4 closes and with the proceeds pay the debts of the said John Scatchard, and also that the same pay the residue to Thomas Scatchard, John Scatchard, William Scatchard and Elizabeth Scatchard, children of the said John Scatchard and the survivers of them, each equally, on attaining 21 years. The interest on the same money is to be paid to John Scatchard the father until the children come of age. Agreed: entry fine of 6s 3d. [mem 5d]

Horbury (*30*) James Speight of le Street in the township of Soothill by William Midlebrough, lord's tenant and sworn, surrendered a close called Longland in Ossett in the graveship of Horbury now occupied by James Speight or his assigns at a lord's rent of 12d and certain fine: to the use of Francis Gill, his heirs etc. Agreed: entry fine of 3s. *Compounded for by Thomas Gill*

Thornes (*31*) Jeremy Mawde of Wakefeld appeared before Thomas, viscount Savile, baron Pontefract, high steward of Wakefeld, and took a parcel of land of half an acre at the end of Kirkegate in Wakefeld at Pennywalls in the graveship of Thornes, occupied by the same, which had been seized for his refusal to pay his entry fine as appeared from an enquiry at Wakefeld court on 14 December 14 Charles [1638]. Proclamation having been made at three different courts according to the custom of the manor, no one offered but Mawde. Agreed: entry fine of 40s. *Fine not compounded, 40s paid*

[A] [Latin] Wakefield Court: 22 October 27 Elizabeth [1585], before Edward Carye esq, high steward.

Horbury: Robert Kay came before Edward Carye esq, high steward of the Queen in the manor of Wakefeld and by virtue of a writing of William Tusser esq, clerk of the duchy of Lancaster directed to the steward, took a house called a Kilnehouse with a garden adjoining of 80 feet and a way and an encroachment on the Queen's waste in Horbury by the mill, now occupied by the same Robert Kay or his assigns: granted under the seal of the duchy of Lancaster, dated 27 February 22 Elizabeth [1580] and enrolled to hold as other ancient tenants at an annual new rent of 7d and an entry fine of 13s 4d.

21 February 1639/40

Wee of the Jury do finde that the above named Robert Kay did dye above two yeares agoe and before three great Courts last and that none came to make fine with the Lord for the same since the death of the said Robert, and therefore the lands above mencioned are forfeited into the Lords hands.

[signed] Thomas Wright/William Gill/Richard Brodbent/Paul Ramsdene

[B] [Latin] Panel for 21 February 1640

[as engrossed, with addition]

Francis Blacker 10s because not present when jury sworn

John Roo 10s amercement

Grave of Sandell because he did not appear

[mem 5 d]

WAKEFIELD: the Court Baron of Gervase Clifton held on 13 March 15 Charles [1640]

Inquisition on the oaths of John Sunderland, Christopher Smith, John Forrest, Robert Clarke, Thomas Metcalfe, Brian Peace, Robert Bargh, Christopher Brooke, Richard Dawson, George Glover, John Walker and Henry Tayler.

Hipperholme: Presentment that John Whitley of Rookes in Hipperholme yeoman by indenture of 10 March last leased to Nathan Drake of Godley in the township of Northowrome yeoman half a rood of land and the buildings thereupon with 4 acres 3 roods by Sinderhills in the graveship of Hipperholme, now occupied by Judith Pannell or her assigns at a lord's rent of 19½d and certain fine, being copyhold, for a period of 21 years, without licence of the court. Order to the grave of Hipperholme to seize the same into the lord's hand.

Horbury: First proclamation by the grave of Horbury that he had seized a Kilnehouse and garden etc in Horbury near the windmill, lately held by Robert Kay, as ordered in the previous court, the same being offered for claimants.

Hipperholme (*32*) Testimony by Robert Bairstowe, lord's tenant, that Jonathan Bairstowe late of Browneshirste and Lucy his wife, she agreeing separately, on 13 February last surrendered a toft called Brig Roid and all lands associated in Northowrome in the graveship of Hipperholme now occupied by Mary Waterhouse and Joseph Waterhouse or either or their assigns at a lord's rent of 3s 6d and certain fine: to the use of Mary Bairstowe of Northowrome, spinster, and her heirs etc. Agreed: entry fine of 10s 6d. *Compounded for by John Bairstowe of Brownesthirst*

Hipperholme (*33*) Appearance of John Brearcliffe, son and next heir of Edward Brearcliffe late of Halifax deceased and Hester late wife of the same, who paid 12s 6d as heriot for a toft called dammhead with the buildings thereon and 9 closes associated in Northowrome in the graveship of Hipperholme, estimated at 5 acres, with another messuage called Adderish gate, a barn, a 'fouldstead', a garden, a croft called Tentercrofte, a close called Greatynge of an acre, another 3 closes called Kilnebutts, Narrbanke, and Farrbanke, containing 4 acres, a close called Litleynge or Johnynge of two acres in Northowrome in the graveship of Hipperholme, now occupied by Sara Hopkinson, widow, and Robert Crowther or their assigns, with the close of land, meadow, pasture and wood called Stubynge of an acre located at Adderishgate in Northowrome, now occupied by Robert Crowther or his assigns, following the death of the said Edward Brearcliffe and Hester his wife, daughter and next heir of John Brearcliffe. Agreed.

Hipperholme (*34*) Appearance of Anne Deane and Grace Dean, daughters and next heirs of Grace Deane, late wife of John Deane late of Overden deceased, before the high steward, who fined as heriot for the toft called Otes Roid and 7 closes and buildings thereon lately of John Sutcliffe deceased, late father of Grace Deane their mother [mem 6] at Amblerthorne in Northowrome in the graveship of Hipperholme, now occupied by Widow Bairstowe, Nicholas Smith, John Mitchell and Richard Moore or their assigns at a lord's rent of 2s 10½d. Of this 2s 7½d is covered by certain fine and the remaining 3d is not so covered. Agreed. *Fine and heriot for land compounded, 7s 10½d, for land not compounded —*

Hipperholme (*35*) Appearance of Anne Deane and Grace Deane, sisters and next heirs of Richard Deane, lately son and heir apparent of John Deane late of Ovenden deceased and Grace his wife, who paid heriot of 12s for the toft commonly called Heslehirst or West heslehirst and the buildings thereon etc in Northowrome in the graveship of Hipperholme, now occupied by Anthony Waterhouse or his assigns at a lord's rent of 4s and certain fine. Agreed.

Wakefeld (*36*) Edward Lowden gen and Anna now his wife, she agreeing separately, by Cotton Horne gen, lord's tenant and sworn, surrendered all the messuages etc in copyhold in the parish of Wakefeld saving the unenclosed land in the field called Cliffe feild in the parish of Wakefeld: to the use of Francis Tindall esq. Agreed.

Wakefeld (*37*) Stephen Bateman and Elizabeth his wife, she agreeing separately, by Cotton Horne gen, lord's tenant and sworn, surrendered so much of a messuage commonly called le Horsehead located in Wakefeld in Westgate as held by copyhold, occupied by Sara Hitchon, widow, with the buildings thereon in the graveship of Wakefeld at a lord's rent of 4s and certain fine: to the use of Francis Stocks, his heirs etc. Agreed: entry fine of 12s.

Holme (*38*) James Grene by John Grene, lord's tenant sworn, surrendered a house and barn and 'le Outshutt' or 'Eelinge' adjoining, consisting of two bays, and part of a fold etc in Holme in the graveship of Holme, now occupied by Edward Hinchcliffe and Elizabeth Earnshawe at a lord's rent of 2d and certain fine: to the use of Godfrey Grene, his heirs etc. Agreed: entry fine of 6d.

Holme (*39*) Testimony by Francis Hinchcliffe, lord's tenant, that John Shawe on 12 November 14 Charles, 1638, surrendered a close called le Nethercrofte at Ewtrees in Austonley in the graveship of Holme, now occupied by Thomas Waterhouse at a lord's rent of 2d and certain fine: to the absolute use of James Mitchell. Agreed: entry fine of 6d. *Compounded for by Grace Sunderland and Grace Cartwright*

Holme (*40*) Testimony by John Hirst, lord's tenant, that John Greene on 7 November 14 Charles, 1638, surrendered 2 closes called le Middledowneshutts and Litledowneshutts at Ewtrees in Awstonley in the graveship of Holme, now occupied by John Shawe, at a lord's rent of 8d and certain fine: to the absolute use of John Shawe. Agreed: entry fine of 2s. *Compounded for by John Sunderland*

Sowerby (*41*) Whereas Richard Deane late of Mixenden in the township of Ovenden deceased was seised in 2 messuages and 7½ acres in Warley in the graveship of Sowerby, previously occupied severally by John Aikroid and Isaac Breare and now by Widow Viccars and Sybil Breare or their assigns, together with the other lands late of Edward Brookesbanke of Bradshawe in Warley in the graveship of Sowerby, lately of the inheritance of Gilbert Brookesbanke deceased, late father of Edward Brookesbanke, at a lord's rent of 2s 4d and certain fine, and the same Richard Deane died seised within the last great court being held at Wakefield on 11 October last. Following this death John Deane as cousin and next heir, viz. as son and next heir of William Deane deceased, late brother of the said Richard, entered the same messuages and died since Michaelmas past, before the date of the court, without making an entry fine. Now Anne Deane and Grace Deane, daughters and co-heirs of the said John Deane deceased appear and pay 14s as heriot for the 2 messuages and 7½ acres in Warley, viz. 7s in respect of the [mem 6d] death of Richard and another 7s in respect of the death of John, whose daughters they are. Agreed.

Sowerby (*42*) Jonas Bordall of Skircote, county York, clothier, and Mary his wife, she agreeing separately, by Martin Milnes, lord's tenant and sworn, surrendered a messuage or house and 2 closes of meadow of an acre and a half known as le Stubbynge in Sowerby in the graveship of Sowerby, lately occupied by Gabriel Bordall deceased, father of the said Jonas or his assigns, and now by William Thomas and Simeon Helliwell or either or their assigns at a lord's rent of 6d and certain fine: to the use of Michael Lomme of Netherwhitelee in Midgley in the same county, clothier, provided that if Jonas Bordall, his heirs, executors or administrators indemnify the said Michael Lomme his heirs etc against John Lomme of Northowrome in the same county, yeoman, etc touching an obligatory letter of the same date as the surrender whereby Michael, when required by Jonas, should pay John Lomme £140 the said surrender should be null and void. The latter payment arises from a bond dated about 31 May 1634 by which John Lomme at the instance of Mary, wife of the said Jonas Bordall and previously the wife of James Holroid deceased, was bound to the archbishop of York and his commissary in £120 touching the education of James Holroid and Susan Holroid, children of the same, and the payment to them of their filial portions of goods, and the legal expenses of John Lomme, his heirs, executors, etc by reason of the said bond. Agreed: entry fine of 18d. *Compounded for by Gabriell Bordall*

Sandall (*43*) Appearance of John Allott, 'grandchild' and next heir of John Allott late of Bentley deceased, viz. the son and heir of George Allott deceased, son and heir of the said John Allott, who fined as heriot for 3 roods in a close called Quarrell close between the lands of the late John Allott deceased on the east and the lands of John Miller on the west, with the 'cow pasture of Horbury' to the north in the township of Criggleston in the graveship of Sandall, now and lately occupied by George Hirst or his assigns at a lord's rent of 3d and no certain fine, these 3 roods having been bought by the late John Allott from Thomas Milner and Elizabeth his wife. Agreed *Fine for heriot not compounded*

Sandall (*44*) Gervase Norton of Newmilnedamme and Elizabeth his wife, who agreed separately, by Josiah Roo, lord's tenant and sworn, surrendered 3 roods lately enclosed in Pledwicke in the graveship of Sandall, now occupied by George Hutchinson of Newbigginhill or his assigns, at a lord's rent of 3d and certain fine: to the use of George Hutchinson, his heirs etc. Agreed: entry fine of 9d. *Compounded for by Henry Grice esq*

Wakefeld, Stanley, Alverthorpe, Sandall, Holme (*45*) John Allott, son and heir of George Allott deceased by Mary his late wife, George being the son and heir of John Allott late of Bentley deceased, came and paid as heriot £3 3s 8½d and half of a farthing for the reversion after the death of Mary, mother of the said John Allott son of George, of all customary messuages, cottages, houses, buildings etc late of the said John Allott deceased and of Joan lately his wife, commonly called Seilcotes or otherwise in Stanley and Alverthorpe and elsewhere in the parish of Wakefeld in the graveships of Wakefeld, Stanley and Alverthorpe at a lord's rent of 12½d, with the reversion after the death of the said Joan of all customary messuages etc being 36 acres 1 rood in Crigleston in the graveship of Sandall at a lord's rent of 10s 11d, and the reversion after the death of the said Joan of that messuage called Butterley with all buildings, closes, wood, scrub, common pasture, commodity, profits etc being estimated at 50 acres and a quarter rood situated in the graveship of Holme at a lord's rent of 19s 6d and all covered by certain fine. Agreed. [mem 7]

Rastricke (*46*) John Fox late of Toothill and now of Boothroid in

the township of Rastrick by Thomas Hanson, lord's tenant and sworn, surrendered that part of a messuage at le Boothroid in the graveship of Rastrick which was lately occupied by Grace Firth, widow, or her assigns and now by John Firth of Boothroid or his assigns, consisting of a kitchen now made into a dwellinghouse with an upper room and a stable adjoining the barn, a parcel of land to the north of the same house of 6½ yards by 5 yards by agreed measure, and part of a fold, and 3 closes in Rastricke now made into 4 closes, commonly known as le Overbackside, le Stones, le Netherbackside of the Stones and le Houghefeild, estimated at 6 acres, at a lord's rent of 2s: and also a parcel of land of 68 yards by 7 yards to the northeast side of the close called Tentercrofte and lying between the fold at Boothroid and the close called Backside-stones; with the parcel of barn called 'an Eelinge' or 'le Outshutt' now held by John Firth or his assigns at Boothroid at a lord's rent of 1d, all covered by a certain fine, together with reversions: to the use of John Firth, his wife and children from 2 February 1640 for 21 years, paying to John Fox, his heirs etc £3 a year at Whitsun and Martinmas in equal portions, on condition that if the rent be unpaid for 40 days or be sublet without the consent of John Fox, his heirs etc the surrender shall be void. Agreed: entry fine of 3s.
Alverthorpe (*47*) John Sturdy of Alverthorpe and Agnes now his wife, she agreeing separately, by Robert Clarke, lord's tenant and sworn, surrendered a parcel of land lately taken from the lord's waste in Alverthorpe with the buildings thereupon of 8 yards by 6 yards abutting on the land of John Scott to the north and east and under Alverthorpe grene to the south and le Pinfold to the west, in the graveship of Alverthorpe at a lord's rent of 4d and no certain fine: to the use of the said John Sturdy and Agnes his wife and their assigns for the term of their lives and to the longer liver, with reversion to Elizabeth now wife of Richard Burrowe of Alverthorpe and Beatrice Scott of Wakefeld, widow, and their heirs and assigns. Agreed: entry fine —, and Elizabeth and Beatrice paid for the reversion —.

[A] Original indenture in English between John Whitley of Rookes in Hipperholme, yeoman, and Nathan Drake of Godley in the township of Northowrome dated 10 March 15 Charles [1640], of a half rood with the buildings thereon and 4 acres 3 roods of land and meadow near Sinderhills in the graveship of Hipperholme now occupied by Judith Pannell leased for 21 years from the date of the deed at a rent of 5s payable at Whitsun and Martinmas

[signed] John Wytley

[Sealed] before James Forreste and Peter Lee

'Wee find that the foresaid lands are demysed contrary to the

Custome of the said Mannor and therefore ought to be seised into the Lords hands.

[signed] John Sunderland
Robart Barghe
Thomas Metcalfe
Christopher Smith [cf. pp. 53–55]

[B] Panel for 13 March 1640

[C] *Wakefeld maner* [Latin] Warrant of Thomas viscount Savile baron Pontefract, high steward of the said manor to the grave of Horbury and his deputy to seize into the lord's hand before the next court at Wakefield a house called a Kilnehouse with a garden and 80 feet encroached from the lord's waste in Horbury near the mill in the late occupation of Robert Kay or his assigns. Given on 21 February 15 Charles [1640] [signed] J. Midgley
[Endorsed] Execucion of possession and seisin was taken of the within named kilnehouse For the use of the Lord of the manor of wakefeild the second day of March Anno Regni Regis Caroli etc .xv.[to] by theis foure men hereunder written.

William Mitchell [M] John Walker
John + Haghe [mark] John Walker jun. [W]
Thomas Leytel greave

[mem 7 d]

WAKEFIELD: the Great Court Baron of Gervase Clifton held on 10 April 16 Charles [1640]
Free tenants William Savile bt, Arthur Pilkington bt, Thomas Middleton kt, *appeared by attorney*, John Savile esq, Thomas Beaumont esq, Thomas Watterton esq *appeared by attorney*, the heirs of Mathew Wentworth esq, John Armitage esq, Henry Grice esq, Thomas Thornhill esq *appeared by attorney*, John Farrer esq, William Savile esq, the heirs of William Ramsden esq, Ashton Stansfeld esq, John Copley esq, Edward Lowden gen, Cotton Horne gen, Ralph Arthington gen, Edward Goodwyn gen, the heirs of John Hanson, John Nayler of Clifton *appeared by attorney*, Henry Barraby, Thomas Pymont, John Wibsey, Richard Pearson *appeared*, Richard Liversedge *essoined*, Thomas Crosland, Thomas Walker *essoined*, William Dodgson *essoined*, Richard Archer *appeared*, Robert Preistley, Michael Foxcrofte, Nathaniel Chadwicke, Jonas Byns gen, John Sprigonell *essoined*, James Foxcrofte, John Drake, Thomas Burnley, Robert Brigge, Robert Mitchell, Edward Boardman *essoined*, Robert Johnson of Dirtcarre *appeared*, Richard Oxley of the same *appeared*, Francis Stockes, Gervase Norton of Newmilnedamme, Thomas Wright of Milnethorpe, Brice Norton and Richard Johnson of Paynethorpe *appeared* owe suit for their free tenements every three weeks by ancient custom and are admitted to fine for release until the next Great Court, viz. Michaelmas, unless their presence is necessary meantime.

Inquisition on the oaths of Gervase Hatfeild gen, Samuel Byns, Richard Kent, Christopher Haldisworth, Richard Johnson, Gervase Norton, Robert Johnson, William Gill, Robert Bargh, Thomas Langfeild, Samuel Thornes, George Firth, Godfrey Mathewman, John Moorehouse, John Wadisworth, Thomas Hanson and Richard Tayler: who testify that William Savile bt *5s*, Arthur Pilkington bt *5s*, John Savile esq *3s 4d*, Thomas Beaumont esq *3s 4d*, the heirs of Mathew Wentworth esq *3s 4d*, John Armitage *3s 4d*, Henry Grice esq *3s 4d*, *Thomas Thornhill esq*, John Farrer esq *3s 4d*, William Savile esq *3s 4d*, the heirs of William Ramsden esq *3s 4d*, John Copley esq *3s 4d*, Edward Lowden gen *2s*, Cotton Horne gen *2s*, Ralph Arthington gen *2s*, Edward Goodwyn gen *2s*, the heirs of John Hanson *6d*, Henry Barraby *6d*, Thomas Pymont *6d*, John Wibsey *6d*, Thomas Crosland *6d*, Robert Preistley *6d*, Michael Foxcrofte

6d, Nathaniel Chadwicke *6d*, Jonas Byns gen *6d*, James Foxcrofte *6d*, John Drake *6d*, Thomas Burnley *6d*, Robert Brigge *6d*, Robert Mitchell *6d*, Francis Stocks *6d*, Gervase Norton of Newmilnedamme *6d*, Thomas Wright of Milnethorpe *6d* and Brice Norton *6d* owe suit and neither appeared nor essoined and are fined as noted.

Sandall: Presentment that Francis Leake of Thorncliffe yeoman and Margaret his wife by an indenture of 10 January last leased to William Copley of Skelmonthorpe, husbandman, 2 acres of land and 2½ acres arable and meadow with their houses, buildings, barns, orchards, gardens, folds, 'backsides', easements etc in Criggleston in the graveship of Sandall and now in the several occupation of Thomas Leake and John Wade or their assigns at a lord's rent of 18d and certain fine for the term of 21 years, without the prior licence of the court. Order to the grave of Sandall to seize the land into the lord's hand before the next court.

Hipperholme: Certificate by the grave of Hipperholme of his seizure into the lord's hand of half a rood and buildings thereon with 4 acres 3 roods land and meadow by Sinderhills in the graveship of Hipperholme, now occupied by Judith Pannell or her assigns at a lord's rent of 19½d and certain fine, this being the first proclamation.

Horbury: Second proclamation regarding a house called a kilnehouse with garden adjoining of 80 feet with a way encroaching on the lord's waste in Horbury near the mill lately occupied by Robert Kay or his assigns.

[Additional, item in draft only viz., *leave to Thomas Grice to fine for 3 closes etc in the graveship of Ossett*]

Holme (*48*) Testimony by Edward Batty, lord's tenant, that John Moorehouse on 10 February 14 Charles [1639] surrendered a messuage occupied by Richard Berry, a garden and a close called Little Newhey, a barn adjacent to the house where James Tayler lived, half a barn in les Modwoods, half le ynge and half les Leyes as lately divided, held in Overthwonge and Cartworth in the graveship of Holme by Richard Berry at a lord's rent of 12½d and certain fine: to the use of the said Richard Berry, to run from 2 February last past before the date of the surrender for the term of 17 years at an annual rent of £4 6s 6d payable to John Moorehouse and Dinah his wife at Whitsun and Martinmas. Agreed: entry fine of 18¾d.

Holme (*49*) Testimony by Edward Batty, lord's tenant, that John Moorehouse on 10 February 14 Charles, 1638/9 surrendered a house at Overbrigge occupied by James Tayler, with a garden, half a barn in les Modwoods, half le ynge, and half les Leyes with the wood and a little close at the west end of the same, [mem 8] lately divided from the other half in Overthwonge and Cartworth in the graveship of Holme and held by the said James Tayler at a lord's rent of 12d and certain fine; to the use of the said James Tayler from 2 February

last past to the date of the surrender for 17 years at an annual rent to John Moorehouse and Dinah his wife of £3 2s 6d payable at Whitsun and Martinmas. Agreed: entry fine of 18d.
Holme (*50*) Joshua Castell and Thomas Roberts by Edward Batty, lord's tenant and sworn, surrendered a house called Newhouse in Cartworth in the graveship of Holme at a lord's rent of ½d, and a close called Lathcrofte with the buildings thereon at a lord's rent of 3d and certain fine: to the use of William Brodehead and Mary his wife. Agreed: entry fine of 10½d.
Holme (*51*) Testimony by Edward Batty, lord's tenant, that Abraham Moorehouse and Susan his wife, she agreeing separately, on 24 November 14 Charles, 1638 surrendered certain land called Five acres abutting water on the north and a close called Watteringfeild on the south, with all wood, scrub, ways, watercourses etc at Wadeplace in the township of Cartworth in the graveship of Holme, occupied by John Charlesworth and Arthur Beardsell or their assigns at a lord's rent of 12d and no certain fine: for the use of the said John Charlesworth and Arthur Beardsell, viz. half to each, on condition that the surrender becomes void if Abraham Moorehouse, his heirs etc pay John Charlesworth, his heirs etc £18 on 2 February 1659/60 at or in the south porch of Holmefirth Chapel between 10 a.m. and 2 p.m. and a similar sum of £18 to Arthur Beardsell, his heirs etc at the same place and times. If default be made in either payment, then the surrender becomes absolute to the use of John Charlesworth and Arthur Beardsell etc. Agreed: entry fine of 3s.
Holme (*52*) Ambrose Hinchcliffe of Mosse edge and Jane his wife, she agreeing separately, by Francis Mathewman, lord's tenant and sworn, surrendered a new house where Ambrose and his wife now live, a fold associated, a backside adjacent, a maltkiln and sufficient access, a garden to the south of a croft called Bentcrofte to the south of le Tentercrofte adjacent to the said Bentcrofte and the lower part of a wood called Mossedgewood with all ways etc at Mosse edge in Cartworth in the graveship of Holme, now occupied by the same at a lord's rent of 6d and certain fine: to the absolute use of David Charlesworth, his heirs etc. Agreed: entry fine of 18d. *Compounded for by Richard Hinchcliffe*
Holme (*53*) Godfrey Cuttell junior by Francis Mathewman, lord's tenant and sworn, surrendered a parcel of land called Jacklanefoote with the buildings thereon in Cartworth now made into 2 little closes, and another little close or 'pingle' adjacent to Intackhead in Woldale in the graveship of Holme, now occupied by Michael Wood or his assigns at a lord's rent of 1d and certain fine: to the absolute use of Thomas Littlewood of Dammehouse, his heirs etc. Agreed: entry fine of 3d. *Compounded for by John Byns and Elizabeth his wife*
Holme (*54*) John Byns of Bankend, clerk, by Francis Mathewman,

lord's tenant and sworn, surrendered an annuity of £5 payable at Martinmas and Whitsun from half a messuage called Wadeplace and from half of 28 acres land, meadow and pasture in Cartworth in the graveship of Holme, now occupied by Arthur Beardsell or his assigns at a lord's rent of 7s and certain fine: to the use of Elizabeth Byns and her assigns for life, with immediate right to distrain in case of default. Agreed: entry fine of 8s 4d.

Holme (*55*) Testimony by Francis Mathewman, lord's tenant, that James Grene alias Roberts on 2 February 1638/9 surrendered that toft in Overthwonge lately inhabited by Luke Swallowe and all houses, barns, gardens, folds, closes and backsides (except the 2 closes called Annottroid and Bynsfeild) at a lord's rent of 2s 2½d [mem 8d] and no certain fine, now occupied by James Batty or his assigns: to the use of the said James Batty, his executors and assigns for the term of 21 years as from the date of the surrender, paying £3 10s a year at Whitsun and Martinmas. Agreed: entry fine — *Fine not compounded*

Sowerby (*56*) Jonathan Mitchell of Ovenden, clothier, by Nathaniel Chadwicke, lord's tenant and sworn, surrendered that messuage and 17 acres ½ rood in Blackwood in the graveship of Sowerby now occupied by Abraham Bothomley or his assigns at a lord's rent of 6s and certain fine: to the use of the said Jonathan Mitchell and his assigns for life and 12 years beyond, with subsequent use to Jonathan Mitchell his son and heir apparent. Agreed: entry fine of 9s paid by Jonathan Mitchell the father, and 9s paid by Jonathan Mitchell the son. *Compounded for by Abraham Brigge*

Horbury (*57*) John Liversedge by William Awdisley, lord's tenant and sworn, surrendered a close of meadow and pasture called Runtynge in the graveship of Horbury at a lord's rent of 8d and certain fine: to the use of Jane Peace, widow, lately wife of Thomas Peace deceased. Agreed: entry fine of 2s.

Ossett (*58*) John Liversedge by William Awdisley, lord's tenant and sworn, surrendered a messuage with all buildings thereon, a croft and garden and 7 roods of land at les Crofte end lately enclosed in the graveship of Ossett at a lord's rent of 6d and certain fine: to the use of Thomas Peace, son and heir of Thomas Peace deceased. Agreed: entry fine of 18d.

Ossett (*59*) William Awdisley of Ossett by William Middlebrooke, lord's tenant and sworn, surrendered a cottage and 'gardenstead' adjoining in the graveship of Ossett, now occupied by George Nayler and John Phillippe of Ossett at a lord's rent of ½d and certain fine: to the use of the said George Nayler of Ossett. Agreed: entry fine of 1½d. *Compounded for by Roberte Finch*

Rastricke (*60*) Appearance of Joshua Brooke of Newhouse gen, son and heir of Thomas Brooke late of the same gen deceased, and paid

– as heriot for 2 messuages in Totehill in the graveship of Rastricke, now occupied by Edmund Fox and Edward Fox or their assigns and all houses etc associated lying in Totehill on the southwest of a lane from Totehill to Bradley yate or Totehillyate, also a close of wood called Dodgewood alias Foxspringe, with ways and passages associated, all at a lord's rent of 7s and certain fine, these and other lands in the graveship of Rastricke being held by Thomas Brooke at his death, together with a twelfth part (it being divided equally into twelve parts) of all the messuages, cottages, houses, buildings, barns, byres, gardens, orchards, tofts, crofts, arable land, meadow, closes, pastures, woods, scrub etc of customary land etc in Rastricke in the graveship of Rastricke with all other commons, commodities, profits, ways, watercourses, etc these twelfth parts coming to John Stanhoppe gen as *nepos*, cousin and third co-heir of Katherine Hanson late of Woodhouse in Rastricke deceased, a fourth co-heiress of John Hanson late of the same deceased. John Stanhoppe previously surrendered and conveyed these to the said Thomas Brooke for his use for life at a lord's rent of 16d and two parts of 2d, two parts of a farthing and a third of a quarter of $\frac{3}{4}$d, representing the rent of a penny (as reasonable part of 18d, for the parcel of lands not yet enclosed) and no certain fine. Agreed.

Wakefeld (*61*) Appearance of Joseph Briggs of Wakefeld, grocer, who gave 12d to fine for the custody of the body of William Preston son of John Preston late of Wakefeld deceased with all the customary lands in the graveship of Wakefeld during his minority, the said Joseph Briggs to make a good and sufficient account to the said William Preston when he attains his legal age.

[A] [Latin] Warrant of Thomas viscount Saville etc to the grave of Hipperholme and his deputy to seize into the lord's hand the half rood with buildings thereon and 4 acres 3 roods of land and meadow by Sinderhills in the graveship of Hipperholme now occupied by Judith Pannell or her assigns at a lord's rent of 19$\frac{1}{2}$d and certain fine and make return at the next court at Wakefeld. Dated 13 March 15 Charles [1640] [signed] J. Midgley

[Endorsed] Aprill 6 1640

This precept was executed by me John Lum Greaue of Hipperholme in the presence of:

Henry Northend/John Lin'/Abraham Sunderland/John Bentley/

[B] Indenture in English dated 10 January 15 Charles [1640] between Francis Leake of Thornecliffe, county York, yeoman, and Margaret his wife, and William Copley of Skelmonthorpe, county York, husbandman, whereby Francis and Margaret 'to thintent to giue a voluntary cause of seisor of the lands and Tenements hereafter mencioned thereby to reduce the same into a perfect estate in Fee simple and to Cutt of remaindors estates intails and all other supposed and surmised titles and rights therein pretended (if any such be) And for diuers other good causes and Consideracions them thereunto moveinge (The said Margarett to be sole confessed and examined by the Steward of the Court of the mannor of Wakefield or his lawfull deputye)' lease to William Copley 2 acres of land $2\frac{1}{2}$ acres arable and meadow, 'with all houses edifices barnes orchards gardens foulds backsides easements and comodityes' associated in Crigleston in the graveship of Sandall now occupied by Thomas Leake and John Wade or their assigns at a lord's rent of 18d and certain fine, to hold by copy of the court roll of Wakefield for the term of 21 years from the date of the indenture, paying to Francis and Margaret Leake a rent of 10s at Whitsun and Martinmas if required.

Sealed etc in the presence of Edward Corsley and others

Francis Leake [seal]

Margaret examined by J. Midgley on 10 January

Margeret Leake [mark] [seal]

Thomas Hanson George Firche
John Morouse [M] Christopher Houldsworth
Richard Tayler
Godfrey Mathewman [M]
John Sandell Francis Mathewman
Gervase Hatfeilds Gervase Norton
Richard Kent [RK] Robert Johnson
William Gill Thomas Langfeild
Richard Johnson Samuel Thornes

The Jury do present and say that the lands above mencioned are demysed contrary to the Custome of the Mannour of Wakefeld and therefore ought to be seised as forfeicted into the lords hands
John Lon
Robert Barghe
John Wadsworth

[C] primo die April Anno regni regis Caroli Anglie etc xv^{to}

Memo. that the day and yeare abouesaid Anthony Charlsworth Godfrey lynley John Yeallott and Francis Mathewman by Thomas morehouse tenant of the lord and sworn have give and surrendred up with a straw into the hands of the lord according to the Custome of the manor of Wakefield and also reuesed releassed and for euer quite claymed vnto James Genn his heires and assigns for euer all that our right title state vse enterest Clayme and demand whatsoeuer which we thaforesaid Anthony Charlsworth Godfrey lynley John Yellot and Francis Mathewman or oar heires have or hereafter might haue of or in our dwelling house in Scoles wherein Agnes Hinchliffe lately dwelt our Closse therevnto adioyning and our other Closse called Broadbutt and twelve dayes work with a plough of our land lyeing and being in the seuerall townefields of Scoles aforesaid with appurtenances in Scoles within the graveshipp of Holme and late in the tenure and occupacion of the said Agnes Hinchliffe deceased and Mathew Berry or their assigns which said premisses are of the yearly rent domino regi of .ij. s. .v. d. and Compounded for: So verely that neither we the said Anthony Charlsworth Godfrey lynley John Yeallott and Francis Mathewman nor our heires nor assigns shall not hereafter make any Clayme title or demand of or into thabouesaid premisses or into any parte or parcell thereof, but from henceforth shalbe vtterly void debarred excluded and shutt out for euer by these presents. given and surrendred the day and yeare abouesaid.

[Straw threaded through]

x° Aprilis 1640

[Latin] *revoked on account of defect*

[D] Panel of jurors

'Wee present for non apparenc

knights	v. s.
Esquires	iij. s. iiij. d.
gentlemen	ij. s.
yeomen men	vj. d.

[Signatures of all jurors except William Gill and Godfrey Mathewman]

[mem 9]

WAKEFIELD: the Court Baron of Gervase Clifton held on 1 May 16 Charles [1640]

Inquisition on the oaths of Francis Mathewman, Robert Cowart, Thomas Metcalfe, Robert Bargh, Robert Clarke, Paul Ramsden, Richard Dawson, Brian Peace, Christopher Brooke, John Swift, John Lindley and Thomas Milner.

Sandall: Certificate of the grave of Sandall of his seisure into the lord's hand of [2 acres land and] 2 acres arable and meadow with all houses etc in Criglestone in the graveship of Sandall now occupied by Thomas Leake and John Wade or their assigns at a lord's rent of 18d and certain fine, as ordered at the previous court. This is the first proclamation.

Hipperholme: Second proclamation for claims to hold half a rood and buildings with 4 acres and 3 roods of land and meadow by Sinderhills in the graveship of Hipperholme, occupied by Judith Pannell or her assigns at a lord's rent of 19½d and certain fine.

Horbury: Third proclamation for claims to hold the house called a Kilnehouse with a garden of 80 feet encroached on the lord's waste in Horbury near the mill, lately occupied by Robert Kay or his assigns.

Sandall (*62*) John Robinson, son and heir of William Robinson of Rile, by William Thornes, lord's tenant and sworn, surrendered to the lord and quit claimed to James Elam of Dawgreene all rights in 6½ acres arable, meadow and pasture with all buildings thereon at Dawgreene in the parish of Great Sandall in the graveship of Great Sandall, now occupied by the said James Elam or his assigns at a lord's rent of 2s 2d (being part of 15s 4½d) and certain fine: to the use of the said James Elam. Agreed: 6d paid for enrolment of the quitclaim. *Compounded for by Robert Carter*

Sandall (*63*) Thomas Beaumont of Whitley hall, Gregory Armitage of Nethershitlington and Henry Grice of Milnethorpe in the township of Great Sandall, county York, esquires, by Thomas Pollard, lord's tenant and sworn, surrendered 3 acres arable and pasture in the graveship of Sandall associated with a cottage in Milnethorpe now occupied by Richard Shillitoe or his assigns, of which one acre lies in le Castle feild, one in le South hill feild, and one in le Woodthorpefeild, with all paths, watercourses etc at a lord's rent of 12d and certain fine: to the use of Francis Nevile of Cheete esq. Agreed: entry fine of 3s.

Sandall (*64*) Thomas Beaumont of Whitley hall, Gregory Armitage of Nethershitlington and Henry Grice of Milnethorpe in the township of Great Sandall, county York, esquires, by Thomas Pollard, lord's tenant and sworn, surrendered 3 acres arable and pasture in Great Sandall, of which one acre is in le South hill feild abutting the land of William Lambert to the north and the land of Ralph Arthington to the south and the highway to the west, and three selions, estimated at one acre, in the same field between the lands of the said Henry Grice to the west and the lands of the heirs of Francis Wood to the east, and 3 selions, containing one acre, lying together in les Lees in Woodthorpefeild, at a lord's rent of 12d and certain fine: to the use of William Lambert of Milnethorpe, yeoman. Agreed: entry fine of 3s.

Sandall (*65*) Henry Grice of Milnethorpe esq by Thomas Pollard, tenant and sworn, surrendered 6 selions of arable, meadow and pasture estimated at 1½ acres lately enclosed by 2 closes lately the land of Francis Wood called les Fowlewells on the north and a baulk (*lira*) on the south, and another selion in the same close estimated at 1 rood in the graveship of Sandall now occupied by the said Henry Grice or his assigns at a lord's rent of 7d and certain fine: to the use of Francis Nevile of Chevett esq. Agreed: entry fine of 21d.

Sandall (*66*) William Lambert of Milnethorpe in Sandall, yeoman, and Elizabeth his wife, she agreeing separately, by Thomas Pollard, lord's tenant and sworn, surrendered a messuage and an estimated 16 acres of land, meadow and pasture sited in Woodthorpe and Milnethorpe in the graveship of Sandall lately occupied by the said William Lambert or his assigns at a lord's rent of 5s 3½d and certain fine: to the use of John Lambert son of the said William Lambert, and Isabella now wife of the said John Lambert, and their assigns for the term of their two lives and the longer liver, with remainder to the use of the legitimate heirs of their bodies, with remainder to the use of the heirs of the said William Lambert. Agreed: entry fine of 7s 11¼d paid by John and Isabella, and another 7s 11¼d paid by John for the remainder.

Sowerby (*67*) Richard Brigge late of Quickstavers in Sowerby and now of Ryton, Lancashire, yeoman, and Martha now his wife, she agreeing separately, by Richard Bentley, lord's tenant and sworn, surrendered that messuage commonly called le Holme and all those closes of land, meadow and pasture commonly called severally le Crofte, le Spowtefeild (previously divided into two parts), le Milnefeild (previously divided into two parts and now into four parts), les Birkes (previously in two parts), le Litlemilnefeild, le Longefeild with Cowgapps and le Moorehey (previously in four parts and now in five) in Sowerby, now severally occupied by John Tilson, Samuel

Hoyle, Daniel Holdisworth and Richard Rawcliffe and their assigns, together with a cottage and close associated, commonly called le [mem 9d] Spowtfeild wood and a lane leading from Ratton Rawe moore to the said messuage called le Holme and thence to a spring called Spowtefeild well in Sowerby now held by Robert Haigh or his assigns, with all houses, buildings, barns, structures, closes, lands, tenements, ways, paths, water, watercourses, woods, scrub etc associated with the same at a lord's rent of 8s 5d and certain fine: to the use of James Robinson of Bowood, yeoman. Agreed: entry fine of 25s 3d. *Compounded for by Richard Wade*

Sowerby (*68*) Richard Fournes of Sowerby, yeoman, by Michael Brigge, lord's tenant and sworn, surrendered that messuage commonly called Booth house and 9 acres estimated appurtenant in Blackwood in the graveship of Sowerby occupied by Isabella Dobson widow or her assigns, also 3½ acres in Blackwood in the graveship of Sowerby now similarly occupied by Isabella Dobson, also 3 acres 1 rood of land, meadow and pasture with buildings in the graveship of Sowerby formerly occupied by John Lomme and Margaret Lomme or their assigns and now by John Wilson or his assigns, and a cottage in Blackwood now occupied by James Crowther or his assigns, all paying a lord's rent of 5s 3d and certain fine: also a messuage commonly called Westfeild, a barn, a garden, a croft, and 4 closes of land, meadow and pasture and 3 acres of land, meadow and pasture commonly called Thorngraves and a close called Overthwart containing an estimated 1 acre in Warley in the graveship of Sowerby now occupied by Thomas Carre or his assigns, also a cottage and 4 other closes of land, meadow and pasture in Warley in the graveship of Sowerby now occupied by Peter Moore or his assigns, also a parcel of land now enclosed containing an estimated 6 yards in length by 14 yards in width with all buildings thereon, previously in the lower part of the close of Thomas Oldfeild of Newland to the north of Harroodwell in Warley in the graveship of Sowerby and now occupied by Samuel Denton or his assigns, all of which land in Warley pays a lord's rent of 3s 3d and certain fine: and a parcel of land used as a lane from the west of the close called Overthwart at a lord's rent of ½d and certain fine: also 2 messuages commonly called Hollings and all houses, buildings, barns, gardens, lands, tenements, closes, pasture, ways, waters, watercourses etc associated, estimated at 20 acres 1 rood in Blackwood in the graveship of Sowerby, now occupied by Richard Wadisworth, John Hopkinson, Joseph Meller and the said Isabella Dobson at a lord's rent of 6s 9d and certain fine: also a messuage and 9 acres 3 roods in estimation in Blackwood in the graveship of Sowerby previously occupied by Richard Brookesbanke deceased and now by Isaac Crowther or his assigns at a lord's rent of 3s 9d and certain fine: also a messuage commonly called Woodlane and all houses etc associated, estimated at 9 acres 3 roods in the graveship of Sowerby lately occupied by Thomas Fournes deceased, and 2 cottages beside the said messuage called Woodlane in the graveship of Sowerby, now severally occupied by Daniel Culpon and Stephen Hoile or their assigns at a lord's rent of 3s 4½d and certain fine: and 6 closes of land, meadow and pasture in the graveship of Sowerby now in 7 closes and all houses and structures thereon, estimated at 3 acres 1 rood, now occupied by James Fawcett or his assigns at a lord's rent of 13d and certain fine: and a fourth part of 3 acres and a half of meadow with the buildings thereon between the land lately of William Oldfeild deceased to the east and the land now of John Crowther to the west and north, now in 2 closes called le ynge in the graveship of Sowerby and occupied by the said Isabella Dobson or her assigns at a lord's rent of 3½d and certain fine: to the use of John Fournes son and heir apparent of the said Richard Fournes. Agreed: entry fine of £3 11s 4½d.

Holme (*69*) William Bray of Hillhouse in Cartworth and Agnes now his wife and Thomas Bray, Agnes agreeing separately, by Francis Mathewman, lord's tenant and sworn, surrendered half a messuage called Hillhouse and all lands etc associated in Cartworth in the graveship of Holme, containing by estimation 11½ acres, (except for a new house in which the said William Bray lives, a garden, half a fold adjacent, and a close called Hillhouse crofte, being a parcel of the said messuage) all of which, saving the exception, pays a lord's rent of 2s 6d and certain fine and now is occupied by the said William Bray or his assigns, with ways, waterways etc: to the absolute use of Anne Harrison of Allhallowse-barkin in county Middlesex, widow, her heirs etc. Agreed: entry fine of 7s 6d. [cf. no. 94]

Horbury (*70*) Francis Nevile of Cheete esq appeared before Thomas viscount Savile etc and took the house called 'a Kilnehouse' with a garden containing 80 feet and a path previously encroached from the lord's waste in Horbury near the mill, lately occupied by Robert Kay or his assigns and seized into the lord's hands after Kay's death as none made fine for the same within the space of three great courts after Kay's death, in accordance with the custom of the manor, as found by enquiry at the court held at Wakefeld on 1 February last, and solemn proclamation was made at three courts held at Wakefeld on different occasions according to custom [mem 10] for claimants, and only Francis Nevile proffered for the same. Entry fine —

[A] [Latin] Warrant of Thomas Savile viscount Savile etc to the grave of Sandall and his deputy to seize into the lord's hand before the next court the 2 acres of land and 2½ acres arable and meadow and

houses etc in Crigleston in the graveship of Sandall now severally occupied by Thomas Leake and John Wade or their assigns at a lord's rent of 18d and certain fine. Dated 10 April 16 Charles [1640] [signed] J. Midgley
[Endorsed] This was executed by me, Josias Ros, bailiff, in the presence of the underwritten: Josias Roo, Gervase Norton, Thomas Pollard, George Allott.

[B] Panel for 1 May 1640
John Sunderland/Thomas Leake/William Harrison/Thomas Ellis/ William Bever/John Morehouse/John Eastwood/

[mem 10]

WAKEFIELD: the Court Baron of Gervase Clifton held on 22 May 16 Charles [1640]

Inquisition taken on the oaths of Francis Mathewman, John Swifte, William Harrison, Thomas Metcalfe, Brian Peace, John Walker, Paul Ramsden, Thomas Milner, Robert Bargh, Richard Dawson, Francis Gill and William Thornes, who testify that (*72*) John Allott late of Bentley deceased held by charter 9 acres in Fulston in the graveship of Holme lately of Robert, late earl of Leicester, and that John Allott is his grandchild and next heir in reversion after the death of Jennett Allott widow of the late John Allott, and he owes in relief 3s, viz. 4d an acre.

Sandall: Second proclamation for claimants for 2 acres with 2 acres of arable and meadow with all houses etc in Crigleston in the graveship of Sandall and now in the several occupation of Thomas Leake and John Wade or their assigns at a lord's rent of 18d and certain fine.

Hipperholme: Third proclamation for claimants for half a rood and the buildings thereon and 4 acres 3 roods of land and meadow by Sinderhills in the graveship of Hipperholme now occupied by Judith Pannell or her assigns at a lord's rent of 19½d and certain fine.

Holme (*73*) Thomas Haigh of Hadfeild in Derbyshire by William Dernilee, lord's tenant and sworn, surrendered a close called Roger Royd and a parcel of land late of the inheritance of John Brodehead of Crosse adjacent, another close called Roger Roydynge and another called Bynnswood with all waterways etc in Overthwonge in the graveship of Holme, now occupied by Andrew Swallowe or his assigns at a lord's rent of 8d and no certain fine: to the use of Nicholas Haigh of Hadfeild his heirs etc after the death of the said Thomas Haigh. Reversion agreed: entry fine — *Fine not compounded*

Holme (*74*) Thomas Haigh of Hadfeild in Derbyshire by William Dernilee, lord's tenant and sworn, surrendered all interest and title in a close of arable called Lathecrofte, another called Rydinge, a house in the same two closes called Pense bothomes, a close called Holme adjoining a fulling mill, a piece of wood and land called Prickmoore banke (now divided into three), another close called Tentercrofte, 2 barns, a little backside adjoining (saving an access way at all times for repair of the fulling mill) and all rents associated in Overthwonge and Cartworth in the graveship of Holme, now occupied by Edward Batty or his assigns at a lord's rent of 2s 6d and certain fine: to the use of Nicholas Haigh of Hadefeild in Derbyshire his heirs etc. Agreed: entry fine of 3s 9d. *Compounded for by Edward Batty, John West and Martyn Allott*

Holme (*75*) Testimony by Francis Mathewman, lord's tenant, that Oliver Robert and Mary Charlesworth, youngest daughter of Godfrey Charlesworth of Mosse edge deceased, on 10 October 1639 surrendered a house, a garden adjoining, a croft called Litlecrofte, a close of arable called Overfeild with all waterways, folds etc in Woldale in the graveship of Holme, now occupied by the same Oliver Robert' and Mathew Berry or their assigns at a lord's rent of 10d and no certain fine: to the use of Godfrey Crosland of Booth house his heirs etc on condition that Oliver Robert', his heirs, executors or administrators pay Godfrey Crosland or his certain attorney etc £60, viz. £10 on 1 January first after the date of this surrender and annually for five years thereafter until the £60 be repaid. The money is to be repaid at the dwellinghouse of the said Godfrey Crosland at Booth house, county York, and should there be any default of payment the surrender stays valid in favour of Godfrey Crosland without any provision, condition or 'mortgage'. Agreed: entry fine of — *Fine not compounded*

Hipperholme (*76*) Henry Moore of Northowrome yeoman and Anne now his wife, she agreeing separately, by Thomas Crosley, lord's tenant and sworn, surrendered a messuage and an estimated 11 acres of land, meadow and pasture at Shugden head in Northowrome, now occupied by the said Henry Moore or his assigns at a lord's rent of 3s 8d and certain fine: to the use of Henry Cockcrofte of Mayroid yeoman and his assigns for the natural life of the said Henry Moore and Anne now his wife and the longer liver. Agreed: entry fine of 5s 6d. [mem 10d]

Hipperholme (*77*) John Lister of Overbrea yeoman and Phebe now his wife, she agreeing separately, by Joseph Lister, lord's tenant and sworn, surrendered a parcel of land estimated at 1½ roods with the buildings thereon commonly called le Hough in Northowrome in the graveship of Hipperholme, now occupied by the said John Lister or his assigns at a lord's rent of 1½d and certain fine: to the use of John Lomme of Westercrofte in Northowrome yeoman. Agreed: entry fine of 4½d. *Compounded for by Robert Hemingway of Overbrea*

Hipperholme (*78*) John Whitley of Rookes in Hipperholme appeared before Thomas viscount Savile and took half a rood and the buildings thereon with 4 acres 3 roods of land and meadow by Sinderhills in the graveship of Hipperholme, now occupied by Judith Pannell or her assigns at a lord's rent of 19½d and certain fine, which was lately seized into the lord's hand because John Whitley by an indenture of 10 March last leased it to Nathan Drake of Godley in

Northowrome, yeoman, for 21 years without fining with the lord, in his contempt and contrary to the custom of the manor as found at Wakefeld court on 13 March when the offence was presented. Proclamation was made at three separate courts for claimants, and only Whitley proffered. Approved at the ancient rent: entry fine of 4s. 10½d.

—— (*79*) Richard Spurre appeared and paid 6d for licence to view by six customary tenants whether the hedge was in the customary place, and where it should be, between the lands of the said Richard Spurre and John Stead called Streetehaggs in the graveship of Ossett. An enquiry by Christopher Awdisley, Francis Gill, William Thornes, Robert Bargh, Richard Fearnley and Christopher Brooke testified 'Wee whose names are abovewritten being chosen to view accordinge to this warrant did find John Steads hedge and his ditch to be too nigh Richard Spurrs ground for in some places from the place where wee thinke the hedge ought to be there is a yard and a halfe with his hedge and his ditch which we thinke too much to be allowed.
Fine for having six tenants, 6d

Holme (*80*) Mary Milnes, daughter of Abraham Milnes deceased, by Godfrey Cuttell, lord's tenant and sworn, surrendered and remitted to William Matson of Holmefirth his heirs etc all interest etc in a close of land and meadow called Childynge in Scoles in the graveship of Holme now occupied by the said William Matson or his assigns at a lord's rent of 4d and certain fine. Agreed: fine for quit claim, 6d.

Holme (*81*) William Matson of Holmefirth appeared before Thomas viscount Savile etc, and with the assent of Mary Milnes, daughter of Abraham Milnes deceased took a parcel of land estimated at 9¼ yards by 6¼ yards and a new house thereon by Holmefirth Chappell, with a close of land and meadow called Childynge estimated at 1 acre in Woldale in the graveship of Holme, lately occupied by John Milnes or his assigns at a lord's rent of 4d and certain fine, which was lately seized into the lord's hand because John Milnes who lately held by copy of the court roll according to the custom of the manor of Wakefeld died and no one made fine for the same within the space of three courts. After it was presented on 1 November only William Matson proffered. Agreed at the ancient rent: entry fine of 12d.

[A] These are to charge and commaund you that you give warninge vnto six Copyholders within your graveshippe and that they do view whether the hedge be made in the accustomed place and where it ought to be betwixt the lands of Richard Spurr and John Stead called Streetehaggs within your graveshippe and that you together with the same Copyholders be at the next Court to be holden at

Wakefeld then and there to certify the Court how and in what manner the same ought to be made whereof faile you not at your perill. given at Wakefeld this first day of May 1640.

To the grave of Ossett his deputy [signed] J. Midgley
and deputyes

[Endorsed] Christopher Audisley, Francis Gill, William Thornes, Roberte Bargh, Richard Fearnley and Christopher Brooke sworn

We whose names are above written [as engrossed]

[Signed]

[B] Panel for 22 May

[mem 10 d]

WAKEFIELD: the Court Baron of Gervase Clifton held on 12 June 16 Charles [1640]

Inquisition on the oaths of Thomas Metcalfe, Robert Bargh, Paul Ramsden, Francis Gill, William Thornes, Richard Dawson, Thomas Milner, John Forrest, John Wade, William Matson, Humphrey Crosland and Robert Whitacres.

Sandall: Third proclamation for claimants for the 2 acres and 2 acres of arable and meadow with all houses etc in Crigleston in the graveship of Sandall now occupied severally by Thomas Leake and John Wade or their assigns at a lord's rent of 18d and certain fine. [mem 11]

Sowerby (*82*) Edward Sutcliffe of Sowerby, county York, yeoman, and Saba now his wife, she agreeing separately, by Jonas Haldisworth, lord's tenant and sworn, surrendered a close of meadow called Littleynge estimated at 2 roods 28 perches at the lower end of a close called Hey estimated at 2 roods 22 perches as measured from the rest of the close, also ½ acre 1 rood 32½ perches of larger measure, as delimited by the metes and bounds on the south of a close called Greatynge in Warley in the graveship of Sowerby, now occupied by William Wade or his assigns, also ½ acre 1 rood 32½ perches by the larger measure at the lower end of the close called Rough hey in Warley in the said graveship, now occupied by Thomas Hartley or his assigns at a lord's rent of 13d, being parcel of half of 31 acres of land, meadow and pasture with buildings etc in Warley paying a lord's rent of 3s 5½d and certain fine: to the use of Daniel Grenewood of Halifax, yeoman. Agreed: entry fine of 3s 3d. *Compounded for by Samuell Haldisworth*

Sowerby (*83*) Richard Tattersall of Warley, yeoman, and Tabitha now his wife, she agreeing separately, by Jonathan Gawkroger, lord's tenant and sworn, surrendered a barn standing at le Waterhill in Warley and all easements, and a garden beside the same, now occupied by the said Jonathan Gawkroger or his assigns at a lord's rent of 2d and certain fine: to the use of Edward Sharples of Warley. Agreed: entry fine of 6d. *Compounded for by Jehocanan Mawde*

Sowerby (*84*) Edward Mawde late of Warley and now of Westbretton in Yorkshire, clothier, and Susan now his wife, she agreeing separately, by Jonas Haldisworth, lord's tenant and sworn, surrendered 6½ roods with buildings in Warley in the graveship of

Sowerby lately occupied by Robert Mitchell or his assigns and now by Robert Fearnley, Agnes Nicholson and Susan Chadwicke or their assigns or subtenants at a lord's rent of 6½d and certain fine: to the use of John Ryall of Halifax, yeoman. Agreed: entry fine of 19½d.
Compounded for by Edward Mawde
Hipperholme (*85*) John Bairstowe of Barlebyebanke in the parish of Hembrough, county York, gen and Jane now his wife, she agreeing separately, by Jonas Holdisworth, lord's tenant and sworn, surrendered a messuage called Northbrigge and 1 rood associated in Northowrome in the graveship of Hipperholme, another messuage in Hayleybanke in Northowrome and 2½ acres of land, pasture and wood, lately of Henry Batt gen, John Batt his son and John Haldisworth of Blackhill, and 6 selions of land and pasture lying in a close called Hartroid in Northowrome in the same graveship (one close now occupied by John Hodgson called Ellingroydynge at a rent of – always excepted) the foregoing being at a lord's rent of 10d and certain fine and now in the occupation of Michael Driver, Michael Freare, Samuel Smith, Anthony Browne, Samuel Bairstowe and Henry Radcliffe or their assigns: to the use of Michael Ramsden of Stoneroid in Southowrome, William Benson of Eland and John Whittell of the same, son of William Whittell of Eland, yeoman. Agreed: entry fine of 2s 6d.

[A] Panel of jurors for 12 June [name of Thomas Metcalfe lifted to top of list from 9th place]

[mem 11]

WAKEFIELD: the Court Baron of Gervase Clifton held on 3 July 16 Charles [1640]

Inquisition taken on the oaths of Joseph Armitage, Peter Andrewe, Thomas Ellis, John Walker, Francis Gill, John Haigh, Richard Dawson, Robert Awdisley, William Collett, Christopher Brooke, William North and Joseph Denton, who present that Francis Tindall gentleman, who lately held that parcel of land at Newton estimated at 44 yards by 14 yards with all houses etc in the graveship of Alverthorpe now occupied by John Richardson or his assigns at a lord's rent of ½d and certain fine forfeited this to the lord and it should be seized. Order for the same to the grave of Alverthorpe.

Sowerby (86) Richard Denton of Warley, county York, clothier, by Thomas Oldfeild, lord's tenant and sworn, surrendered those messuages, gardens etc in Warley in the graveship of Sowerby now severally occupied by Robert Craven, Richard Shawe, Henry Howker, Ambrose Grenewood, Jane Earnshawe and the executors or assigns of William Craven at a lord's rent of 1d and certain fine: to the use of Abraham Wade of Warley, clothier. Agreed: entry fine of 3d. *Compounded for by Richard Denton* [mem 11d]

Sowerby (87) James Kinge of Bairstow in Skircote by Thomas Oldfeild, lord's tenant and sworn, surrendered that messuage called le Cawsey and all houses etc associated estimated at 3 acres ½ rood in Warley in the graveship of Sowerby now occupied by the said James Kinge and Daniel Gawkroger and Martha Hopkinson widow and their assigns or subtenants at a lord's rent of 18d, and a close of land and meadow called Mawdeholme estimated at 1½ acres in the graveship of Sowerby now also occupied by the said James Kinge or his assigns at a lord's rent of 6d and certain fine: to the use of John Kinge of Skircote son of Henry Kinge deceased immediately after the death of the said James Kinge and for 12 years following in accordance with an indenture made between the said James Kinge and John Kinge, on condition that if James Kinge pay John Kinge 6d before two or more honest witnesses the surrender becomes null. Agreed: entry fine of 3s. *Compounded for by Samuel Kinge*

Sowerby (88) Elias Mawde of Warley yeoman and Mary now his wife, she agreeing separately, by John Bentley, lord's tenant and sworn, surrendered half a cottage called les Yatestoopes with barns etc and a garden in Warley in the graveship of Sowerby now occupied by the said Elias Mawde or his assigns (saving half of 5 closes of land, meadow and pasture estimated at 4 acres appurtenant to the cottage in Warley in the graveship of Sowerby now occupied by the said Elias Mawde or his assigns, and half of all paths, watercourses, commons etc), at a lord's rent of 6d and certain fine: to the use of Martha Northend, younger daughter of Michael Northend late of le Feild in Northowrome deceased. Agreed: entry fine of 18d. *Compounded for by —*

Sowerby (89) Elias Mawde of Warley yeoman and Mary now his wife, she agreeing separately, by John Bentley, lord's tenant and sworn, surrendered half a cottage called Yatestoopes with barns etc and a garden in Warley in the graveship of Sowerby now occupied by the said Elias Mawde or his assigns, and half of 5 closes of land, meadow and pasture estimated at 4 acres and now occupied by the said Elias Mawde or his assigns and half of all ways etc at a lord's rent of 6d and certain fine: to the use of Grace Northend, younger daughter of Michael Northend late of le Feild in Northowrome deceased. Agreed: entry fine of 18d.

Alverthorpe (90) Thomas Nayler and John Nayler sons of Christopher Nayler gen deceased and Gilbert Barrett, administrators of the goods and chattels of the same Christopher Nayler, by John Rodes, lord's tenant and sworn, surrendered all interest in a close estimated at 3½ acres now occupied by the said Thomas Nayler, John Nayler and Gilbert Barrett in the graveship of Alverthorpe: to the use of Cotton Horne gen. Agreed: entry fine of —.

Hipperholme (91) Michael Bentley of Siddallhall, yeoman, Michael Bentley of Hipperholme, yeoman, son of the said Michael, and Michael Bentley of Hipperholme his grandchild by Martin Milnes, lord's tenant and sworn, surrendered that messuage in Northowrome commonly called Symercarre now occupied by the said Michael Bentley senior of Hipperholme or his assigns with all houses, tofts, closes, paths, watercourses etc in Northowrome estimated at 4½ acres, and another close of land, meadow, wood and pasture called Symer roid (lately divided into two closes) sited at Aderishgate in Northowrome and now occupied by Michael Bentley senior of Hipperholme or his assigns at a lord's rent of 2s 3d and certain fine: to the use of Elias Mawde of Warley clothier on condition that if Elias Mawde, his heirs etc do not fulfil or pay to the said Michael Bentley senior of Hipperholme, his attorney etc the sum of £105 on 2 February coming after 25 April last past in the south porch of Halifax parish church the surrender is void. Agreed: entry fine of 3s 4½d. *Compounded for by Michael Bentley* [mem 12]

Holme (92) Appearance by Godfrey Roberts, brother and next heir of Dorothy Roberts late of Longley deceased, who gave 1½d as fine for the heriot of a little parcel of land with a cottage thereon estimated at 6½ yards by 4 yards in Woldale in the graveship of Holme at a lord's rent of ½d and certain fine. Agreed.

Holme (*93*) John Allott of Bentley, son and heir of George Allott late of the same deceased, by Thomas Ellis, lord's tenant and sworn, surrendered all that messuage called Butterley and all houses, closes, woods, commons etc estimated at 50 acres ¼ rood held by copy in the graveship of Holme and now occupied by William Rowley of Butterley or his assigns at a lord's rent of 19s 6¼d and certain fine: to the use of the said William Rowley and his assigns as from the death of Jennett Allott widow, late wife of John Allott late of Bentley deceased, for the term of 21 years at an annual rent to John Allott son of George, his heirs etc of £10 at Whitsun and Martinmas, together with 'one yane of shearers' (*tres tonsores*) in harvest for one day, 'one gallon of honey' (*unum brocum mellis*) at Michaelmas [29 September], two capons and 14 cockerels on 24 June if required, together with certain lands leased to the said William Rowley by the said John Allott by an indenture of the present date, Allott having the right to distrain for arrears after 30 days of default. The surrender becomes void if the land or any part of it be occupied other than by the said William Rowley, his wife or children. Agreed: entry fine of 29s 3¼d and half a farthing. *Compounded for by John Allott deceased*

Holme (*94*) Anne Harrison of Allhallowes-barkin, Middlesex, widow, by Francis Mathewman, lord's tenant and sworn, surrendered half a messuage called Hillhouse and all lands etc in Cartworth in the graveship of Holme estimated at 11½ acres (except a new house now occupied by William Bray, a garden, half an adjoining fold and a close of land called Hillhouse crofte) at a lord's rent of 2s 6d and certain fine and now occupied by William Bray or his assigns: to the use of William Bray, Agnes his wife, and their heirs, paying to Anne Harrison widow her heirs etc an annual rent of £5 at Martinmas and Whitsun or within 20 days, with her right to re-enter if the rent is in arrears, when the surrender becomes void. Agreed: entry fine of 7s. 6d. *Compounded for by* — [cf. no. 69]

Holme (*95*) Robert Beever and Sara now his wife, she agreeing separately before John Midgley gen, deputy steward, surrendered out of court and quitclaimed to Gabriel Blakey who is now in seisin all title in that parcel of land called Shough (now divided by a wall into two) sited at Fosterplace in Hepworth in the graveship of Holme and now occupied by Christopher Kay and Godfrey Jackson or their assigns at a lord's rent of 6d and certain fine. Agreed: fine of 6d for enrolment. *Compounded for by Samuel Bever*

[A] We lay in paine that no person shall put in any more Cattell into Woldale Feilde then his right in peine of xxxix. s.

[signed]	Robert Awdsley	Joseph Armitage
	Francis Gill	William North

[B] Panel of jurors for 3 July 1640

George Lee	(2)	cancelled	Thomas Ellis	(5)	added	
Thomas Leake	(4)	,,	John Haigh	(8)	,,	
Richard Fearnley	(7)	,,	Christopher Brooke	(11)	,,	
Christopher Smith	(12)	,,	John Forrest	(12)	,,	& cancelled
			Joseph Denton	(13)	,,	

[mem 12 d]

WAKEFIELD: the Court Baron of Gervase Clifton held on 24 July 16 Charles [1640]

Inquisition by Richard Birkhead, Robert Coward, Brian Peace, John Ibbotson, Robert Bargh, Francis Gill, Paul Ramsden, William Thornes, Christopher Brooke, Edward Pickard, Richard Wormall and Brian Tayler, who present that Henry Northend of Quarlers in Northowrome yeoman and Samuel Northend his son and heir apparent by indenture of 21 July last leased to one John Lomme of Westercrofte in Northowrome, yeoman, all that close of land, meadow and pasture commonly called Landymer estimated at 2 acres (divided now into two parts) at a lord's rent of 9½d and a parcel of land lying to the west side of the same and now enclosed in the same, lately of the inheritance of Richard Batt gen at a lord's rent of ¼d in Northowrome, now occupied by the said Henry Northend or his assigns, and all that messuage and a garden in Northowrome now occupied by the said Henry Northend or assigns, also all that croft adjoining the said messuage estimated at ½ acre, a close called les Leyes estimated at one acre and two other closes of land, meadow and pasture called Nethercrofte and Midlefeild estimated at 3 acres in Northowrome in the graveship of Hipperholme now occupied by the said Henry Northend or his assigns at a lord's rent of 2s and certain fine for a term of 21 years. As no fine was made to the lord nor licence obtained from the court, an order was made for the seizure of the same by the grave of Hipperholme.
Alverthorpe: Certificate by the grave of Alverthorpe of his seizure of a parcel of land at Newton estimated at 44 yards by 14 yards with houses etc in the graveship of Alverthorpe now occupied by John Richardson at a lord's rent of ½d and certain fine, this being the first proclamation.
Sandall (96) John Sprigonell of Paynthrope and John Sprigonell his son by Thomas Norton of Chappellthorpe, lord's tenant and sworn, surrendered a close of land and pasture lately divided into several closes commonly called Emmottrodes with all buildings estimated at 12 acres in the graveship of Sandall lately of the inheritance of Luke Sprigonell deceased at a lord's rent of 4s and certain fine and now occupied by William Whitehead, clerk, or his assigns: to the use of Francis Sprigonell of Paynethorpe, son and heir apparent of the said John Sprigonell the father. Agreed: entry fine of 12s. *Compounded for by John Sprigonell* [cf. no. 100]
Alverthorpe (97) John Lewes son and heir of Christopher Lewes by

Paul Ramsden, lord's tenant and sworn, surrendered a parcel of land of 11 yards by 17 yards with all buildings thereon in the graveship of Alverthorpe at a lord's rent of 1½d now occupied by the said John Lewes at certain fine: to the use of the said John Lewes and Agnes Howle, daughter of Robert Howle of Wakefeld (whom he soon intends to be his wife) during their two lives and the longer liver and their procreated heirs, with reversion to the heirs of the said John Lewes. Agreed: entry fine of 4½d. *Compounded for by Robert Killingbecke*

Horbury (98) Testimony on the oath of William Middlebrooke, lord's tenant, that Francis Gill of Ossett and Anne his wife, she agreeing separately, on 12 June 16 Charles, 1640, surrendered that close of meadow and pasture in the graveship of Horbury now occupied by one Cockin Tonge or his assigns at a lord's rent of 12d and certain fine: to the use of Cockin Tonge from 25 March last past for 12 years paying annually to Francis Gill 37s 4d at the Annunciation [25 March] and Michaelmas [29 September], with the right to distrain for arrears after 14 days. Agreed: entry fine of 18d.

Alverthorpe (99) Christopher Naylor esq by Joseph Waterhouse, lord's tenant and sworn, surrendered a close called Clayton close in the graveship of Alverthorpe and abutting on Westgatemoore between the close called le Eleinge on the west and the close called Troughsteele close on the east, with 3 selions at le Toppe of the said close called Clayton close in the close called les Fourelands in the graveship of Alverthorpe: to the use of Cotton Horne of Wakefeild gen. Agreed. *Fine* —

[A] Panel of jurors for 24 July

[B] Wee lay in payne that no person shall put in any more Cattell into Wooledale feild then his right in payne of xxxix. s

We find that James and Josua Robarts haue put into Woodalefeild bye the consent of Richard Robarts their father one Cow contrary to this payne

George Roberts

[endorsed] Richard Birkhead/Paule Ramsden/William Thornes/
Richard Wormall/Francis Gill/

[C] This Indenture made the One and twentith day of July in the Sixtienth yeare of the Raigne of our sovereigne Lord Charles by the Grace of God Kinge of England Scotland Fraunce and Ireland Defender of the faith etc Betwene Henry Northend of Quarlers in Northowrome in the County of Yorke yeoman and Samuel Northend sonne and heire apparant of the said Henry of thone party And John Lomme of Westercrofte in Northowrome aforesaid in the said County yeoman of thother party Witnesseth that the said Henry

Northend and Samuel Northend to thintent to give a voluntary cause of seisour of the lands and tenements hereinafter mencioned thereby to reduce the same into a perfect estate in Fee simple and to cutt of all Remanders and estates intayle for this end and purpose that the same may be regaunted (sic) from the Lord in manner and forme followinge (that is to say) the Close called Landymer hereinafter mencioned and the parcell of land now inclosed in the same vnto Thomas Lister of Shibdenhall gent. and his heirs and assignes for ever In consideration of the somme of Fifty five pounds of lawfull money of England by him in hand paid to the said Henry Northend and Samuell Northend or to thone of them And that the Messuage and tenement and all the residue of the Closes lands and tenements herein after mencioned to the said Henry Northend and his heires for and dureinge the tearme of his naturall life and from and ymmediately after his deceasse then to the same Samuel Northend and his assignes for and dureinge the tearme of his naturall life and from and ymmediately after the deceasse of the longer liver of them the said Henry Northend and Samuel Northend then to the first sonne of the body of the said Samuel Northend lawfully to be begotten and the heirs of the body of the same first sonne lawfully to be begotten and for default of such issue to the second sonne of the said Samuel Northend lawfully to be begotten and to the heires of the body of the same second sonne lawfully to be begotten And for default of such issue to euery other sonne and sonnes for the tyme beinge of the body of the said Samuel Northend lawfully begotten and to be begotten seuerally and successively and to the seuerall and successive heirs males of the body of euery such seuerall sonne and sonnes lawfully begotten and to be begotten the elder of such sonne and sonnes of the body of the said Samuel Northend lawfull to be begotten and hereafter to be borne for the tyme beinge and theirs males of his body beinge euer preferred before the younger and theirs males of his body And for default of such issue then to all and euery the daughter and daughters of the body of the said Samuel Northend lawfully to be begotten and to theirs and assignes of the same daughter and daughters for euer and for default of such issue to thuse of Nathan Northend and theirs of his body and for default of such issue To thuse of David Northend and of his heirs and assignes for euer and for diuers other good causes and consideracions them therevnto moveinge Have demised graunted leassed and to farme letten and by this Indenture for and from them their heirs and assignes do deuise graunt leasse and to farme lett vnto the said John Lomme All that one close of land meadowe and pasture Commonly called Landymer conteyning by estimacion two acres now divided into two closes or parts beinge of the yearly rent to the Lord of Nine pence ob. And also all that one parcell of land heretofore lyinge on the west side of the said Close called Landymer and now inclosed in the same close beinge late thinheritance of Richard Batt gent. and of the yearly rent to the Lord of one q[a] with all their appertenances lyinge and beinge in Northowrome aforesaid and now in the tenure and occupacion of the said Henry Northend or his assignes And also all that one Messuage or Tenement and one garden to the same belonginge with thappertenances in Northowrome aforesaid and now in the tenure or occupacion of the said Henry Northend or his assignes And also all that one Crofte of land adioyninge to the said Messuage conteyninge by estimacion halfe an acre One close of land called the Leyes conteyninge by estimacion one acre and two other closes of land meadowe and pasture Called Nethercrofte and Midlefeild conteyninge by estimacion three acres with all their appertenances lyinge and beinge Nothowrome [sic] within the Graveshippe of Hipperholme now in the tenure or occupacion of the said Henry Northend or his assignes beinge of the yearly rent to the Lord of Two shillings and for all which premisses Composicion is made for the certeynty of the fynes thereof To Have and to hould the said Messuage or tenement closes and parcell of land lands tenements and hereditaments and all and singuler of the premisses before by these presents mencioned to be demised with all their appertenances vnto the said John Lomme his heirs and assignes from the date and makeinge hereof for dureinge and vntill the full end and tearme of Twenty one years from thence next followinge and fully to be complete and ended Yeildinge and payinge therefore yearly and euery yeare dureinge the said tearme vnto the said Henry Northend and Samuel Northend their heirs or assignes the yearly rent of Five shillings of lawfull money of England at the Feasts of Pentecost and St. Martin the Bishopp in Winter by even porcions (if the same be demaunded). In witnesse whereof the partyes abovenamed to the parts of these Indentures Interchaungably have sett their hands and sealls. Yoven the day and yeare first above expressed.

Sealled signed and delivered in the presence of vs to the hands of Thomas Lister to the use of the abovenamed John Lomme

Henry Northend [seal]
Samuell Northend [seal]

Thomas Lister John Richardson [overwritten] J. Midgley

[Endorsed] Wee of the Jury do find that the lands within mencioned are demissed contrary to the Custome of the Mannour and therefore ought to be seised as forfeited vnto the Lords hands

[Signed] Richard Birkhead
Paule Ramsden
William Thornes
Richard Wormall
Francis Gill

[D] Warrant in Latin to the grave of Alverthorpe and his deputy to seize into the lord's hand for the court at Wakefeld that parcel of land at Newton estimated at 44 yards by 14 yards with all houses etc in occupation of John Richardson or his assigns at a lord's rent of ½d and certain fine. Given on 3 July 16 Charles [1640]

J. Midgley

[Endorsed with return of performance on 23 July, signed by Christopher Naylor, grave in Alverthorpe]

[mem 13]

WAKEFIELD: the Court Baron of Gervase Clifton held on 14 August 16 Charles [1640]

Inquisition on the oaths of John Swift, Thomas Baynes, Brian Peace, Thomas Milner, Paul Ramsden, Robert Awdisley, John Walker, William Matson, Christopher Brooke, William Thornes, William Harrison and Francis Gill.

Hipperholme Certificate by the grave of Hipperholme of his seizure of a close of land, meadow and pasture called Landymer estimated at 2 acres now divided into 2 closes at a lord's rent of 9½d with that parcel on the west side of the close called Landymer and now enclosed in the same, lately of the inheritance of Richard Batt gen and all annual rents etc in Northowrome now in the occupation of Henry Northend or his assigns, with a messuage and garden in Northowrome now occupied by the said Henry Northend or his assigns, also a croft adjacent to the messuage of ½ acre, a close called les Leyes estimated at 1 acre, 2 other closes called Nethercrofte and Midlefeilde of 3 acres in Northowrome in the graveship of Hipperholme, now occupied by Henry Northend or his assigns at a lord's rent of 2s and certain fine, this being the first proclamation.

Alverthorpe Second proclamation of a parcel of land in Newton of 44 yards by 14 yards with all houses etc in the graveship of Alverthorpe now occupied by John Richardson or his assigns at a lord's rent of ½d and certain fine.

Sandall (*100*) Francis Sprigonell of Paynethorpe in person surrendered a close of land and pasture (lately divided into several closes) commonly called Emmottrodes, with all buildings estimated at 12 acres in the graveship of Sandall lately the customary holding of Luke Sprigonell deceased at a lord's rent of 4s and certain fine, now occupied by William Whitehead, clerk, or his assigns: to the use of Francis Nevile of Chevett esq on condition that if Francis Sprigonell, his heirs etc pay Francis Nevill (sic), his attorney etc £150 at Chevetthall at Whitsun 1651 the surrender will be void. Agreed: entry fine of 12s. [cf. no. 96]

Sowerby (*101*) William Denton of le Slacke in Huddersfeild yeoman and Grace now his wife, she agreeing separately, by Thomas Crosley, lord's tenant and sworn, surrendered 3 closes of land, meadow and wood commonly called Deyneynges and le Wood in Soyland in the graveship of Sowerby estimated at 5 acres, now occupied by

Anthony Byns and Simeon Bates or their assigns at a lord's rent of 20d and certain fine: to the use of John Marsden of le Pule in Marsden, yeoman. Agreed: entry fine of 5s.
Sowerby (*102*) William Horton of Barkinsland gen by Thomas Crosley, lord's tenant and sworn, surrendered the reversion after the death of William of a messuage in Sowerby and all houses . . tofts . . lands estimated at 14 acres in the graveship of Sowerby now occupied by Henry Leigh or his assigns at a lord's rent of 5s. 6d. with the reversion of another messuage called Sheene in Sowerby with all houses . . .watercourses etc estimated at 10 acres in the graveship of Sowerby now occupied by Nicholas Waddington or his assigns at a lord's rent of 3s 9d: also the reversion of 2 other cottages in Sowerby and a garden associated now occupied by Jacob Earnshawe and Robert Walton or his assigns and 2 closes of land, meadow and pasture called les Overthwartes in the township fields of Sowerby, containing by estimation 1 acre, now occupied by Brigett Haigh widow or her assigns at a lord's rent of 4d, parcel of an annual rent of 3s payable by John Hoile for other lands lately acquired from the same by William Horton and covered by an agreement by John Hoile, grandfather of John Hoile, together with the reversion of two messuages and 8 acres of land, meadow and pasture at Goodgreave in the graveship of Sowerby and 3 acres of land meadow and pasture by estimate and all buildings thereon at le Goodgreave head in the graveship of Sowerby now occupied by Joseph Preistley or his assigns, also an annuity of 6s 8d from a parcel of land with buildings by Ribbonden in the graveship of Sowerby and now occupied by John Walkden, clerk, or his assigns and all other lands etc held by copyhold covered by the surrender of the said Joseph Preistley at a lord's rent of 3s 8d: also the reversion after the death of William Horton of a messuage and 2 cottages in Sowerby and all lands, watercourses and hereditaments lately occupied by William Horton through the surrender by Samuel Tattersall at a lord's rent of 2s 2d: and 3 roods with buildings at le Milnebanke in Sowerby lately occupied by Nathan Hoile, Samuel Rayner, Edith Hill and Samuel Leavens or their assigns at a lord's rent of 3d: and 3 roods now occupied by the said Samuel Leavens or his assigns and 3½ acres of land and meadow and buildings commonly called le Steele in the graveship of Sowerby and now occupied by Isaac Bates or his assigns at a lord's rent of 3d: and all are covered by certain fine: to the use of Joshua Horton the youngest (*minimus*) son of the said William Horton and his heirs. Agreed: entry fine of 24s 3½d.
—— (*103*) Appearance of John Batty of Alverthorpe, who paid 12d for licence to have the wardship of Robert Smith son of William Smith late of Seile Cotes deceased and of all his lands in the graveships of Alverthorpe and Wakefeild during his minority. Agreed

on condition that he account to Robert Smith when he reaches his majority.

[A] [Latin] Warrant to the grave of Hipperholme and his deputy for the seizure of the close called Landymer containing by estimation 2 acres and now subdivided into two at a lord's rent of 9½d, with the parcel of land lying on the west of the close called Landymer and now enclosed in the same, lately of Richard Batt gen paying a lord's rent of ¼d in Northowrome in the occupation of Henry Northend or his assigns, with a messuage and garden in Northowrome now occupied by the same, also a croft and land adjoining estimated at ½ acre, and 2 other closes called Nethercrofte and Middlecrofte estimated at 3 acres in Northowrome in the graveship of Hipperholme and now occupied by Henry Northend or his assigns at a lord's rent of 2s and certain fine. Given on 24 July 16 Charles [1640] [signed] J. Midgley [seal]
[Endorsed with execution by John Lum, grave of Hipperholme in the presence of John Lister, John Clay, John Mellin, John Whiteley [mark]]

[B] Panel for 14 August, 1640

[mem 13 d]

WAKEFIELD: the Court Baron of Gervase Clifton held on 4 September 16 Charles [1640]

Inquisition by Francis Mathewman, Brian Peace, Robert Clark, Robert Bargh, Christopher Brooke, Godfrey Morton, Timothy Denison, Thomas Baynes, Peter Moxon, Robert Sharpe, William Lamberte, and John Hirst.

Hipperholme: Second proclamation for claims to a close of land, meadow and pasture called Landymer estimated at 2 acres divided into two at a lord's rent of 9½d, also a parcel of land on the west of the same and now enclosed within it, lately of the inheritance of Richard Batt gen at a lord's rent of ¼d in Northowrome now occupied by Henry Northend or his assigns, also a messuage and a garden in Northowrome now occupied by the said Henry Northend or his assigns, also a croft adjoining estimated at ½ acre, a close called les Leyes estimated at 1 acre, and 2 other closes of land, meadow and pasture called Nethercroft and Midlefeild estimated at 3 acres in Northowrome in the graveship of Hipperholme now occupied by the said Henry Northend or his assigns at a lord's rent of 2s and certain fine.

Alverthorpe: Third proclamation for claims to a parcel of land at Newton estimated at 44 yards by 14 yards with all houses and buildings thereon in the graveship of Alverthorpe now occupied by John Richardson or his assigns at a lord's rent of ½d and certain fine.

Hipperholme (*104*) Whereas Michael Slater late of Hipperholme deceased surrendered in writing at the court leet at Brighouse on 16 October 8 James [1610] by Edward Hanson of Netherwoodhouse, lord's tenant and sworn, a belowmentioned messuage, lands and tenements to the use of John Cowper of Deanehouse and Edward Slater of Woodhouse and their heirs in trust for the said Michael Slater and Michael Slater his son and heir apparent and Jennett Rawnsley, daughter of Robert Rawnsley, the intended wife of Michael Slater junior, for the life of Michael Slater senior and thereafter to Michael Slater junior and the heirs male of him and Jennett Rawnsley, with reversion to the male children of Michael Slater and full reversion to his heirs general, and the trustees were admitted: Edward Slater later died, then John Cowper. Furthermore Michael Slater senior and Michael Slater junior are now dead, the latter having as male issue Michael Slater minimus, also now dead without further male issue. William Cowper is son and heir of the said John Cowper the surviving feoffee, and in settlement of the trust he by Jonas Haldisworth surrenders the messuage with all houses and buildings and 2 acres of land, meadow and pasture in Hipperholme, occupied by Michael Brodeley and Thomas Feilden or their assigns at a lord's rent of 2s [rectius 8d] and certain fine: to the use of Sara Richardson wife of Thomas Richardson, daughter and next heir of the said Michael Slater senior. Agreed: entry fine of 2s.

Rastricke (*105*) Appearance of Samuel Hoile son and heir of Elizabeth Hoile late of Brigroid in Rastricke deceased, late wife of Samuel Hoile late of the same deceased, and fined 5s 0¾d as heriot for a messuage called Brig Royd and all 'houseinge' and buildings associated and 5 closes of land, meadow and pasture now in 6 closes commonly leased therewith in the graveship of Rastricke lately occupied by the deceased Samuel Hoile and by the said Elizabeth Hoile and now by the said Samuel Hoile the son or his assigns, estimated at 6 acres, and all other lands of the late Elizabeth in the same at a lord's rent of 20¼d and certain fine made after the death of Elizabeth, whose son and heir Samuel Hoyle is. Agreed. *Compounded for by Gilbert Hoile*

Holme (*106*) Richard Hirst and Humfrey Hirst by John Hirst, lord's tenant and sworn, surrendered a close of land and meadow called Overbothome with all buildings thereon, another close of land and meadow called Netherbothome now in two closes, and all paths, watercourses, easements etc now occupied by Thomas Charlesworth, with 2 closes called Litlefeild, parcel of a messuage at Overthwonge, lately occupied by Robert Brodhead, and a little house now occupied by James Hirst or his assigns in Austonley and Overthwonge at a lord's rent of 18d and certain fine: to the use of Anne Greene, widow, intended wife of Humfrey Hirst for life as jointure should she survive the said Humfrey. Agreed: entry fine of 2s. 3d.

Wakefeld (*107*) Testimony on oath by John Story gen, lord's tenant, that the Lady Sara Mounson of Horbury, county York, widow, on 2 May last past surrendered a little close at the bottom of le Cliffefeild of Wakefeld, sometime Fleemings and now occupied by Richard Poole or his assigns at a lord's rent of 2d and certain fine: to the use of William Savile, grandchild of the said Sara Mounson and his heirs. Agreed: entry fine of 6d. *Compounded for by John Fleeminge*

[A] The sixteenth day of Martch 1639

Memo that I John Righton of Wakefeild in the County of Yorke yeoman haue surrendred and giuen vpp into the hands of the Lord of the Mannor of Wakefeild by John Story tenant of the Lord and sworne All that my howse in Wakefeild whearein I liue with all the shopps Chambers and sellors to the same belonging One shopp and one Chamber in the occupacon of Symeon Watkinson And one acre of Land Lyeng in the westfeild of Owtchthorp To the vse and behofe of John Righton my sonne and to his heires and assignes for ever. In wittness Wheareof I haue hearevnto put my hand and deliuered the same as abouesaid the day and yeare first aboue written

John Righton

[comment] respited because part is freehold
[Endorsed] John Righton: Surrender

[B] Panel of jurors for 4 September 1640 [the names of John Hirst, George Roberts, Richard Fearndley, Thomas Leake and Thomas Lea deleted]

[mem 14]

WAKEFIELD: the Court Baron of Gervase Clifton held on 25 September 16 Charles [1640]

Inquisition on the oaths of Francis Mathewman, Paul Ramsden, Thomas Metcalfe, Christopher Brooke, Brian Peace, Peter Andrew, Robert Carter, John Walker, Richard Dawson, Robert Bargh, Samuel Byns and Thomas Ellis.

Hipperholme: Third proclamation for claimants to a close of land, meadow and pasture commonly called Landymer estimated at 2 acres now subdivided into two at a lord's rent of 9½d, also a parcel of land on the west of the same and now included in the same, lately of the inheritance of Richard Batt gen at a lord's rent of ¼d in Northowrome, now occupied by Henry Northend or his assigns, also a messuage and garden in Northowrome now similarly occupied, also a croft adjacent estimated at ½ acre, a close called les Leyes estimated at 1 acre, and 2 other closes of land, meadow and pasture called Nethercrofte and Midlefeild estimated at 3 acres in Northowrome in the graveship of Hipperholme, now occupied by the said Henry Northend or his assigns at a lord's rent of 2s and all at certain fine.

Holme (*108*) George Roberts of Woldale by Francis Mathewman, lord's tenant and sworn, surrendered all his doles of arable and meadow in a close or field called Wellcroft and other doles of arable and pasture in the town fields of Woldale consisting of 6 days' work with a plough, viz., one day-work in le Westfeild, another in Midlefeild, one in Northcrofte, one in Kirkroide, one in Oldhouse, one in Wheatcrofte, in Woldale in the graveship of Holme, in whosesoever occupation they may be, reputed to be the seventh part of lands of the said George Roberts, lately bought by him from John Ramsden, knight, at a lord's rent of 10½d and certain fine: all to the absolute use of Thomas Ellis of Woldale. Agreed: entry fine of 2s 7½d. *Compounded for by William Ramsden Esquier*

Holme (*109*) Abraham Bever son and heir of Samuel Bever late of Fosterplace deceased by Francis Mathewman, lord's tenant and sworn, surrendered all the houses, barns and buildings, gardens and folds at Fosterplace now occupied by Godfrey Jackson or his assigns which are parcel of a messuage called Fosterplace in Hepworth in the graveship of Holme at a lord's rent of — and certain fine, with all paths etc: to the absolute use of Gabriel Blakey and his heirs. Agreed: entry fine of 6d. *Compounded for by Samuel Bever*

Sandall (*110*) Francis Stocks of Thornes and Elizabeth his wife, she agreeing separately before John Midgley gen, steward of the court of Wakefeld, surrendered out of court 2½ acres arable in a field of Sandall called le Castle feild in the graveship of Sandall and now occupied by the said Francis Stocks or his assigns at a lord's rent of 10d and certain fine: to the use of Ralph Arthington of Milnethorpe gen. Agreed: entry fine of 2s 6d. *Compounded for by Richard Norton*

Sandall (*111*) Appearance of Thomas Burton junior, son and heir apparent of Thomas Burton senior of Methley and brother and next heir of John Burton, second son of the said Thomas Burton senior deceased, before the steward of the court to pay 13½d. as heriot for the reversion on the death of Robert Wright of Milnethorpe and Mary his wife of 9 selions of arable and pasture in the graveship of Sandall in a place called Shawshutt containing 9 roods and lying between the lands of Thomas Booth on the south and the lands of Robert Johnson junior on the north, now occupied by the said Robert Wright or his assigns at a lord's rent of 9d and certain fine. The reversion is his, following the death of the said John Burton of whom he is brother and next heir. Reversion approved. *Compounded for by Robert Wright*

Hipperholme (*112*) Richard Ramsden of Halifax, county York, yeoman, and Judith now his wife, one of the five sisters and co-heiresses of John Deane late of Blackhillend in Northowrome deceased, she agreeing separately, by John Bentley, lord's tenant and sworn, surrender the fifth part of that messuage called le Auncient old house at Blackhill in Northowrome and all houses and buildings thereon being a barn and threshing floor called le Overbarne of 17 yards with half a fold to the north of the house door with free passage through the other half as necessary, with a fifth of all closes of meadow, wood and pasture below named, viz. le kilne crofte on the north of the barn, another subdivided into two called Sholebrodes, another of arable and pasture called Rye Pighel, another of the same called Overchurlebothome, the north half of a meadow called Crawewoodynge and a third close of land and pasture called les Overblackhillbanks, adjoining the land late of Abraham Wood to the south and of Samuel Haldisworth to the north with all paths, watercourses, commons etc estimated at 10 acres now occupied by the said Richard Ramsden or his assigns with any reversions at a lord's rent of 6d and certain fine: to the use of John Bairstowe of Mixenden in the township of Ovenden. Agreed: entry fine of 18d. *Compounded for by John Haldisworth of Blackhill*

Hipperholme (*113*) Denis Illingworth of Mixenden in the township of Ovenden and Isabel now his wife, one of the five sisters and coheiresses of John Deane late of Blackhillend in Northowrome deceased, younger son of Robert Deane late of Jackroid in Ovenden deceased, Isabel agreeing separately, by Robert Bairstowe of Northowrome, lord's tenant and sworn, surrendered the fifth part of the messuage called le Auncient old house at Blackhill in Northowrome and all houses etc and a part of a barn and area of threshing floor called le Oldbarne 17 yards land and half a fold to the north of the door [mem 14d] with free passage across the other half as necessary, with a fifth of all closes as above: to the use of Prudence Deane of Ovenden, another daughter of the said John Deane deceased. Agreed: entry fine of 18d. *Compounded for by John Haldisworth of Blackhill*

Hipperholme (*114*) Henry Northend of Quarlers in Northowrome yeoman, Samuel Northend his son and heir apparent, and Thomas Lister of Shibdenhall in Southowrome gen appeared before Thomas, viscount Savile, baron Pontefract, chief steward of the manor of Wakefeld, and took of the lord that close of land, meadow and pasture called Landymer of 2 acres, now subdivided into two at a lord's rent of 9½d, also that parcel on the west of the same now enclosed within it lately of the inheritance of Richard Batt gen at a lord's rent of ¼d in Northowrome and now occupied by the said Henry Northend or his assigns, also that messuage and garden in Northowrome now occupied by the said Henry Northend or his assigns, also that croft adjoining the same, estimated at a half acre, a close called les Leyes estimated at 1 acre, and 2 other closes of land, meadow and pasture called Nethercrofte and Midlefeild estimated at 3 acres in Northowrome in the graveship of Hipperholme now occupied by the said Henry Northend or his assigns at a lord's rent of 2s and certain fine, lately seized into the lord's hands because Henry Northend and Samuel Northend by indenture of 21 July last leased the same to John Lomme of Westercrofte in Northowrome yeoman for a term of 21 years without fine with the lord of the manor or the leave of the court in contempt of the lord and against the custom of the manor as shown by an enquiry at Wakefeld on 24 July. There had been public proclamations at three courts and none but Henry Northend, Samuel Northend and Thomas Lister had offered for the same, viz. the close called Landymer and the parcel of land therein enclosed, lately bought with the messuage etc by Thomas Lister from Henry and Samuel Northend as a life interest for Henry Northend with remainder to Samuel Northend for life, then to the eldest son of the same Samuel Northend and his children, with remainder to the second son of the same Samuel Northend and his children and so on, being male heirs, failing which to Samuel's sons and daughters and their heirs, with remainder to Nathan Northend, younger son of the said Henry Northend and his heirs, with remainder to David Northend, another younger son of the same and his heirs and assigns:

excepting the lease of John Mellin of Northowrome of the close called Landymer and its enclosure from Henry Northend, and the lease of Robert Brodeley of Norwood greene in Hipperholme covering the remaining land from the same. Thomas Lister paid an entry fine of 2s 5¼d, Henry Northend paid 3s, and Samuel Northend paid for the remainder 3s. *The .ij. s. rent is Compounded for by Henry Northend, the .ix. d. ob. rent by John Boys, and the farthinge rent by Richard Batt*

——(*115*) Reginald Wood yeoman and Elizabeth Wood, his mother, appeared in court before Thomas viscount Savile, baron Pontefract, chief steward, and by the consent of Francis Tindall and Edward Lowden gen, took that parcel of land at Newton containing an estimated 44 yards by 14 yards with all houses and buildings thereon in the graveship of Alverthorpe now occupied by John Richardson or his assigns at a lord's rent of ½d and certain fine, lately seized into the lord's hands because Francis Tindall the late tenant and his heirs refused to pay the due rent to the lord, as found by enquiry at the court at Wakefeld on 3 July past, and proclamation was made publicly at three courts at Wakefeld and only Reginald Wood and Elizabeth Wood made proffer. Elizabeth Wood is to have the land for life, with reversion to Reginald Wood. Entry fine of ¾d paid by Elizabeth Wood, and another ¾d by Reginald for the reversion.

[A] Whereas cause of seisure is given into the hands of the Lords of the Mannour of Wakefeld of a parcell of land lyinge at Newton conteyninge by estimacion Fourty and foure yards in length and Fourtiene yards in Bredth with all houses and buildings therevpon-builded lyinge within the graveshippe of Aluerthorpe in thoccupacion of John Richardson or his assignes of the yearly rent to the Lord of a halfe penny and compounded for Wee Francis Tindall and Edward Lowden gent' are well contented that the same shalbe regraunted to Elizabeth Wood widow duringe her life and the remainder to Reginald Wood and his heirs for ever. In testimony whereof wee the said Francis Tindale and Edward Lowden have herevnto sett our hands and sealls the nynthenth day of September 1640.

Witnesses hereof — [signed] Fran: Tindall
William Tyndall — Edward Lowden
George Holmes
George Twisleton — [seals]

[B] Panel for 25 September [Richard Johnson deleted]

[C[1]] *Sex* Septimo die Maij Anno regni domini nostri Caroli regis Anglie etc. xv[to] 1639

Memo. that the day and year abouesaid Abraham Bever sonne

and heir apparent of Peter Bever of Fosterplace by Francis Mathewman tenante of the lord and to be sworne hath giuen and surrendered vp with a straw into the hands of the lord according to the custome of the manor of Wakefield, the reuercion after the Sixt day of May next Comeynge after the date hereof and in one litle Closse of land and medowe called barnesyde lane ynge with appurtenances in hepworth within the graveship of Holme and now in the tenure and occupacion of thaforesaid Abraham Bever or his assigns which said premisses are of the yeares rent domino regi of .ij. d. and Compounded for, with all wayes easements watercourses and Comodityes whatsoeuer to the same belongeinge vsed or occupyed, to the absolute vse and behooffe of John Tyas of Oxlee and of his heires and assigns for euer. Giuen and surrendred the day and yeare abouesaid.
Abraham Bever [mark]
Compounded for by Peter Bever [Latin] *Respited on account of defect*
[C2] [Sewn to dorse] Appearance of Robert Broadley of Norwoodgreene in Hipperholme on the third proclamation who sued his right to a messuage, a garden, a croft estimated at $\frac{1}{2}$ acre, a close called les Leyes estimated at 1 acre, 2 other closes of land, meadow and pasture, now subdivided into four, called les two Nethercrofts and les two Midlefeilds otherwise Grenelanefeild estimated at 3 acres, and a close called Wilkin in Northowrome, now occupied by Samuel Deane or his assigns these lands being excepted in the concession to Henry and Samuel Northend of customary land lately seized into the lord's hand on account of an indenture of lease made between Henry Northend of Quarlers in Northowrome, yeoman, and the same Robert Brodeley on the other.

Appearance of John Mellyn of Northowrome on the third proclamation who sued his right in a close in Northowrome commonly called North Landymier, now occupied by the said John Mellin being excepted in the concession of the above lands lately seized into the lord's hands as result of an indenture of lease between Henry Northend of Quarlers in Northowrome, yeoman, and the said John Mellin.

[mem 15]

WAKEFIELD: VIEW OF FRANKPLEDGE AND COURT LEET WITH TOURN: 12 October 15 Charles [1639]

Inquisition taken for the King on the oath of William Yarbrough gen, John Mawde gen, Thomas Royston gen, Richard Birkhead, Thomas Tayler, William Waller, Robert Killingbecke, Peter Moxon, John Nayler, William Lambert, Henry Hutchinson, William Hustler, William Awdisley, Francis Redman, Thomas Bradley and Robert Nayler, who presented:

that Elizabeth Petty made affray and drew blood from Margaret Rider *10s*

that the inhabitants of Alverthorpe did not made a gate called Kirkamyate in accordance with a previous pain *former pain, 39s*

that Stephen Bateman tethered his horses in le Cliffefeild *10s*

that William Hill *3s 4d* Arthur Simpson *3s 4d* Emmott Kelshaw *3s 4d* Elizabeth Godfrey *3s 4d* Mary Burrowe *3s 4d* and John Nayler *3s 4d* let their pigs go in the graveyard of Wakefeld *20s*

that – Hitchon made a rescue against the pinder *3s 4d*

KIRKGATE: Robert Totty, constable, and his fellows presented that Robert Thompson was chosen as constable this year.

that John Swifte and Gervase Norton did not make the pavement at Winde end *3s 4d*

that Joseph Waterhouse did not repair the pavement between his houses in Kirkgate *3s 4d*

that John Riley did not make the pavement before his house *3s 4d*

that the Governors of the Free School did not make the pavement before a house in Wrengate belonging to the Free School *3s 4d*

WESTGATE: Edward Horncastle, deputy of John Ellis, constable, and his fellows presented that Thomas Garnett was chosen as constable this year.

that Sara Hitchon widow *3s 4d* Cotton Horne gen *3s 4d* John Keysar gen *3s 4d* Ashton Stansfeild esq *3s 4d* Elizabeth Jenkinson *3s 4d* Abraham Haworth *3s 4d* Wife Moorehouse *3s 4d* James Fraunce *3s 4d* John Beeston *3s 4d* Francis Tayler *3s 4d* Richard Worrall and his mother *3s 4d* Wife Thompson and her son *3s 4d* and Barnabas Mawde *3s 4d* did not make the pavement before their several houses *43s 4d*

that William Jenkinson *3s 4d* and Thomas Bayne *3s 4d* baked bread severally contrary to the statute *6s 8d*

that Allan Noble *3s 4d* Thomas Somerster gen *3s 4d* Robert Beeston *3s 4d* William Andrew *3s 4d* Anne Walker widow *3s 4d*

John Beeston *3s 4d* Francis Tayler *3s 4d* James Lambe *3s 4d* and Thomas Richmond *3s 4d* Miles Sandisford *3s 4d* Wife [Widow] Hardwicke *3s 4d* and William Lewis *3s 4d* Richard Tailesforth *3s 4d* Thomas Roydes *3s 4d* Peter Hodgson *3s 4d* John Burnley *3s 4d* William Hudswell *3s 4d*, Christopher Nayler esq *3s 4d*, Robert Kay gen *3s 4d*, Thomas Roiston *3s 4d*, William Thompson *3s 4d*, John Ellis *3s 4d*, James Prince *3s 4d* and William Thompson of the Corner *3s 4d* Anne Symme [widow] *3s 4d* and Stephen Walton *3s 4d* did not repair the high street in Wakefeld *£4 6s 8d*

NORTHGATE: Robert Speight, deputy of John Nayler, constable, and his fellows presented that Thomas Baskervile was chosen constable this year who made Robert [sic] Speight his substitute

that Andrew Hargreaves *3s 4d*, William Lee *3s 4d*, Thomas Lee *3s 4d*, John Fleemeinge *3s 4d*, Robert Gamble *3s 4d* did not make bread according to the assize *16s 8d*

that John Smith failed to remove rubbish and timber from before his door *3s 4d*

that Thomas Walker *3s 4d*, – Waugh clerk *20d*, Thomas Baskervile *20d*, Amor Rishton *3s 4d*, John Fleeminge *3s 4d*, and Edward Smith *3s 4d* did not repair the pavement before their houses

STANLEY, ALVERTHORPE, THORNES: William Holtby, constable, and his fellows presented that William Wadisworth was chosen as constable this year

SANDALL John Lee, constable, and his fellows presented that Denis Hirst was chosen constable this year

that William Lambert did not make his gate in the Parke lane *3s 4d*

that Wife Lee did not ring and yoke her pigs *4d*

that John Morris of Agbrigge put his goods on Sandall common *former pain, 5s*

that – Burdett gen and Thomas Wright did not make gates at Carrsome Lane *10s*

that – Gawthorpe the fisherman broke the lord's fold *3s 4d* [Ten groats in draft]

CRIGLESTON: George Allott, constable, and his fellows presented that William Baxter was chosen as constable this year

that Paul Brownell kept a cow contrary to the pain previously levied *12d*

WALTON: Thomas Healey, constable, and his fellows presented that William Pell was chosen as constable this year

BRETTON: William Bretton, constable, and his fellows presented that William Robinson was chosen as constable this year

HORBURY: Thomas Haigh, constable, and his fellows presented that Robert Thornes was chosen as constable this year

that William Dick of Nethershittlington kept his goods on the commons of Horbury *10s* that Robert Jagger of Horbury kept his goods on the fields and commons of the township of Horbury contrary to statute *1s*

that the wife of Richard Batty broke hedges *1s*

that Edward Lockwood did not scour the ditch beside his croft *1s*

OSSETT: Anthony Curtis, constable, and his fellows presented that John Haigh was chosen constable this year

that George Allen *3s 4d* and Brian Brooke *3s 4d* broke the lord's fold at Ossett

that George Feild made affray on the constable of Ossett *6s 8d*

that Robert Crofte did not cut hedges in Little Lane *1s*

that Edward Langfeild did not scour his ditch according to a pain previously levied *former pain, 1s*

that Brian Brooke did not scour his ditch at Shawyate 1s

that Dorothy Medley let her pigs in le Hardcornefeild unyoked *1s*

EMLEY: Richard Clayton, deputy of John Gleidhill, constable, and his fellows presented that Richard Clayton was chosen constable this year.

that John Woffenden junior made affray on Robert Hobson *3s 4d*

that Robert Hobson or his wife drew blood from John Wooffenden *6s 8d*

that John Copley, 'locksmith', made affray and drew blood from James Child *10s*

that Thomas Issott made affray on Thomas Bedford *3s 4d*

FLOCKTON: Christopher Moulson, constable, and his fellows presented that Richard Eastwood was chosen constable this year

that John Swallow and Elizabeth Bilcliff made affray and drew blood from John Dixon *10s*

NORMANTON: Henry Barraby, constable, and his fellows presented that William White was chosen constable this year

that Robert Hitch clerk *12d*, Richard Denton *12d*, and Wife Frobisher *12d* did not severally make their parts of the pinfold adequately

that Richard Overinge failed to make his rigg abut on Sandall feild *4d*

that William Garlicke kept a pig unringed, contrary to a previous pain *4d*

that Wife Garlicke kept an unringed pig *4d*

that Robert Spinke did not make his rigg abut on the common in le Highfeild *4d*

that William Crawshawe did not make his rigg abut at Longland *4d*

SOYTHILL: Richard Archer, constable, and his fellows presented that John Tilson was chosen as constable this year

that William Speight *40s* and Anthony Fearnley *40s* refused to be constable of Soythill this year.

that Thomas Ashton broke the hedge of James Speight *12d*
that Thomas Grave put scabbed horses on the common of Soythill – [10s]

WESTARDISLAWE: William Scott, constable, and his fellows presented that John Allerton was chosen as constable this year
that Thomas Thornill of Fokisby esq did not scour his ditch about Spinkwelcroft *3s 4d*
that William Linley did not come to work on the repair of the highways in the township *20s*

DEWISBURY: Michael Bentley junior, constable, and his fellows presented that James Fearnley was chosen constable this year and put in his place Michael Whelewright
that Wilfred Peele demolished the commons' walls and carried the stones to his own house *39s 11d*
that Wilfred Peele put his goods on the commons of Dewsbury where he had no right *10s*
that Michael Wheatley neither ringed nor yoked two pigs *2s*
that James Fearnley *5s* and John Milne *5s* divulged the deliberations of the jurors at the last tourn
that Richard Dawson let his hedge lie open between his own ground and that of Michael Bentley *3s 4d*

ECCKLESHILL: John Boothman, constable, and his fellows presented that Abraham Ogden was chosen constable this year
that George Booth put a scabby mare on the commons of Ecckleshill *10s*
that George Booth did not yoke a pig *4d*

The jurors present that all the above is true
Peter Hodgson was chosen to seal hides
Ralph Robucke was chosen to be pinder of Sandall

[A] Wakefield view, 12 October 15 Charles [1639]

Kirkegate: Robert Tottie, constable, Robert Howle, Richard Roome, Robert Leeke and John Snawdon, sworn, say that Robert Thompson is elected constable there this year. Sworn.

Westgate: Edward Horncastle, deputy of John Ellis, constable, Richard Lumm, John —, Edward Byns and Stephen Walton, sworn, say that Thomas Garnett is elected constable etc.

Northgate: Richard Speight, deputy of John Nayler, constable, William Scrowby, William Lancaster, William Shauue and Richard Brodebent, sworn, say that Thomas Baskervile is elected constable etc. He substitutes Robert Speight, who is received and sworn.

Stanley, Alverthorpe, Thornes: William Holtby, constable, John Rose, Roger Massie, John Clarkson and John Leake, sworn, say that William Wadisworth is elected constable etc.

Sandall: John Lee, constable, Edward Musgreave, Thomas Hill,

Brian Longley and Joseph Beatson, sworn, say that Denis Hirst is elected constable etc.

Crigleston: George Allott, constable, John Sprigonell, Robert Johnson, Edward Awdisley and Thomas Booth, sworn, say that William Baxter is elected constable etc.

Walton: Thomas Healey, constable, William Arnold, and Thomas Wright, sworn, say that William Pell is elected constable etc.

Bretton: William Bretton, constable, Robert Wright and Thomas Arnold, sworn, say that William Robinson is elected constable etc.

Horbury: Thomas Haigh, constable, John Walker, Richard Roberte, William North and Thomas Donne, sworn, say that Robert Thornes is elected constable etc.

Ossett: Anthony Curtis, constable, William Thornes, John Sugden, Thomas Bargh and Thomas Awdisley, sworn, say that John Haigh is elected constable etc.

Emley: Richard Clayton, deputy of John Gleidhill, constable, Thomas Bedford, Robert Hewett, William Haigh and John Perry, sworn, say that Richard Clayton is elected constable etc.

Flockton Half: Christopher Moulson, constable, William Mountayne and Francis Walshay, sworn, say that Richard Eastwood is elected constable etc.

Normanton: Henry Barraby, constable, Robert Sympson, Robert Brewister, George Standish and Brian Watson, sworn, say that William White is elected constable etc.

Soythill: Richard Archer, constable, Richard Dawson, James Speight, William Kitson and John Tailer, sworn, say that John Tilson is elected constable etc.

Westardisley: William Stott, constable, John Wilby and Paul Sharpe, sworn, say that John Allerton is elected constable etc.

Dewisbury: Michael Bentley junior, constable, John Dawson, James Clayton, Henry Barber and Robert Barber, sworn, say that James Fearnley is elected constable. He substitutes Michael Wheelewright, who is received and sworn.

Eccleshill: John Boothman, constable, Christopher Gill and Abraham Baraclough, sworn, say that Abraham Ogden is elected constable etc.

Peter Hodgshon is elected sealer of hides and sworn.

Ralph Robuck is elected pinder of Sandall and sworn.

[B^1] Panel of jurors: headed by William Yarbrough gen, and bracketted 4, 4, 4, 3

[B^2] We whose names are here vnder written being sworne on the Jury at the Kings Majesties Courte leete have agreed on this our verdite this .xviij.th day of October 1639

[signed by all jurors except Lambert and Hutchinson, who made their marks]

[C] Rogger Watson for makin afray and drawin of blod vpon Nickolas Anyeard .x. s.

Traversed [signed] William Yarburghe/Robert Killingbeck/
Thomas Rishtone/William Waller/

[D] Margrit Rider being sworne came and presented Elizabeth Pettie wife to Bryon Pettie for a blood and afray vpon her the said Margrit

[signed] William Yarburghe/Robert Killingbeck/
Thomas Rishtone/Richard Birkhead/
John Maude *examined by bailiff of Wakefield*

[E]

The Punder of Wakefeild

present the inhabitants of olverthorp for not makinge kerkcum yeate according to a payne 39s
Item Steune Batman for teathering his horses in the Cleffeild 10s
Item William Hill for his swine going into the Churchyearde 3s 4d
Item Athure Simson for the like . . . [as engrossed]

by enquiry by bailiff of Wakefeild

[endorsed] William Yarburghe/Robert Killingbecke/Thomas Rishton/Richard Birkhead/John Maude/

[F]

Kirkegate

Imprimis a paine layd that euery houshoulder in kergate shall repaire and keepe theire dorestead and causey before theire dores in good repaire in paine of euery default 3s 4d

Item we lay in paine that euery houshoulder in Kirkgate doe dress theire dore euery saturday in paine of not so doing 12d

Item that Edmond Sikes shall take away his floed yate at his croft end so that the water may haue fre passage downe the sciterické in paine of 3s 4d

Item we lay in paine that euery houshoulder in wrengate doe paue theire dores and drese theires dores euery saturday in paine of not so doing 3s 4d

Item that noe Alhouse keper shall keepe any mans seruant drinking after eight of cloke at night in paine of euery time so doing 3s 4d

Item that noe man shall sufer any mastife dog to goe vnmusled in paine of 12d

Item that noe man shall suffer his swine to goe abrood vnyoaked or vnringd in paine of 3s 4d

Item that noe inhabitants of wakefeild shall dig or get any sand nere the hie way between the goat runing from the corne mill and the riuer of colder in paine of euery time soe donne 5s

Item that no man shall dig vp any earth or make any morter of this sid bridge at pennewals in paine of euery time 12d

Kirkegate

[dorse]

wee doo present John Swift and Jeruis Norton or either of them whom it doth concerne for not making their pauement at winde end 3s 4d

we doe present Joseph Watterhouse for not repaireing his causey before his houses in kirgate 3s 4d

we doe present John Riley for not making his causey before his house 3s 4d

we doe present the gouernorns of the fre scoole for not making theire pauement before the dore of one house in the sayd wrengate belonging to the fre scoole 3s 4d

[signed]	William Yarburghe	Robert Totty
	John Maude	Robert Howley
	Robert Killingbecke	Richard Roome
	Richard Birkhead	Robert Lee
	William Hustler	John Snawden

[G]

Westgate

Item that noe man keepe or suffer any swine vnringe or vnyoake 3s 4d

Inprimis A paine layde that euery one thatt keepeth any mastiffe doge shall keepe them musled in paine of 3s 4d

Item that euery Inhabitant shall sweepe there doores and bear away the sweepings in paine of 3s 4d

Item that noe persons shall take any Clay forth of the backe laine in Westgate to the hurt of the Common way in paine 3s 4d

Item that none shall cast any Carryon into the backe laine in Westgate which shalbe any way anoyance in paine 3s 4d

Item that noe man shall tether or Tent any horsse or mare in the Cliffeild and St. Johns Feild of wakefeild after they haue mowne and shorne there corne and grasse that grewe there of in paine of 3s 4d

Mrs Hickinge wee present for not making her pafement before her dore, according to a paine laid 3s 4d

[as engrossed]

Examined by bailiff of Wakefeld

Richard Lumm [RL]	we finde that 2 laine ends in westgate the
John Hyrst [IH]	one goeing into the Ings and the other
Stephen Walton [SW]	Joyneing to the house of Correction vn-
Edward Bynns [mark]	mercyed but put to the Juryes discrettion
John Ellis [JE]	because it is not desyded of whome it
	belongeth to

[dorse]

We present Edward Jenkinson for baking bread lesse then the statute alloweth 3s 4d

Item William Baynes for the like 3s 4d

[as engrossed]

John Ellis [I]	[signed] William Yarburgh
Richard Lumme [RL]	Robert Killingbecke
John Hurst [I]	William Waller
Edward Binnes [mark]	Thomas Rishtonne
Stephen Walton [SW]	John Maude

[G²]

Westgate presentments October the — 1639

Wee whose names are here vnder written doe present these partyes following for these defects vizt.

Imprimis Allan Noble for not repairing his part of the high cawsey 3s 4d

[as engrossed]

[marks of Edward Binnes, Richard Loumme, John Hurst and Stephen Walton]

[endorsed with signatures of Yarburghe, Rishtone, Maude, Birkhead, Nayler, Killingbecke, Waller, Redman, Hustler and Awdssley, and marks of Lambert, Hutchinson and Tellier]

[pinned on] Item I lay in paine that Steuen Bateman be twix this and martinmas next doe scoure his *Goutter* Backe and cut his hedge that leadeth to the lau feild that passingeres may haue fre passage on the bancke or stand in pane of not soe doeing 20s

[signed] Laurance Browne

[G³]

Westgate peyns October 1639

We lay in payne that Thomas Couerter shall make a sufficient porll or Wall betwixt the Back houis fould and the streete betwixt this time and the next Ladyday 30s

Item wee lay in payne Thomas Souester, Allan Noble, John Dalle, Widow Harwicke, John Ellisemough, Henery Tellir, Robart Beston, John Bertom, George Proctor, John Briche, Robart Townend, Thomas Whitle, Gerog Becket, William Tate shall sufficiently make and keepe the Backe Lane betwixe John Elismough Crofte end and the house of Correction and scourre there Dikes and keepe there sewers and fill all there houles at ther Croft ends that men may pase on Fote In payne of every one not soe Doeing *39s* 6s 8d

[H]

Northgate

Wakefeld Visus Franci Plegii ... 12 October 15 Charles [1639]

Robert Speight, deputy of John Nayler constable

Northgate

William Scrowby
William Lancaster
William Shauue
Richard Brodebent } sworn

Item wee present Andru Hargrave for not makeing his bred according to the sise 3:4

Traverse made at this tourn

Item we present John Clarson of Woodside for siling vnlaufull buter for want of wight 20:0

Item wee present William Lee for not makeing his bred according to the sise 3:4
,, Thomas Lee ,, 3:4
,, John Michell ,, 3:4

Traverse made at this tourn

,, William Oslar for a Rescue in the markit about his bread 10:0

Traverse made at this tourn

,, John Flemin for not makeing his bred according to the sise 3:4
,, Robert Gamell ,, 3:4
,, John Smith for not drifing away the Rubis and the timbe before the house in Northgate 3:4
,, Thomas Walker for not mending his Pauement before his house 3:4
,, Mr Waugh and Thomas Baskirvile for not mending there dore before there house 3:4

[as engrossed]

examined all but theise that are traversed

[Marked or signed as above] signed by Yarburghe Rishtoun, Maude, Birkhead, Waller, and Killingbecke

[I]

Panes for Stanley

Imprimous wee lay in payne that all the Occupiars of the landes in the Churchfeld doe scoure thare land Endes agoying vpon Northey layne frome Bromnshay yeate to the seuares going in to Northey and allsoe that the ouarseores of the hiewayes doo poull vp those seuares and lay them so that that watar may haue passege in to Northey before and Crossmes day nexte in payne of not so doing of 10s

Item wee lay in payne that the inhabetants of Wakkefeld do make the foute way anence the fre scoulle and make passege that the wattar do not stand to troubbell the Kinges popell to Church and market before and Crossemes day nexte in pane of not so doing of 39s

Item wee lay in payne that all the Occoupiares of the Grounddes betwene netharfeild and Colldar do scoure there watarcource betwene and Crossmenmes nexte in pane of not so doing of 10s

Item that Euery person that hath any ground adioyninge to the hieghwayes betweixt Colldar and the Crosstreted tre of Thornes do scoure there diches before and Anders day nexte in pane of Euere one note so doinge in pane of 10s

Item wee lay in pane that John Flathar do scoure his dyke at his yete end in smawellay lane before and Crossmes nexte in payne of note so doing of 3s

Item that no person do driue any goodes through hawroyd feild betwixe the owte wood and Stanlay in pane of euery so doing 10s

Presentements

Imprimus wee presente Jereme Maude for putting a scabbed horse or nage into the Oute Wood 10s

Item we presente Thomas Norfocke far driuing Goodes ouar the Panroyd feld Contrary to a pane therein 3s 4d

Stanley

[attached] Item wee lay in payne that the Ouerseeres of the hiewayes for Stanlay do lay the gottere trese and the foute brige in hanroydefeild layne before and Andars day nexte Coming in note so doing in payne of 20s

[signed] William Yarburghe/Robert Killingbecke/Thomas Rishtoune/John Maude

[endorsed] William Howltbe/John Rose/Roger Masse/John Clarkson/John Leake [mark]

Peter Moxson layed a payne of .xx. s on John Mitchell that he make a flodyate at his Close head a Joyneing to the layne betwene Stanley and the outwoods betwext this and the first day of March next and soe keepe the same from time to time, and also Cower all his dikes adioyneing to the same highway

Peter Moxon

[J[1]]

presentments made by the counstable and fouremen of the towneshipp of Sandall

first they present William lambart for not making his yate in the parke layne 3s 4d

Item they present Robert gamball and William lambart for not making theire yeate in the straite layne end 3s 4d

[as engrossed]

Edward Musgrave [mark]   John Lee
Brian Longley [mark]   Joseph Beatson
Thomas Hill [TH]

[signed] William Yarburghe/Robert Killingbecke/William Waller/Richard Birkhead/John Maude

Sandall

[J[2]]

Certaine paines laide by the cunstable and foure men of the township of Sandall

Att the sheriff turne holden at Wakefeild 12 of October 1639 in manner and form as followeth:

First they lay in paine that euerieman make their yeats and hedges aboute the hardcorne feild betweene thes and Thursday at night next in paine of euerie yeate then not made 03^{s} 4^{d} and euerie side hedge 03^{s} 4^{d} and euerie gapp or land end 12^{d}

Item they lay in paine that euerie one ring theire swine betweene this and Thursday next in paine of not soe doeinge for euerie swine 4^{d}

Item they lay in paine for euerie one that hath anie grounde betweene the towne well and the brooke that they scowre theire ditches well and sufficiently betweene this and Martlemass day next of paine of euerie one not soe doeinge for euerie close of 05^{s}

Item they lay in paine that euerie one that hath anie lands on the kilne hill that they scowre theire ditches well and sufficiently in paine of euerie land end vndone betweene this and Martlemass next 12^{d} and alsoe that euerie one that hath anie ground betweene the rounde inge bridge and the greene dike bridge that they scowre theire ditches well and sufficiently betweene this and martlemass day next in paine of not soe doeing euerie close 05^{s}

Item they lay in paine Mr Burdett and Thomas Wright that they hange a goode and sufficient yeate [at] Carsoune layne and soe keepe it at all times [a]t paine not soe doeing 10^{s}

Item alsoe that the inhabitants of Walton hang a goode and sufficient yeate at Walton greene end and soe keepe at all times in paine [not soe doeing] 10^{s}

Sandall

[endorsed] Cunstable and foure men: Edward Musgrave/Joseph Beatson/Brian Longley/Thomas Hill/

[K[1]] Criglestone October 12 1639

We doe present Paull Brownell who hath made a common costome of keeping of his cowe contrarie to our paine 12d

[signed] George Allott Constable *ex' ball' de Wake*

John Sprigonell/Robert Johnson/Edward Awdesley/
Thomas Booth, fowre men

William Yarburghe/Robert Killingbecke/William Waller/John Maude

Crigleston

[K[2]]

Criglestone

Imprimus we doe laie in pane that euery one do make their yates and hedges about the hard Corne feldes betwixt this and saint Luke day next in pane of not so doing for euery yate 3s 4d

Euery side hedge 3s

Item Euerie gappe and land end 12d

Item that Euerie one doe yoke and ring their swine betwixt this and All saints day next in paine of euery one making defalt therein for euery swine 4d

Item we doe laie in paine that euery one do scoure their ditches from neusane lane to mile brooke betwixt this and Martine Mase in paine of not soe doing 3s

Item we do laie in paine that Robbert Gamble and Samuell Feilding doe set two stayes ouer crimbles brigde [sic] and ouer kelder close bridge either of them not so doing 3s 4d

Item we doe laie in paine that Henery Brooke and John Spetch do take in the water betwixt Pease and Baulke and haueroodend betwixt this and Martinmas next in paine of not so doing 3s 4d

Item we doe laie in paine that Richard Wade and Thomas Boyne doe take the water out of the stonieland in paine of not so doing betwixt this and Martinmas 5s

Item we doe laie in paine that John Clarke doe take the water out of the bokeland betwixt this and martinmas next in paine of not so doing 3s 4d

Item we do laie in paine that Thomas Denton do remoue away the dunghill betwixt this and saint Luke day in paine of not so doing 5s

Item we do laie in paine that John Knutton take the water out of the way into his close betwixt this and Thursday in paine of not so doing 5s 4d

Item we do laie in paine doe take in the water at hendlemore yate in paine of not so doing 3s 4d

October the twelfe day 1639

[signed] William Baxter Constable

John Sprigonell/Robart Johnson/Thomas Booth/Edward Awdesley

[L]

the Constable and 4 men for Walton Cum Brettan

omne Bene *Constables bill*

[signed] Thomas Healey/Thomas Arnold/Thomas Wright/Robert Wright/William Arnold

Walton cum Bretton

[M[1]]

presentments made by the constable and foure men of Horbure at the sherife turne houlden at Wakefeld the 12 day of october 1639

Item we present Mr Bilclif of Flocton the ouner of the house at Lidgate 10s

Item we present William Diche of Nethershitinton for keping his goods of Horbure Comon 10s

Item we present Robert Jayer of Horbure a younge man for keping goods within the tounefelds and Comons of Horbure Contrare to the statute 1s

Item we present Thomas Edge of Ossit for keping sheepe in the Stanshill 10s

Item we present Richard Batlie wife of hedge breking 1s

Item we present Edward Lokwood for not scouring his dich after his crofte side 1s

[signed] Thomas Haighe Constable
John Hunte John Robert [JR] Richard Robert [R]
Horbury

[endorsed] William Yarburghe/Robert Killingbecke/John Maude/ Thomas Rishtoune

[M²]

paines laide by the Constable and foure men of Horbure at the sherifturne houlden at Wakfeld the 12 day of October 1639

Imprimis we lay in paine that no man in our towne do kepe any Inmates Contrarie to the statute in paine of euere month 10s

Item that all the Watercourses in and about the toune be well and sufficientlie scoured and so kept that the water may be kept in the right course in paine of 20s

Item that all the foote wayes in and aboute the toune be well and sufficienly kept with good stiles as formerly hath bene in [paine] of euere default 10s

Item that no young man in our toune doe kepe any sheepe or other Cattell in the tounefeldes or Comons of Horbure which is not a househoulder in paine of euere default 10s

Item that no person do breake any mans hedge or carie wood forth of any man ground vnles it be their oune in paine of euere default 3s 4d

Robert Thaurns Constable [T]
John Walker [mark] William North
Horbury

[N¹]

Robert Tompson Pinder of Osset

George Allin for breakin the pinfould at Osset 3s 4d

Brian Brooke for the like 3s 4d

William Yarburghe
William Awdssley

[N²]

Ossett Bill

we present

George Feild for smiteing downe our Constable 6s 8d

Robert Croft not switchinge his hedg in litle laine 1s

[as engrossed]

Dorothy Medley for her swine taken in the hardcorne feild in the corne and unyoked 1s

[signed] Anthoni Courtise [A]
William Thornes
John Sugdin
Thomas Awdslay
Thomas Barghe [mark]

[examined] John Rishtoune
John Maude

Ossett

[endorsed] William Yarburghe
Robert Killingbeck
John Maude
Richard Birkhead

By the Constable of Ossett

[N³]

Paynes layde at the Sheriffe turne houlden at Waiekefeild the xij th day of October by the Constable and Sworne men as followeth, Anno Domini 1639

Imprimis we lay in paine that all the yeates and fences aboute our feilds be well and sufficiently made betwixt this and wedensday next and soe keept from time to tyme in paine of every yeate not sofficiently kept 3s

And be likewise every gapp not well made and kept sofficient vntill the feild Ridd 12d

● Item we lay in payne that every one that hath any swine within our Towne keepe them well yoaked and ringed in payne of every default 12d

● Item we lay in payne that noe person do breake any hedges except they be theire owne in payne of every default 12d

● Item we lay in payne that noe person doe receive any hedge wodd of any person that is suspected for hedge breakeing in paine of every default 12d

● Item we lay in payne that noe person doe digg for any stones in our highe streets vnless the Constable and sworne men and other neighbours give consent there vnto in payne of 10s

● Item we lay in payne that widdow Peace doe keepe a sufficient yeat at Haygate laine from Tyme to tyme in payne of 3s 4d

● Item we lay in payne that Josua Hepworth doe make a sufficient fence adioyneing to the same yeate and so kepe yt from tyme to tyme in paine of 12d

● Item we lay in payne that Richard Hemingway Thomas Hemingway Robert Whittakers and Thomas Akeroyd doe kepe a sufficient yeate hunge betwixt the lordshipp of Chikingley and the Township of Ossett from tyme to tyme in payne of 6s 8d

Item we lay in payne that William Gill doe take the water into the Brear ynge which of right he ought to doe betwixt thys and

Martynmas day next in payne of 3s

Item we lay in payne that Thomas Langfeild and William Gill doe scovre theire ditches in the bottom of Healey laine and alonge the wash yng side in payn of either of them offendinge 3s

Item we lay in payne that Thomas Awdslay doe take the water out of the Rieroyde laine betwixt this and Martynmas day next and soe kepe yt from Tyme to tyme in payne of every default therein 5s

Item we lay in payne that James Speight scovre his ditch alonge his longe lands close side where any nede is betwixt this and the last day of this instant October in pain of 5s

Item we lay in payne that George Lee and Josua Hepworth doe plowe as many furrows back againe to Ripling balke as they have plowed from yt betwixt this and martinmas Day next in payne of either of them refuseing so to doe —

Item we lay in payne that William Gill and Thomas Hepworth doe either of them restore as much to Sowdell balke as they have plowed from yt betwixt this and martinmas day next in [pay]ne of either of them 5s

Ossett

[dorse]

Item we lay in payne that Robert Roods do plow as much back againe to over morecroft balke as he hath plowed from yt betwixt this and mids[umm]erday next in paine of —

Item we lay in payne that Richard Brooke and John Jagger scovre theire ditches adioyneing the Towneyate so deepe as yt kepe the water that yt rune not into the Towneyate betwixt this and alsaints day next in paine of 5s

Item we lay in payne that Christopher Awdsley and Christopher Broke doe scovre theire ditches in Oxley laine betwixt this and alsaints day next in paine of 5s

Item we lay in payne that William Midlebroughe William Hall Thomas Wilbe or William Milner Christopher Broke Edward Langfeild and William Beatson do scoure their ditches in Back laine and bringe yt vnder the Brigstone before William Beasons dore betwixt this and alsaints day next in paine of every one of them offending 2s

Item we lay in paine that all those that have any land adioyneing to maplewell laine doe switche theire hedges and scoure theire ditches there betwixt this and alsaints day next in paine of every one offending herein 2s

Item we lay in paine that all those persons that hath any land adoyneing the Bridle stye in Healey betwixt stonyroyde yeate and wastynge do switch theire hedges there and make the[m] good so as passengers may kepe the way betwixt this and alsaints day next in paine of every one offending therein 3s

Item we lay in payne that noe person doe make any way any more from lanes yeate over those lands to Riplinge way in [paine] of every one offending therin 2s

Item we lay in payne that those that have any land adioyneinge the litle laine doe switch theire hedges there betwixt this and alsaints day next in paine of every one offendinge herein 2s

Item we lay in paine that Robert Bradforth doe scovre his ditch alonge his houneley cole close side and alsoe over the end thereof and kepe the water for cominge out of his close into the highway betwixt this and alsaints day next in paine of 6s 8d

Item we lay in paine that all the inhabitants of Gawthorp that hath any land adioyneing to the kings high way doe scovre their ditches betwixt this and alsaints next in paine of every one offendinge herein 3s 4d

Item we lay in paine that John Dishforth do take the water out of the strete at bottome of Ten lands betwixt this and alsaints next in paine of 3s 4d

Item we lay in paine Brian Broake doe take the water out of strete at Hayyeate betwixte this and alsaints next in paine of 3s 4d

[N4]

Item we lay in paine that all the inhabitants of Gawthorp that hath any adioyneinge to the Bridle sty betwixt Gawthorp and Chidsell doe scoure there ditches there betwixt this and Martinmas day next in [payne] of every default therein 2s

[signed] John Haighe constable [mark]
William Thornes/John Sugdin/Thomas Awdsley/Thomas Barghe [mark]

[O]

The presentments made by the Constable of Emley and foure men the twelute of october 1639

First we present John wooffenden Junior for afray made vpon Robert Hobson *3s 4d* and Robert Hobson or his wife for a bloode made vpon John wooffenden 10s

we present John Copley Locksmith for a fray and a bloode made vpon James Child 10s

we present Thomas Issott for a fray made vpon Thomas Bedforth 3s 4d

John Gledhill ould Constable
Richard Clayton deputye

Thomas Bedforth
Robert Hewett
John Perry
William Haige
} fouremen

[signed] William Yarburghe
Robert Killingbeck
Thomas Rishton
John Maude
William Hustler

Emley

[P]

Flockton halfe bill

Affray was made by John Swallowe and Elizabeth Bilcliffe of John Dixon and blood drawne

[signed] Christopher Mowlson Constable   William Yarburghe
Francis Wolshaw   John Maude
Robert Killingbeck
William Waller

Flocton di.

[Q]

Normanton Bill

Presentments made by the Constable and fower men the 12 daie of October AD 1639

we present Robert Hitch Clarke for his parte of Pinfold beinge not sufficientlie maide 12d

we present Richard Denton and vxor forbisher for thare part of the Pinfolde beinge not sufficientlie maide, either of them 12d 2s

we present Richard Overinge for one lande end buttinge of Sandall feild being not maide 4d

we present William Garlicke for one Swyne being not Rynged Contrayrie to our paines 4d

we present vxor Garlick for one Swine beinge nott Rynged 4d

we present Robert Spinke for one land end beinge not maide buttinge of our Common in the high feild 4d

we present William Crawshay for one Land end Lyinge of Longlands lying open to our Common 4d

[signed] Henrie Barrabie Constable *extract'*
Peter Godsone [mark]   Robert Simpson
Robert Brewster   William Blewitt [mark]

[signed] William Yarburghe/Robert Killingbecke/William Awdssley /John Maude

Normanton

[R]

Soothill Bill, the 12 October 1639

Thomas aston presented for brakinge James Speight heidgg 12d

Thomas grave for putinge scabed horses vpon oure Commons 6s 8d

10s

[signed] Richard Dawson   James Speight [I]
John Tayler [I]   William Kittson
Richard Archer [R]

[signed] William Yarburghe/Robert Killingbecke/Richard Birkhead /William Waller/John Maude

Soythill

[S]

Presentments for ardsley west

Imprimis We presente Mr thornhill of fixbye for not scouring his dicke about spinkwell Close 3s 4d

we presente William lynley of duninglay for wante of sixe Common day works with a draught £1 0s 0d

[signed] Willyam Stott [mark]
John Wilbye [I]
Paull Sharpe [mark]

[signed] William Yarburghe/Robert Killingbecke/Richard Birkhead /Thomas Rishtone/John Maude

Westardislawe

[T]

Dewsburye Bill

Inprimis We present Wilfrey Peele for pullinge downe our Common walle and Carriinge the stones away and makeinge a way to his house where hee falleth none 39s 11d

Item we present the same Wilferey Peele for putting his goods to our Common where he hath noe righte vnto 10s

Item we presente Michaell Wheatley for not yoakinge and ringinge two Swine 2s

Item we presente James Fearnley and John Milnes for relateinge what was done at the last Sheiriffe torne for either of them 10s

Item we presente Richard Dawson for letting his hedge lie open betwene his owne ground and the ground of Michaell Bentley 3s 4d

[signed] Michaell Bentley [M] Constable
John Dawson/James Clayton/Henry Barbar/Robart Barbarr/

[signed] William Yarburgh/Robert Killingbecke/Thomas Rishtone/ John Maude/

Dewisbury

[U]

West Eckleshill bill

presentments made by vs named are heare vnder written

Imprimus George Booth for lettinge a inffected mare with scab goe othe Comon 10s

Item George Booth for one Swyne beeinge vnyoked 4d

[signed] John Boothman *ex' bailiff of Wakefeld*
Abraham Barroclough [mark]/Christopher Gill

Ecckleshill

[endorsed] William Yarburghe/Robert Killingbecke/William Awdssley/Richard Birkhead/John Maude/

[mem 15d]

HALIFAX VIEW OF FRANKPLEDGE AND COURT LEET WITH TOURN: 14 October 15 Charles [1639]

Inquisition taken for the King on the oath of Abraham Parkinson yeoman, Roger Bolton, John Crosland, John Milner, Richard Bentley, Michael Brigge, Michael Longbothome, John Horsfall, William Walker, John Whelewright, John Utley, John Grenewood, John Knowles and Abraham Sunderland, who present that James Cowper, butcher, made affray and drew blood from Robert Briar *10s*

that William Sutcliffe, tailor, made affray and drew blood from Richard Robinson *10s*

Jonathan Lumm	,,	,,	Lambert Towler	,,
Joseph Lomme	,,	,,	,,	,,
James Wood, hotepresser	,, on William Thomas			*3s 4d*
Henry Wadsworth	,, Peter Lefaver			,,
Peter Lefaver	,, and drew blood from the said Henry Wadsworth			*10s*
Mark Farrer	,,	,,	Hugh Haworth	,,
Isabel Ottiwell	,,	,,	,,	,,
Jarrett Denton made affray and drew blood from Henry Crowther				,,
Samuel Sladen	,,	,,	Sara Thomas	,,
John Hellewell	,,	,,	said ,,	,,
John Lister	,,	,,	Joseph Fairbanke	,,
Nathan Wood	,,	,,	said ,,	,,
Joseph Fairbanke	,,	,,	John Lister	,,
,,	,,	,,	Nathan Wood	,,
Stephen Dixon	,,	,,	Jonathan Bairstowe	,,
,,	,,		Michael Hailey, blacksmith	,,
said Michael Hailey	,,	,,	Stephen Dixon	,,
Jonas Tasker	,,	,,	Jonathan Bairstowe	,,
,,	,,	,,	Richard Gibson	,,
Richard Longbothome	,,	,,	Jonathan Bairstow	,,
John Crosley	,,	,,	Henry Kershaw	,,
,,	,,	,,	Abraham Kershaw	,,
,,	,,	,,	John Utley	,,
Henry Sutcliffe	,,	,,	James Grenewood	,,
James Grenewood	,,	,,	Henry Sutcliffe	,,
Thomas Rishton	,,	,,	Michael Bentley	,,
Grace Dobson	,, on Isaac Heape			*3s 4d*
,,	,, William Whitwham			,,
Ambrose Grenewood	,, and drew blood from Thomas Crosley			*10s*

John Widdopp of Wadsworth killed 100 fish in the Calder, against statute *20s*

Henry Horsfoll diverted water course in the field called Longe Lane *3s 4d*

the maid of John Boy contaminated the water *1s*

Richard Worrall, Judith his wife and Jane Worrall made affray and drew blood from Henry Greaves, Thomas Gleidhill and John Hartley *10s*

HALIFAX Henry Riley and William Parkin, deputies of John Smith mercer and Abraham Mitchell, constables, and their fellows present that Christopher Robinson and John Smith of Hallend were chosen constables this year

that Miles Croysedall made a nuisance under the window of John Crosland *3s 4d*

SKIRCOTE Simon Rigge, deputy of John Bawmforth, constable, and his fellows present that Richard Waterhous was chosen constable this year

SOWERBY Henry Wilson, constable, and his fellows present that Richard Bentley was chosen constable this year. He deputes Josiah Stansfeild, who was accepted.

WARLEY John Holdsworth, constable, and his fellows present that Thomas Oldfeild of Cliffehill was chosen constable this year. He deputes Simeon Otes, who was accepted.

that John Dodgson drew blood from John Crowther *6s 8d*

OVENDEN: William Bollinge, deputy of Samuel Tasker, constable, and his fellows present that Edward Ridinge was chosen constable this year

WADISWORTH: James Harwood, constable, and his fellows present that John Pighell was chosen constable this year

MIDGLEY: John Padgett, deputy of Gregory Padgett, and his fellows present that John Hellewell was chosen constable this year

that Richard Midgley and Samuel Midgley of Midgley failed to repair the vennel called Bradfordlane in Midgley according to a previous pain *former pain, 10s*

that Samuel Midgley of Midgley failed to mend the highway from the lower end of Bradfordlane in Midgley to Holmhousebridgend, as previously laid on him *former pain, 5s*

that James Oldefeild of Warley failed to mend the highway from le Holmhousebridgend in Warley to the lower end of the vennel called Bankhouselane in Warley, as previously laid on him *former pain, 10s*

that Brian Crowther of Warley failed to repair the walls adjoining the lands occupied by him on the highway in Warley and let stones lie in the highway, and did not throw open his watercourses, as previously laid on him *former pain, 5s*

RISHWORTH: John Bothomley, constable, and his fellows present that Abraham Batchler was chosen as constable this year. He deputes John Barrow, who was accepted.

STANSFEILD: Thomas Halme, constable, and his fellows present that John Stansfeild was chosen constable this year

HEPTONSTALL: Thomas Draper, constable, and his fellows present that Thomas Grenewood was chosen constable this year that John Longley twice broke the lord's fold *6s 8d*

William Whitwham ,, ,, ,,

Brian Bentley made an affray on James Bentley *3s 4d*

[mem 16]

LANGFEILD: William Farrer, constable, and his fellows present that Jeremy Ingham was chosen constable this year

AIRINGDEN: John Bordall, constable, and his fellows present that Samuel Hanson was chosen constable this year.

Sowerby (*116*) James Murgatroid of Bankehouse in Warley and Sara now his wife, she agreeing separately, by John Haldsworth, lord's tenant and sworn, surrendered into the lord's hand and quitclaimed to Abraham Stansfeild of Warley, clothier, now in peaceful possession, all their rights in that messuage and 6 acres land and pasture in the midst of les Withens in Warley in the graveship of Sowerby, lately occupied by Abraham Croyser or his assigns and then occupied by one Gilbert Sladen and Thomas Hartley or their assigns, and now by the said Abraham Stansfeild, at a lord's rent of 2s and no certain fine, where James Murgatroid and Abraham Stansfeild lately had the surrender of the said Gilbert Sladen of Warley, mason, and of Isaac Sladen his son, and of Grace, lately deceased wife of the said Gilbert, who was the daughter and heiress of Abraham Croyser deceased: to the use of the said Abraham Stansfeild. Abraham Stansfeild fines 6d. *Quit claim, 6d: not compounded*

Sowerby (*117*) Samuel Wade, younger son of Anthony Wade late of Peelehouse in Warley deceased, by John Banaster, lord's tenant and sworn, surrendered that messuage commonly called le Oversnape in Sowerby and all houses, buildings and easements, and 5 closes of land meadow and pasture in the township and graveship of Sowerby now occupied by John Mitchell or his assigns, and all paths, water, water courses, liberties etc at a lord's rent of 15d and certain fine, representing 4 messuages known commonly as le Lowersnape, Oversnape, le Heyend and le Myriewall in Sowerby with all houses etc, lately occupied by Richard Longbothome, Alexander Bradshawe, Alice Londe, George Holmes and Ralph Haworth or their assigns at a lord's rent of 7s 9d: to the use of the said John Mitchell and Tabitha his wife from 1 May past as to the messuage, and from 2 February next as to the closes, for a term of 13 years each, paying annually to Samuel Wade £6 at Whitsun and Martinmas, provided that if the rent be in arrears for 40 days, or if any other person than John Mitchell or his wife occupy the same without the special consent of Samuel, written under his hand and seal, the surrender becomes void. Agreed: entry fine of 22½d. *Compounded for by Anthony Wade*

Sowerby (*118*) John Hoyle of Sowerby and Ruth now his wife, she agreeing separately, by Thomas Crosley of Stainland lord's tenant and sworn surrendered 2 cottages in Sowerby and a garden associated, now occupied by Jacob Earnshawe and Robert Walton or their assigns and the reversion after the death of Brigett Haigh, widow, 'natural mother' of the said John Hoile, of 2 closes of land meadow and pasture called Overthwart in le Townefeild of Sowerby estimated at 1 acre and occupied by the said Brigett Haigh or her assigns, and all paths, watercourses etc at a lord's rent of 4d, being part of the 3s payable for this and other land, and certain fine; to the use of William Horton senior of Barkisland gen. Agreed: entry fine of 12d. *Compounded for by John Hoile*

Sowerby (*119*) Testimony on the oath of Michael Oldfeild, lord's tenant, that Edward Bolton of Skircote, co. York, clothier, on 16 May 14 Charles [1638] surrendered the west end of a house commonly called le Cawsey and the east of a croft of land and meadow now separated by metes and bounds estimated at 1½ roods, and a half rood in Warley in the graveship of Sowerby now occupied by John Bolton or his assigns and a water mill used to grind shears, with all ways, paths, watercourses, stews and easements associated with the mill in Warley in the graveship of Sowerby now occupied by the said John Bolton at a lord's rent of 2d and no certain fine: to the use of John Bolton of Warley, shearmaker, from 1 May last past for 21 years at an annual rent of £3 10s payable at Whitsun and Martinmas, with repossession if the rent falls into 40 days arrears. Agreed: entry fine [illegible, blank in draft] [mem 16d]

Sowerby (*120*) Thomas Oldfeld [of the Cawsey in Warley] by Michael Oldfeild [lord's tenant and sworn,] surrendered the west side of a croft now divided from the east side estimated at 1½ roods of land meadow and pasture, also the west end of a barn, now divided, in Warley in the graveship of Sowerby now occupied by the said Thomas Oldfeild or his assigns at a lord's rent of ½d: to the use of John Cotes of Halifax, co. York, badger, for the natural life of Susan Oldfeild, wife of the same Thomas Oldfeild, paying to Thomas and Susan during her lifetime 15s a year at Whitsun and Martinmas with their right to distrain for immediate arrears. *Not compounded*

Sowerby (*120*) [*sic*] Richard Brigge of Quickstavers yeoman and Martha now his wife, she agreeing separately, by Ambrose Grenewood, lord's tenant and sworn, surrendered 2 messuages and all houses, buildings, lands, closes, meadow, pasture and hereditaments in Sowerby now occupied by Abraham Hanson and Michael Riley or their assigns at a lord's rent of 2s 6d and certain fine: to the use of John Fournes of Sowerby yeoman. Agreed: entry fine of 7s 6d

Sowerby (*121*) Jonas Hellewell of Sowerby, clothier, younger son of Richard Hellewell late of Norland deceased and Edith now his wife, she agreeing separately, by John Illingworth, lord's tenant and sworn, surrendered that close commonly called Astley bothome estimated at 1½ acres in the graveship of Sowerby now occupied by the said Jonas Hellewell or his assigns at a lord's rent of 6d and certain fine, the close being part of 12 acres belonging to 2 messuages in Sowerby called Longedgend: to the use of Henry Bentley of Turvyn in Sowerby yeoman. Agreed: entry fine of 18d. *Compounded for by Jonas Hellewell*

Sowerby (*122*) William Walker of Midgley yeoman by Simon Wade, lord's tenant and sworn, surrendered the reversion immediately after the death of the said William Walker of that messuage and all the lands estimated at 8½ acres of land meadow and pasture in Warley in the graveship of Sowerby now occupied by the said William Walker and a Henry Walker or their assigns at a lord's rent of 2s 10d and certain fine: to the use of John Walker *alias* Stead, reputed son of the said William Walker and to his lawful heirs, with remainder to Mary Walker, daughter of the said William Walker and to her lawful heirs, with remainder to the right heirs of the said William. Agreed: entry fine of 4s 3d [altered in the draft from 3s 5d] *Compounded for by William Walker*

Holme (*123*) Margaret Brodeley of Halifax widow, late wife of Robert Brodeley deceased and previously wife of John Haigh late of Skircote deceased, by George Fairbanke, lord's tenant and sworn, surrendered all the crofts, closes and parcels of land called le Crofte, Croftbothome and Wood in Holme in the graveship of Holme, lately occupied by a Luke Swallow and now by a Joseph Denton or his assigns at a lord's rent of 8d and certain fine: to the use of William Lowther of Leeds gen. Agreed: entry fine of 2s. *Compounded for by Edward Haigh*

Francis Moxon, Brian Gleidhill and William Ramsden sworn as examiners of hides and Robert Gleidhill as sealer

[The draft roll commences with surrender (116) and continues with the presentation of constables, viz:]

Halifax: Henry Riley and William Parkin, deputies of John Smith mercer *dead* and Abraham Mitchell, constables, Thomas Wood, Henry Heape, Stephen Standeven, Mathew Calvert, Richard Lightollers, Samuel Farrer, John Simson and John Wilkinson, sworn, say that Christopher Robinson and John Smith of Hallend are elected constables

Skircote: Simon Rigge, deputy of John Bawmforth, constable, Richard Wood, Ambrose Grenewood, Henry Gill and Edmund Hoile, sworn, say that Richard Waterhouse is elected constable

Sowerby: Henry Wilson, constable, John Dickson, Nathan Carter, John Illingworth and John Crosley of Smallees, sworn, say that

Richard Bentley is elected constable. He deputes Josiah Stansfeild, who is accepted and sworn.

Warley: John Holdsworth, constable, Elias Mawde, James Halstead, Thomas Deane and Jonathan Gawkroger, sworn, say that Thomas Oldfeild of Cliffehill is elected constable. He deputes Simon Otes, who is accepted and sworn.

Ovenden: William Bollinge, deputy of Samuel Tasker, constable, John Scott, Thomas Rawlinson, Samuel Akeroid and Richard Longbothome, sworn, say that Edward Rydinge is elected constable

Wadisforth: James Harwood, constable, Edward Hoile, John Wiggan, Henry Parker and Adam Sutcliffe, sworn, say that John Pighells is elected constable.

Midgley: John Patchett, deputy of Gregory Patchett, constable, Richard Smith, William Deane, John Shawe and Laurence Oldfeild, sworn, say that John Hellewell is elected constable

Rishworth: John Bothomley, constable, John Godley, Martin Firth, Robert Wood and Gabriel Bentley, sworn, say that Abraham Batchler is elected constable. He deputes John Barrowe, who is accepted and sworn.

Stansfeild: Thomas Halme, constable, Samuel Brigge, Thomas Crosley, Michael Bentley and John Speake, sworn, say that John Stansfeild is elected constable

Heptonstall: Thomas Draper, constable, Jeremy Sutcliffe, Ambrose Grenewood, Josua Bentley and John Awsten, sworn, say that Thomas Grenewood is elected constable

Langfeild: William Farrer, constable, Robert Sutcliffe, John Ogden, John Crosley and Henry Wilson, sworn, say that Jeremy Ingham is elected constable

Ayringdon: John Bordall, constable, Abraham Farrer, Henry Cockcroft, Richard Horsfall and Richard Cockcroft, sworn, say that Samuel Hanson is elected constable

Francis Moxon, Brian Gleidhill and William Ramsden are sworn as searchers of hides, and Robert Gleidhill as sealer

[The surrenders continue, (117)–(123)]

[A[1]]

Halifax Pannell for the King 14 October 1639

Abraham Parkinson 4:4:5

[A[2]]

Item James Cowper Butcher for makinge a fray against Robert Briar of Hallifax and drawinge blood

Item William Sutcliffe Taylor for makinge afray and drawing the blood of Richard Robinson

[etc as engrossed to Richard Longbothome]

[signed] Abraham Parkinson we finde as above written by the
Roger Boulton Othes of Daniell Gibson

John Croslande [IC] | John Millnes
Michaell Brigge | Henry Ridinge
Richard Bentley

John Milnar/Michaell Loungbothom/John Horsfall [IH]/William Walker/John Wheelewright [W]/John Utlay/John Grenewod/John Knowles [I]/Abraham Sunderlaund

[endorsed] by enquiry

[A3]

present

In primas John Crosley for making an afray and dreying bloyd vpon John Kershaw

John Crosley for the Lyke vpon Abraham Kershaw

[etc as engrossed to John Widdopp of Wadsworth]

[signed] Abraham Mitchell/Abraham Parkinsone/Roger Boulton/Richard Bentley/Abraham Sunderland/Michaell Longbothom

by enquiry for the bailiff of Heptonstall

[A4]

Presentments per Thomas Hoult

Imprimis I present Henery Horsfald for setting the water out of the Course in A field which hee Occupieth Lying by the side of Long John Lane 00–03–04

Item I present John Boye for his Mayden defileing the water Courses 00–01–00

we find by the Oth of Thomas Houlte as aboue written

[signed] Abraham Parkinson/Roger Bentley/Michaell Longbothom/John Milnar/John Utley/John Grenewood/William Walker

by enquiry

[A5]

Richard Wormold, Judeth his wife and Jane Wormald for Blood and fray vpon Henrie Greaves, George Litlcliff and John Hartlay

we finde by the Oth of John Hartleay as aboue written

[signed] Abraham Parkinson/Richard Bentley/Roger Boulton/Michaell Lond

by enquiry

[A6]

October 14 1639

Paynes Laide per the presenters of Hallifax as followeth

Imprimis wee present Richard Richardson for Richard Hargreaves his Tennant abuseing the water Course within the house wherein the said Richard Hargreaves now dweleth in 00–10–00

Item wee present Mary Nayler de Hepton Brigge widow for suffering A walle to falle downe on the backside of Hugh Fawcett Whereby the water Course of Bowerum is stoped in 00–10–00

Presentments laide as followeth

Imprimis wee present Richard Richardson if hee doe not suffitiently amend the Water Course as aboue writen before the first of December next in 01–00–00

Item wee present Mary Nayler widow if shee doe not Suffitiently amend her walle before this and the first of December next as is aboue written 01–00–00

[signed] Henry Riley   Thomas Woodd
William Parkin   Stephen Standen

He the said John Crossland de Hallifax beeing one of the Jury dothe present Miles Croysdale and his wife of the same for A noyance done vnto him vnder his parler widow (*sic*) 3s 4d   Henery Heape [mark]   Mathew Calverd [mark]

[signed] Abraham Parkinson/Roger Boulton/Abraham Sunderland/ Michaell Brigge/William Walker/Michaell Longbotham

Halifax

[B]

Skircoates 15° sep: 1639   Constable with the presenters heere vnder-written doe subscribe as Followeth

Viz; The stockes, Whipstockes, Buttes, Pinfold and all high Wayes are in good Repaire   Rest Omnia bene

[signed] John Balmeford/Ambrose Grenewood/Simon Rigge/ Edmund Hoile [EH]/Henry Ghill/Richard Woode [R]

[signed] Abraham Parkinson/Roger Boulton/Michaell Brigge/ William Walker/Michaell Longbothom/John Grenewood/ John Utlay/John Milnar

Skircote

[C]

Sowerby Bill

Court Leete houlden att Hallifax the 14th day of October 1639

We whose names are vnderwritten lay in paine Henery Crosley for not takeinge the water in att the ordinary course nigh vnto his yate aboue the loynehead, which water course if it be not amended within this two moneths, we paine it in twenty shillings

Also we lay in paine Robert Hargraues and Samuell Hanson for not takeinge in the water att their ordinary courses att a place called delues in Crowell Lawes, which water courses if they be not amended within this six weekes wee paine either of them in fyue shillings.

Also we lay in paine John Banister and George Banister of Stake or the occupiers thereofe, for not takinge in the water att the ordinary courses beinge great annoyance to the high way, which water course if it be not amended within this two moneths we paine it in six shillings eight pence.

Also we lay in paine William Bramfitt of Pynest in Skircoote for turninge the water downe the loyne as also for not repairinge that way aboue Pynest and beneath as far as his ground reacheth, which way if it be not amended within this six weekes we paine it in twenty shillings.

Also we paine the Inhabitants of the towne of Wadsworth for not *repairinge* amendinge the high way betwixt Blagden Bridge and widdopp crofte, which way if it be not amended betwixt this and the first of January we payne it in twenty shillings.

Sowerby

[endorsed] John Dickson/Nathan Carter/John Crosley/John Illingworth/Henrie Wilson

[signed] Abraham Parkinson/Roger Boulton/Michaell Longbothom/William Walker

[D]

October the 14th 1639

Presentments for Warly

we present John Dogan for drainge blood of John Crouthar

for hiee wayes and butes and – and stockes, these are all in good Repare and for other thinges we know non

ex' 6s 8d

[signed] James Halsted/Elias Mawde [mark]/Thomas Deane [T]/ Jonathan Gawkroger

[signed] Abraham Parkinson/Roger Boulton/John Holdsworth/ Richard Bentley/Abraham Sunderlaund

Warley

[E]

14 die October AD 1639 At the Court Leet att Halifax

Ovenden

We lay in paine that Abraham Wilkinson John Tetlow and Nathan Braysett of Ovenden shall before the first day of November next open the water course in the land and ground in Ovenden aforesaid in their respectiue Seuurs, all along their seuerall lands in paine of euery of them not so doing 6s 8d and shall thence forth keepe the same contynually open in paine of euery weeke they neglecte to do it after, each mann of 3s 4d

The stocks, whipstocke, and Buttes are in good repair

[signed] Samuell Tasker, constable

John Scott

Thomas Rowllaindson

Samuell Aikeroid [S]/Richard Longbothom [R] presenters

[signed] Abraham Parkinson/Roger Boulton/Michaell Brigge/ William Walker/Michaell Longbothom/John Milner/ John Grenewood/John Utley/

Ovenden

[F]

15 die Octo: 1639 Att the Court Leet att Halefax

Wadsworth

Wee lay in paine that the Inhabitants of Midgley shall before the last day of November next sufficiently amend the highway from the Holme house bridge to the Rate-house in Midgley in paine of 20s and shall henceforth for euer keepe the same way in good repair in paine of each weeke wherein the same way is vnrepayred 3s 4d

Wee lay in paine that the Inhabitants of Warley shall before the last day of November next sufficiently repayre the highway from the Bankehouse lane head in Warley to the Holmehouse bridgend in Warley aforesaid in paine of 20s and shall henceforth for euer keepe it in good repair in paine of each weeke wherein it is not so done 3s 4d

Stocks, Whipstock', Cuckstoole, pinfold and Butts are all in good repair

James Harwod Constable

[signed] Edward Hoyll'/John Wiggan [I]/Henry Parker [mark]/ Adam Sutlefe [mark]/presenters

[signed] Abraham Parkinson/Roger Boulton/Richard Bentley/ Michaell Longbothom/John Milnar/John Vtlay/John Grenewod/William Walker/

Wadsworth

[G]

14 die Octobris 1639 At the Court Leet att Halifax

Midgley in Com: Ebor'

Traversed Wee find that Richard Midgley and Samuell Midgley of Midgley haue not repayred the lane called Bradfordelane in Midgley abovesaid according to a paine formerly laid, and therefore wee amercy them 10s

Item Wee find that the said Samuell Midgley of Midgley hath not amended the highway from the Lowerend of Bradfordelane in Midgley aforesaid to the Holmehousebridgend in Midgley abouesaid according to a paine formerly laid, and therefore wee amercy him 5s

Item we find that James Oldfeild of Warley in the County of Yorke yeoman hath not amended the highway from the Holmehouse-bridgend in Warley aforesaid to the lowerend of one lane called Banckehouse lane in Warley abovesaid according to a paine formerly laid, and therefore wee amercy him in 10s

Item wee find that Bryan Crowther of Warley abovesaid hath not repayred thes walls of thes lands in his occupacon adioyning vpon the hyway in Warley abovesaid, but suffered the stones thereof to ly in the hyway there to and hath not opened his watercourses, according to a paine formerly laid, and therefore wee amercy him in 5s

Item Wee lay in paine that the said Richard Midgley and Samuell Midgley shall sufficiently amend the hyway called Bradfordelane in Midgley aforesaid all along their lands there before the last day of

November next in paine of 30s and shall thenceforth for euer keepe the same in good repaire in paine of euery weeke wherein it is not so kept of 3s 4d

Item wee lay in paine that the said Samuell Midgley shall amend the hyway in Midgley all along his land there from Holmehouse-bridgend to the lowerend of Bradfordlane before the first of December next at paine of 20s and shall thenceforth keepe the same in good repair in paine of each weeke wherein it is not so sufficiently repaired of 2s *traversed*

Item wee lay in paine that James Oldfeild of Warley shall sufficiently amend the hyway all along his lands in Warley aforesaid from Holmehousebridgend to the lowerend of the lane called Banckehouselane before the first day of December next in paine of 10s and shall thenceforth for euer keepe the same sufficiently repaired in paine of euery month wherein it is vnrepayred of 3s 4d

Midgley

[dorse] Item wee lay in paine that Bryan Crowther of Warley aforesaid shall sufficiently amend the highway aboue the land in his tenure in Warley aforesaid by removing the stones and rubbish of the walls of his said land out of the said hyway wherein now they ly, before the 15th day of November next in paine of 20s

[signed] John Patchett Constable
Richard Smyth/Laurence Oldfeild [L]/William Deane [W]/
John Shaw [I]/Presenters

[signed] Abraham Parkinson/Roger Boulton/Richard Bentley/
Abraham Sunderlaund/John Grenewod/William Walker/

[H]

the Constable of Risworth com Norland John Bothomley
his Fower men John Godley, Martin Firth, Robert Woodhead, Gabriell Bentley
for boots and stokes wee haue: for other Misdemayners wee knowe none

[signed] Abraham Parkinsoun/Roger Boulton/Richard Bentley/
Michaell Brigge/William Walker/Michaell Longbothom/
Rishworth cum Norland

[I]

Stanesfeld bill

we paine John Whitwham and William Binglay [added] In twentie shilinges If he do not amend sufesently one way lyinge betwene William Binglayes and a place called the mosse before the second day of februarie next.

Item we paine Robert Croslay Abraham Clege and Samewell Bridge If the[y] do not amend a way lying betwene the banke head and a place called Mathew house in Stanesfeld If it be not ame[n]ded before Candelmas next In twente shillinges.

Item we paine William Suctcliffe and Martin Wilkinsonne In twentie shilinges If they do not amend one way lying betwene Mathew house and the yate next aboue In twentie shillinges If it be not amended before candelmas next.

Item wee paine Luke Horesfall and John Horesfall In thirtie shillinges If the[y] to not amend sufecently one way lying betwene Ratanstall wood and callis brig If it be not amended before Chrisenmas next.

[signed] Thomas Halme Constabell
[marked] Samewell Bridge/Micaell Bentley/John Spake/Thomas Croslay/
[signed] Abraham Parkinson/Roger Boulton/Richard Bentley/ Michaell Brigge/William Walker/Michaell Longbothom/ John Milnar/John Vtley/John Grenewood

Stansfeild

[J]

14th of October 1639 Thomas Draper Constable of Heptonstoll

Jeremy Sutcliffe and Ambrose Greenewood } old presenters
John Bentley and John Austine } new presenters

Inprimis wee doe payne Jonas Thomas, John Crabtree, Richard Naylor, Widowe Sutcliffe, John Ingam, Richard Smyth, John Sutcliffe, and John Longley, if they wash any *foule* clothes or Defile the water in one well called Smyth well for every fault 5s

Item Wee doe present John Langley for breakeing the Lords folde two seuerall tymes 6s 8d

Item Willium Whitwham for the like two seuerall tymes 6s 8d

Item wee present Gidion Stansfeild for makeing vse of the buttering stones of Hepton that parte of Hepton bridge adjoyneing to Wadisworth, in the payne of 39s 11d

Item wee payne the inhabitants of Wadisworth if the said end of the same bridge be not amended before martinmas next 39s

Item we present Bryan Bentley for makeing an affray vpon James Bentley

	Thomas Draper
[signed] Abraham Parkinson	Jeremy Sutcliffe [mark]
Roger Boulton	Ambrose Greenewood [A]
Richard Bentley	Josua Bentley [IB]
Michael Longbothom	John Austine [I]

Heptonstall

[K]

the xiiij day of October 1639

the Constable of Langfeld Thomas Sutcliff and four men

Robartt Sutcliff/James Ogden/John Crosley/Henry Willsone/

as for butes and stockes we haue in good Repear and as for other misdemeners we known none

[signed] Abraham Parkinson/Roger Boulton/Abraham Sunderland/ Michaell Brigge/Michaell Longbothom

Langfeild

[L]

15 die Octobr' 1639

The Butts, and stocks are in good repair

And whereas Henry Helywell was payned att the last sherifs turne that if hee did not sufficiently amend before the 24th of June last the highway from the east end of his house in Eringdon aforesaid along his garden there, hee should forfeit 39s and for euery month after that hee did not amend it 3s 4d

Wee find that the same way was sufficiently amended before the 24th day of June last according to the said pain.

John Boardall Constable [B]

Abraham Farrer [A]/Richard Cockcroft [R]/

Richard Horsfall [R]/Henery Cockcroft presenters

[signed] Abraham Parkinson/Roger Boulton/Abraham Sunderlaund /Michaell Brigge/William Walker/Michaell Longbothom/ John Milnar/John Grenewood/John Utlay/

Eringden

[mem 16d]

BRIGHOUSE: VIEW OF FRANKPLEDGE AND COURT LEET WITH TOURN: 15 October 15 Charles [1639]

Inquisition taken for the King on the oath of Richard Ramsden, yeoman, John Hemmingway, Henry Brighouse, Michael Slater, Thomas Hanson, William Gleidhill, Edward Nicholls, John Mellyn, Francis Jackson, Henry Savile, Anthony Orage, Thomas Preistley, Charles Turner and John Whiteley: who present that James Otes made an encroachment on the road between Northowrome greene and Barmeshill, being a nuisance to neighbours and travellers. *20s*

that the inhabitants of Fekisby failed to mend the road called le Heyland according to a previous pain *former pain, £10*

HIPPERHOLME: Isaac Brodeley, constable, and his fellows present William Walker as chosen constable for this year and he is sworn

RASTRICK: Henry Hanson, deputy of James Londe, constable, and fellows present Thomas Flather as chosen constable ...

that Thomas Flather broke the lord's fold in Rastrick *3s 4d*

FEKISBY: Thomas Reyner, constable, and fellows present Joseph Lockwood as chosen constable ...

NORTHOWROME: Nathan Hoile, deputy of Joseph Butterworth, constable, and fellows present George Longbothome as chosen constable ...

SHELFFE: Robert Lea, constable, and fellows present Robert Birkhead as chosen constable ...

QUARMBY: William Haigh, constable, and fellows present Michael Haigh as chosen constable ...

that Nicholas Colson	made	affray	and drew	blood of	Richard Crosland	*10s*
Joseph Walker	,,	,,	George Helliwell			*3s 4d*
Thomas Dawson	,,	,,	and drew	blood of	Susan Ball	*10s*
Edward Dawson	,,	,,	,,	,,	Susan Ball	,,
Thomas Dawson	,,	,,	,,	,,	James Sykes	,,
William Firth	,,	,,	,,	,,	George Shaw	,,
John Hey	,,	,,	,,	,,	George Hellewell	,,
Henry Hudson	,,	,,	,,	,,	George Hellewell	,,

[mem 17]

DALTON: Thomas Dyson, deputy of Richard Brooke of Lees, constable, and fellows present John Horsfall as chosen constable for this year, who puts in his place Richard Brooke, accepted and sworn.

that Richard Stringer	made	affray	on Roger Brooke			*3s 4d*
Thomas Rawson	,,	,,	Roger Brooke			,,
Thomas Frudd	,,	,,	and drew	blood of	Anthony Orage	*10s*

CLIFTON: Richard Reyner, constable, and fellows present Robert Drake, cardmaker, as chosen constable ...
HARTSHEAD: James Flather, constable, and fellows present Miles Clayton as chosen constable ...
STAINLAND: George Gleidhill, deputy of Humphrey Ramsden, constable, and fellows present Thomas Cordingley as chosen constable ...
BARKISLAND: John Deane, constable, and fellows present James Cordley as chosen constable ...

The jurors present that all above is true.

[A[1]]
Hipperholme: Isaac Brodeley, constable, Arthur Emsall, John Scolefeild, George Wilson and Joseph Thorpe present William Walker as constable etc
Rastricke: Henry Hanson, elect and deputy constable, James Lome, constable, John Crosley, Arthur Hirst, Abraham Farrer and William Steeton present Thomas Flather as constable
Fixby: Thomas Reyner, constable, Robert Haigh, Thomas Stansfeild, Edward Brooke and William Dysonn present Joseph Lockwood as constable
Northowrome: Nathan Hoyle, deputy of Joseph Butterworth, constable, Marmaduke Hall, John Wadisworth, Samuel Hargett and Edward Hodgson present George Longbothome as constable
Shelffe: Robert Lea, constable, John Sunderland, John Firth, John Otes and Edward Slater present Robert Birkehead as constable
Quarmby: William Haigh, constable, Edward Hanson, Nicholas Hirst, George Walker and John Clay present Michael Haigh as constable
[A[2]]
Dalton: Thomas Dyson, deputy of Richard Brooke of Lees, constable, John Spivie, Roger Hirst, Mathew Hirst and William Brookesbanke present John Horsfall as constable, who deputes Richard Brooke.
Clifton: Richard Reyner, constable, Robert Hyley and Robert Drake present Robert Drake, cardmaker, as constable
Harteshead: James Flather, constable, Edward Reyner and John Walker present Miles Clayton as constable
Stainland: George Gleidhill, deputy of Humphrey Ramsden, constable, Richard Bothomley, Richard Preistley, Barnard Denton and Thomas Pighells present Thomas Cordingley as constable
Barkisland: John Deane, constable, George Ramsden, James Scolefeild, James Grene and John Townend present James Cordley as constable

[B]

Brighouse Pannell pro domino Rege xv october 1639
Richard Ramsden etc [4:4:5]

[C]

we *present* laye in payne Thomis Drake or the owners or ockopier of shibden mill to make A Sufficient bridge ouer against a place Called Damhead in 5^{l}

Item we paine Joseph Furnis to mack a sufficient way at A place Called the gumblle in 2^{l}0–0

Item we *present* lay in payn henry Crabtre of Damhead to mend the hye way betwen his groundes betwis his owne house and Mickel Houldesworth in blackes side in 5^{l} 0 0

Item we *present* lay in pain that John Drake of Northourom and henry northend of the sam shall amend wone hie way Called Hoolley liget beneath northorom and mack A suficant wainway and A Horseway and Cut their heges that hangs ofer the said way betwen this and the frist of May next in pain of 5^{l} 0 0.

[dorse] Item we *present* payne John Mellin Edward northend John Clay henry norrie Samuell Hargit Jeremy Holdsworth Giles Tenant the occupiers of the lands of John Thorpe to make a sufficient footway as hath bene vsuall betwixt this and Cristmas next vpon payne of fiue pounds.

we present John Drake and Henrie Northen ether of them 10s for not cuttinge ther hedges but suffers them to grow over the hie way contrary to the statute.

[signed] Richard Ramsden/John Hemingway/Henry Brighouse/
Michaell Slater/ *examined 20s*

[D]

Item we present James Otes thelder for makinge an incroachment vpon the *hie* way leadinge betwixt Northowrome Greene and Barmeshill, beinge a greate annoyance to neighbours and passingers 20s

And we lay in payne that the said James Otes shall cast out the said encroachment betwixt this and Martinmas next or sufficiently amend the said way before Martinmas next in paine of 40s

[signed] Richard Ramsden/John Hemingway/Henry Brighouse/
Edward Niccoll/John Mellin/

[E]

Item we present the Inhabitants of Fixbie for not mendinge a way called the heyland according to a pain formerlie laid of 10^{l}

Wheras Thomas flather is elected Constable this day for Rastricke beinge a man of good estate that either he or a sufficient debiti by him to be provided shall repaire before some of his majesties Justice of peace befor the end of six daies next cominge and there to take his corporall oathe to performe the said office of a Constable for this yeare next followinge vpon paine of 10^{l}

[signed] Richard Ramsden/John Hemingway/Henry Brighouse/ Michaell Slater/Edward Niccoll/John Mellin/Charles Turner/francis Jackson [F]/Thomas Hanson [TH]/John Whiteley [I]/Thomas Prestley [mark]/Anthony herrige [AH]/ Willyam Gledhill [W]/Henry Savill [mark]/

[F]

Hipperholme cum Brighouse bill, October 17th, 1639

Paines laid at the Sherifs turne by the Constable Isaak Brodley, Arthur Empsell, John Scholefield, George wilson Joseph Thorpe

Item we lay in payn that no manner of persons turn out anie Swine unyoked or vnrigged in paine of euerie time so doinge to forfeit 12d

Item we lay in pain that Mr Higginson and Christopher Steuenson do mend one paunde called henroyd' pavnde betwixte this and Martinmesse nexte in pain of either them 20s

Item we lay in paine that Christopher Steuenson doe mend the way betwene his house and the spoute house betwene this and Christmas nexte in paine of 3s 4d

Item we lay in pain that John Nicholl Robert Barocloughe James Wilkinson Edword Baraclough do mende ane laine betwene norwod' grene and horse close brigge betwixte this and Andermesse in paine of 39s

Item we lay in paine that Thomas flother doe remowe his spiggis forth of Angrame dicks ofer the hie way side betwixte this and mortinmesse in paine of 20s

[signed] Richard Ramsden/John Hemingway/Michaell Slater/ Henry Brighouse/Charles Turner

[G¹]

1639

Thomas Mallinson the Constabell of Rastricke and his fower men Arthur Hirst John Crosley Abaram Farra Willeam Steton

Item wee presente Thomas Flatther for a foulld breke 3s 4d

Richard Ramsden/John Hemingway/Henry Brighouse/Michaell Slater/Edward Niccoll

Rastricke

[G²]

Brighouse XV October 1639

Wee laye in paine that the Inhabitants of Fekisbie doe sufficientlie repaire the kings heigh way now in greate decaye called Hey lane in Fekisbye betwene the Hey yate adioininge to Rastrickmore and the yate deuideinge the same lane from the Lordshipp of Bradley beinge parte of the Roadway leadinge betweene Wakefeild and Eland and soe to Rachdale before the First day of Aprill next in paine of Tenn pounds.

Item we laye in paine that the Inhabitants of Fekisbie doe well and sufficienty repaire that parte of the Common hie waye in Fekisbie called the vpperwaye leadinge betweene Huddersfeild and Eland alonge by Fekisbie hall' (towitt) that parte thereof which lyeth betwene the over Coate and Wind-Milne close before the First day of Aprill' next in paine of Five pounds.

Item wee lay in paine that the Inhabitants of Fekisbie doe well and sufficiently make and repaire that parte of the kings heighe waye in Fekisbye leadinge betweene Barnesley and Halifax which doth lye betwene the Heyyate and Lightridge Cloughe before the first daye of Aprill' next in paine of five pounds.

[signed] Richard Ramsden/John Hemingway/Michaell Slater/
Henry Brighouse/Charles Torner
Rastricke

[H]

The Constable of Northowrom with his foure men videlicet Joseph Butterworth Constable Samuell Hardger' marmaduke Hall [H] Edward Hodson [E] John wadsworth

Inprimis we lay in paine Henery more that he kepe the water in shofden land in the ould acostomed course betwixt this and all sants day in paine of ten shilinges.

Item we lay in paine George whyteley and Lawrance Whiticar to mend a way at colear sike betwixt this and all sants day in paine of ether of them fiue shilinges.

Item we lay in paine that no manar of person or persons shal at any time heare after make any foote way our any of the grounds being in the ocupation of mare rawlin widow lyinge on the north side of her now dwelinge house in Northowrom in paine of euery one so ofendinge to forfit for euery time so doinge *ten shilinges* 12d.

Item we lay in paine the ouners and ocupiars of part of the lands belonginge to the tan house and mare rawlin that they make the way soficient betwixt there lands in the end of the north lane betwixt this and al sants day in payne of ether of them fiue shilinges.

Item we lay in paine vido Hopkinson that she mend one foote way lyinge betwixt the damheade and atearish Gate in one Close called Ion Inge betwixt this and all sants day in paine of Thirtene shilinges foure pence.

[signed] Richard Ramsden Northowrome
John Hemingway Michaell Slater
Henry Brighouse Edward Niccoll

[I] October 15th day
1639

paynes layd by the Constable of Shelfe and Foure men
all our paynes layd at the last Court well amended

Imprimis we lay in payne that Edmond wood do amend a place on this side wadhouse Brooke, anent is ground, where he gate stones, betwixt this and martenmise next sufficiently in payne of 10s

Item we lay in payne that Abraham Sunderland do fill his delf Holles, anent his new intake betwixt this and martenmise next in payne of 10s

[signed] Robert lea/John Sunderland/John Firth/John Oates/ Edward Slater/

[signed] Richard Ramsden/John Hemingway/Michaell Slater/ Henry Brighouse/Edward Niccoll/John Mellin/ Shelffe

[J]

Quarmby Bill: presenters

The Constable William Haighe with the foure men Edwarde Hanson Nicholas Hirste George Walker John Claye.

Item presente vpon the oathe of Richard Croslande Nicholas Coulson for makeinge afraye and draweing of Bloode vpon the said Richarde Croslande

Item presente vpon the oathe of George Walker Josephe Walker for makeinge afraye vpon George Heallewell

Item present vpon the oathe Susay Ball Thomas Dawson for makeinge afraye and drawinge of Bloude vpon the said Susay Ball

Item presente Edwarde Dawson for makeinge afraye and drawinge of Bloude vpon the abouesaid Susay Ball

Item present vpon the oathe of Susay Ball Thomas Dawson for makeinge afraye and drawinge of Bloade vpon James Syckes

Item presente vpon the oathe of George Shawe William Firth for macking afraye and draweinge of Bloude vpon the said George Shawe

Item present vpon the oathe of James Fraunce John Hey for makeinge afraye and draweinge of Bloude vpon George Heallewel

Item present vpon the oathe of James France Henery Hudson for makeinge afraye and draweinge of Bloude vpon George Heallewel

examined Isaak Worm:

Quarmby

[dorse]

Item presente vpon the oathe of William Haigh James Dyson for makeinge afraye and draweinge of Bloude vpon Nathan Whyteley

Item Wee laye in paine That William Aneley doe make suffitient fence from John firthe Betwene this and alsants daye next in paine of 10s

Item wee laye in paine that James Dyson and George Shawe doe make suffitiente waye in a lane nere vnto the Heighwestwode Betwene this and the seconde of februarie nexte in paine of 20s

[signed] Richard Ramsden
John Hemingway
Henry Brighouse
Michaell Slater
Edward Niccoll
John Mellin

Quarmby

[K]

1639 October the 15th day Richard Brooke Constable
presentments mad by the Constable of dalton

Imprimis, we present Richard Stringer for makeing a fraye vpon Roger Brooke

Item, we present Thomas Rasonn for makeing afray vpon Roger Brooke

Item, we present Thomas Frudd for makeing a blood and afray vpon Anthony Orage

Item, we present William Gissop and John Dison for makeing afray vpon John Disson ether of other

Richard Broake [mark]/Roger Hirst [R]
Mathew Hirst [I]/John Spivie [mark]/
William Brockesbanke [mark]/

Dalton

[signed] Richard Ramsden/John Hemingway/Henry Brighouse/
Michaell Slater/Charles Torner

[L]

As for presentments there is none Clifton cum Hartishead

Omne bene

[signed] Robert Hylie Robert Drake/John Walker Edward Reiner
[signed] Richard Ramsden/John Hemingway/Henry Brighouse/
Michaell Slater

Harteshead cum Clifton and Fixby presents nothing but omne bene

[M]

Richard Bothomley and Richard Preistley beinge presenters of offences given in charge doe present

Stainland vpon the oath of John Mallinson that John Bentley of Slaghwaite did make a blood and afray at Stainland within the Iurisdiction of this Court vp the said John Mallinson since the last Court

Wee the Inhabitants of Ould Linley doe lay in paine that wee [*added*] owners and occupiers of a close called Newhey within Ould lynley doe make their fences sufficient betwene the said close called Newheye and the comon towne feildes in Ouldlynley aforesaid betwene the 25th of march and Michaellmus in paine of euerie defect 39s 11d.

We alsoe lay in paine that euerie of the Inhabitants within Ould lynley aforesaid doe make their Comon Fences sufficient before the 25th of March in paine of euerie person or houshould hauing any fence theer in the some of 6s 8d

We laye in paine that the owners or occupieres of certaine groundes called Rawbancke doe repaire and [dorse] Make the way sufficient theer before the first of November next in paine of 10s

[signed] Richard Ramsden Richard Preistley/Richard Bothomley/
John Hemingway Barnard Denton/Thomas Pickles/
Henry Brighouse George Gleidhill/*Henry Brighouse*/
Michaell Slater *Michaell Slater*/

Item we lay in paine the ocupier of a parcel of land called Newhey in ould linley mak their fens 20s. Item we lay in pain that all the Inhabetant of ould linleay make theire fenc befor the xxv day of march in pain of euery man 3s 4d

[N[1]]

Barksland bille

Item we lay in paine that Michell Helewel Roberd hansonne Daue prestley John Helewell Henerrie walton Ralfe Bothomley doe mend the way betwixt Ralfe bothomley yeate and the yeate that openeth to stainland greane betwixt this and martinmis Daye in paine of Eueri one 6s 8d

George Ramsdin [R] James greane [I]
James Scalfeld [I] John townend [mark]
John Deane

Barkisland

[endorsed] Richard Ramsden/John Hemingway/Henry Brighouse/ Michaell Slater/

[N[2]]

Brighouse the xvth day of October 1639

We lay in payne that William Horton thelder and Michaell Earnshaw of Barkisland doe well and sufficiently repayre the Common waye leadinge betweene Bothomley and Barkisland in a place lyinge betweene Bothomley yate and the house in the tenure of the sayd Michaell Earnshaw, before the first day of Aprill next cominge in payne of 5 li

Item we lay in payne that William Horton yonger of Firthehouse doo lay forth of his incroachment by him lately made vpon Bothomley greene the watercourse and common way leadinge through the same for the vse of the inhabitants of Bothomley for wateringe of their cattell and wayes and passages for the same before the first day of Aprill next coming in payne of 5 li

Barkisland

[no endorsement]

[Mem 17]

KIRKBURTON: VIEW OF FRANKPLEDGE AND COURT LEET WITH TOURN: 16 October 15 Charles [1639]

Inquisition taken for the King on the oath of Francis Mathewman yeoman, Thomas Lockwood, Henry Jackson, Thomas Coldwell, Mathew Moorehouse, John Kay, Humphrey Robucke, Thomas Lockwood, Abraham Horne, Thomas Tincker, John Brooke, Joshua Brodehead and William Matson, who declare that (*124*) John Byns of Bankend, clerk, and Elizabeth his mother by charter dated 29 October 14 Charles [1638] granted to one Godfrey Cuttell of Holmefirth his heirs etc 3 acres 1 rood of land and all buildings thereon and all watercourses in Woldall and Cartworth in the graveship of Holme lately held by Michael Wood and Thomas Chappell or their assigns, parcel of the lands late of Robert earl of Leicester, which brings to the lord a relief of 13d viz. at 4d an acre *Relief from lands lately of Earl of Leicester 14d*

that John Linley and John Marsden hunted and killed hares in the snow against the statute *13s 4d*

that John Robucke made affray and drew blood from Humphrey Hobkin 10s

Henry Hill ,, against Humphrey Hobkin 3s 4d

BURTON: Robert Senior, deputy of Thomas Senior, constable, and his fellows present Edward Haigh as constable this year. He deputes Robert Senior, who is received and sworn.

SHELLEY: John Armitage, constable, and his fellows present Mathew Nicholls as constable this year

that John Mosley of Shelley made affray on Edward Wood *3s 4d*

SHEPLEY: Thomas Moorehouse, constable, and his fellows present John Rowley as constable this year

CUMBERWORTH: Robert Lockwood, constable, and his fellows present John Moorehouse as constable this year

THURSTONLAND: Henry Gillott, constable, and his fellows present Thomas Archer as constable this year

HOLME: Thomas Moorehouse, constable, and his fellows present James Genne as constable this year

FULSTON: township present that Abraham Moorehouse, lately constable of Holme, failed to account for last year according to the pain previously laid *39s*

SCOLES: township said 'all well'

WOLDALL: ,, ,,

CARTWORTH: township said 'all well'
AUSTONLEY: ,, ,,
HEPWORTH: ,, ,,
THWONGE: ,, ,,

The jurors present that all above is true [mem 17d]

Holme (*125*) Testimony on the oath of James Genne, lord's tenant, that John Booth of Hayslacke and Isabella his wife, she agreeing separately, on 13 June 1639 surrendered half an acre half a rood called Overmeasure and all houses and buildings thereon and another half acre adjoining to the north of a close of the said John Booth called Hayslacke at Hayslacke in Hepworth in the graveship of Holme now occupied by the said John Booth or his assigns at a lord's rent of 4½d and certain fine: to the use of William Marsh of Lookehouse from the feast of the Purification next [2 February] for 21 years at an annual rent to John and Isabella of 27s at Whitsun and Martinmas, and the houses, buildings, fences and ground to be kept in good repair and culture. Agreed: entry fine of 6¾d *Compounded for by John Tincker*

Holme (*126*) Testimony on the oath of Francis Mathewman, lord's tenant, that Laurence Roberte on 26 June 15 Charles [1639] surrendered a house in which Godfrey Morton now lives, an 'amistall' at the west end of a barn, now divided, a fold, a garden, a close of land and meadow called Crofte, a close called Leyfeild, three closes called Thwongeshirst, a close called Whynnes and Whynnynge and a close of land and meadow called Cowperynge in Woldall in the graveship of Holme and now occupied severally by Robert Ellis, Thomas Robucke, and John Batty or their assigns at a lord's rent of 3s 6d and certain fine: to the use of Robert Brodehead of Holmefirth Chappell from 2 February 1644 for three years (provided that Laurence Roberte live so long) at an annual rent to Laurence Roberte of 20s at Whitsun and Martinmas, with the right to re-enter and distrain if the rent falls two days in arrears. Agreed: entry fine of 4s 9d *Compounded for by John Roberte and Elizabeth his wife*

Holme (*127*) Testimony on the oath of Francis Mathewman, lord's tenant, that Richard Firth, son and heir apparent of Luke Firth of Boothhouse on 2 May 15 Charles [1639] surrendered all those houses and buildings, barns and structures sited at Hogley in Awstonley now occupied by Richard Waterhouse or his assigns, a fold, a garden and easements and all closes of arable, meadow and pasture at and above Hogley, viz. from the west of the same, and now occupied by the said Richard Waterhouse or his assigns, and another close called Roid held by copy of the court roll now occupied by the said Luke Firth or his assigns, estimated at 12 acres, in Awstonley in the graveship of Holme, with all reserved rents, paths, water, watercourses, easements, common pasture etc at a lord's rent of 3s and certain fine (saving the life interest of Luke Firth in the same): to the use of the said Richard Firth until his brother Michael Firth return from the King's service in the war and army against the Scots now in 1639, and then to the use of the said Michael Firth and no other use. Agreed: entry fine of 9s *Compounded for by Luke Firth*

Holme (*128*) Testimony on the oath of Humphrey Hirst, lord's tenant, that Joshua Earnshaw on 26 October 14 Charles [1639] surrendered a messuage in Holme and all houses, holdings, etc (saving a close called Cliffe ynge in Holme in the graveship of Holme now occupied by William Mitchell or his assigns at a lord's rent of 2s 5d and certain fine: to the use of the said William Mitchell from 2 February last for 19 years at an annual rent to Joshua Earnshaw of £6 13s 4d at Whitsun and Martinmas. Agreed: entry fine of 3s 2½d (*Compounded for by William Ramsden Esq. and Nicholas Fenay gen*) [mem 18]

Holme (*129*) Testimony on the oath of John Hirst, lord's tenant, that John Grene on 29 April 15 Charles [1639] surrendered a messuage called Overhouse at Barnside and all houses, a garden used with the same, a parcel of land called Litlecrofte and a third part of the maltkiln on the east end of the croft as now agreed, a close called Roidheald, a close called Roid, another called Shirt Cliff ynge, a close called Acre, one called Wilkinynge, one called Mouldclough, one called Appletreelee and one called Appletree Leewood belonging to the same in Hepworth in the graveship of Holme and now occupied by Abraham Roids or his assigns at a lord's rent of 8s 8d and certain fine: to the use of the said Abraham Roids from 2 February past for 13 years at an annual rent to John Grene of £9 10s at Whitsun and Martinmas. Agreed: entry fine of 13s *Compounded for by William Roydes*

[A[1]]

[In the draft roll surrenders are interrupted after (125) by the elections of constables]

Burton: Robert Senior deputy of Thomas Senior, constable, George Sikes, John Robucke, Thomas Chappell and Gervis Booth present Edward Haigh, who deputes Robert Senior, who is accepted and sworn *paid 1d*

Shelley: John Armitage, constable, Richard Nicholls junior, Edward Wood, John Hutchinson and Mathew Wood present Mathew Nicholls *paid 1d*

Shepley: Thomas Moorehouse, constable, Samuell Beardsell, Richard Copley, Robert Hepworth and Edward Moorehouse present John Rowley *paid 1d*

Cumberworth Half: Robert Lockwood, constable, Thomas Coldwell and William Oxley present John Moorehouse *paid 1d*

Thurstonland: Henry Gillott, constable, John Lockwood, Henry Beaumount, Godfrey Barnsley and Robert Pitts present Thomas Archer *paid 1d*
Holme: Thomas Moorehouse, constable, Joseph Denton and William Mitchell present James Genne *paid 1d*
[A²]
Fulston: William Newton Godfrey Mathewman Henry Robucke and John Fitton – *paid 1d*
Scoles: John Brooke and Oliver Roberts – *paid 1d*
Wooldale: George Firth, William Marshall, John Brodehead and Christopher Oldham – *paid 1d*
Cartworth: Thomas Charlesworth, William Bray, Gilbert Cartwright and William Hanson – *paid 1d*
Austonley: Thomas Litlewood and William Charlesworth – *paid 1d*
Hepworth: Francis Tinker, John Ibbotson, Edward Beever and Richard Batty – *paid 1d*
Thwonge: Andrew Swallowe and James Backsters – *paid 1d*
[B]

Panel of jurors: Burton 16 October 1639

Francis Mathewman 4:3:5 [Henry Jackson substituted for Francis Tinlee, and Joshua Brodhead transferred from second to third subdivision]

[C]

Item we present John Linley and John Marsden for tracinge and killinge hares in the snowe contrary to the statute by the othe of George Tias

ex. 6s 8d George Tyas

[signed] Francis Mathewman/Thomas Lockwood/Abraham Horne/
Humfrey Robucke/Thomas Locwood

[D]

By the Jury paine the xvjth day of October 1639

Item we say in paine that the Inhabitants within Shelley shall make sufficient the wayne waye betwixt Shelley and Burton accordinge as they vse and Fall For the Repaire of the hie wayes att or before the last day of this month in paine of 30s.

[signed] Francis Mathewman/Henry Jackson/Thomas Lockwood/
John Kay/Abraham Horne *essoin for Jo: Tynker*
Shelley by inquest

[E]

John Robuck for makinge of a fraye and a blode of Homfray Hobkine

Henry Hille for makinge of a fraye of the said Homfray Hobkine 3s 4d

[signed] Francis Mathewman/Henry Jackson/Thomas Lockwood/
Thomas Lockwood/Hunfrey Robucke/Abraham Horne/

The Jury doth lay in payne thus:

Thomas Morehouse do mak his accounts of what Money he hath received and how he hath disburst the same at or before the xxv^th day of December next in payne of 20s

Francis Mathewman/Humfrey Robucke/Henry Jackson/Abraham Horne/Thomas Lockwood/Thomas Lockwood/

[F]

Paines laide att our Kings Majesties Courte healden att Burton the xvj^th day of October 1639 by the Constable and Sworne men of Burton as followeth

Inprimis we lay in paine that noe maner of person take or Carrie either greene or drie wood out of other mens ground without licence of the owner in paine of euery default 3s 4d

Item wee lay in paine that all the househoulders within the Townshippe of Burton shall make theire Fences aioyninge to hard Corne att or before the first day of nouember in paine of every default 10s

Item we lay in paine that noe maner of person goe ouer other mens ground where there is noe vsuall way in paine of euery default 12d

Item we lay in paine, that all the househoulders within this Townshipe shall Ringe theire swine att or before the last day of this month and soe Keepe them vntill the next Court day in paine of euery default 4d

Item wee lay in paine that Edward Haighe and Edward Coggin shall before Martinmis day Remoue Certaine Earth and mire lyinge betweixt Hallinge yate and greate ditch in paine of either of them 30s

Item wee lay in paine that John Kaye yonger shall Remoue Certaine Earth and meaner forth of the greatt dich side forth of the hieway att or before Martinmis day in paine of 10s

Item wee lay in paine that William Smith shall scoure his dich betwixt his paddock and Thomas Robucke Hallowe where therr is hard Corne att or before Martinmis day in paine of 10s

[signed] Francis Mathewman/Abraham Horne/Thomas Lockwood/ Thomas Lockwood/

Burton

[G]

Paynes laid at the Kings Majesties Court holden at Kirkburton the 16th of October 1639 by the Constable and sworne men of Shelley as followeth

Imprimis we lay in payne that noe manner of person or persons whatsoeuer shall cut or cary away either grene wood or dry out of other mens grownds without lycence of the owner thereof in payne of euery default so sene knowne or taken 12d

Item we lay in payne that noe manner of person or persons shall putt any scabbed or infectious horse or meare to any of the Commons of Shelley in payne of euery tyme soe seene knowne or taken 10s

Item we lay in payne that all the inhabitants within the said towne and towneship shall make their fences adioyneinge to hard Corne betwene this and the 11th day of November next Comeing in payne of euery default 10s

Item we lay in payne that Richard Nicholls thelder and Richard Nicholls yonger shall cast out one encroachment taken of the Comon adioyneinge to one of their closes called horse crofte otherwise called farr side before the xxv[th] day of December next in payne of 39s 11d

Item we lay in payne that noe manner of person or persons whatsoever shall make any way ouer one close of Edward Wood called Farrside where noe vsuall way is in payne of euery tyme so sene knowne or taken 12d

Item we present John Mosley of Shelley for affray made vpon Edward Wood the 24th day of September last past 3s 4d

[signed] Francis Mathewman/Humfrey Robucke/Thomas Lockwood/Thomas Lockwood/

Shelley

[H]

Paines laid att our Kings maieaties Court houlden att Burton the xvj[th] day of October 1639 by the Constable and Sworne men of Sheapley as Following

Inprimis wee lay in paine that noe maner of person take or Carrie either greene or drie wood out of other mens ground without licence of the owner in paine of euery default 3s 4d

Item wee lay in paine that all the househoulders within the Townshipe of Sheapley shall make theire Fences aioyneinge to hard Corne att or before the First day of the next month in paine of euery default 10s

Item wee lay in paine that all the househoulders within Sheapley shall Ringe their Swine att or before the last day of this month and so Keepe them Ringed vntill the next Court day in paine of euery default 4d

Item we lay in paine that noe maner of person goe ouer other mens ground where there is noe vsuall way in paine of euery default 12d

[signed] Francis Mathewman/Humfrey Robucke/Abraham Horne/ Thomas Lockwood/Thomas Lockwood

Shepley

[I]

Paynes layd at the kings Majesties Court holden at Kirkburton the 16th day of October 1639 by the Constable and sworne men of Comberworth halfe as Followeth

Imprimis we lay in payne that noe manner of person or persons whatsoeuer shall cutt or Carry away either grene wood or dry out of other mens grownds without lycence of the owner thereof in payne of euery tyme so seene knowne or taken 12d

Item we lay in payne that noe manner of person or persons whatsoeuer shall putt any scabbed or infectious horse or meare to the Comons belonging to the said Comberworth halfe in payne of euery tyme so sene knowne or taken 10s

Item we lay in payne that all the inhabitants within the said Comberworth halfe shall make their fences adioyneing to hard Corne before this and the 11th day of Nouember next and soe keepe them in payne of 10s

Item we lay in payne that Henry Copley Edward Copley and John Child shall fill that stone pitt which they made at Dan roide stile before this and the first day of *Nouember* December next in payne of 10s

Item we lay in payne that Mr Francis Birdell Es[r] and Mr Thomas Wentworth gent shall fill or cause to be filled all those Cole pitts of the Common of Comberworth halfe betwene this and the xxv[th] day of December next Comeinge in payne of 30s

Item we lay in payne that noe manner of person or persons whatsoeuer shall make any way ouer Thomas Coldwell wood called Whitherwood in payne of euery tyme so sene knowne or taken 12d

[signed] Francis Mathewman/Abraham Horne/Thomas Lockwood/ Thomas Lockwood/

Cumberworth half

[J]

Paines laid att our Kings Majesties Court houlden att Burton the xvj[th] day of October 1639 by the Constable and Sworne men of Thurstonland as Followeth

Inprimis wee lay in paine that noe maner of person take or Carrie either greene or drie wood out of other mens ground without licence of the owner in paine of euery default 3s 4d

Item wee lay in paine that all the househoulders within the Township of Thurstonland shall Ringe theire Swine att or before the last Day of this month and soe Keepe them Ringed vntill the next Courte Day in paine of euery defaulte 4d

Item wee lay in paine that all the househoulders within the Townshippe of Thurstonland shall make theire Fences aioyninge to theire hard Corne att or before the First day of the next month in paine of euery default 10s

Item wee lay in paine that noe maner of person goe ouer other mens ground where therr is noe vsuall way in paine of euery default 12d

Item wee lay in paine that Roberte Hirst and Widdow Heye of Woodend shall scoure the diche in the newe Inge betwixt John

Lockwood of lum hay and them att or before Martinmis day in paine of 10s

[signed] Francis Mathewman/Thomas Lockwood/Thomas Lockwood/Humfrey Robucke/

Thurstonland

[K]

Houlme

At the Court leete or sheriffe turne houlden at Burton the xvth day of October 1639 paynes layd by the swornemen of houlme Joseph Denton and William Micheill

Imprimis we doe lay in payne that noe person nor persons do carie green wood nor drie without licence of the right owner in payne of euery deafolte 12d

Item that euery person doe keepe the watter in the right accustomed course in payn of euery defolte 3s 4d

Item that euery person doe keepe the right accustomed foote pathes within the sayd touneshipe in payn of euery deafolt 3s 4d

Item that euery househoulder doe keep thear swyne well ringed in payn of euery defaulte 12d

Item we lay in payne that euery householder doe come or send a sufficient labourer to the mending of the high wayes and turfe gates vpon indifferent warning giuen them in payne of euery defolt 12d

Item we lay in payne that John Hinchcliffe of Holme doe remoue James Haigh and his wyfe out of his howse before the feast of All Saints next in payne of 13s 4d

Item we lay in payne that euery person doe make his fence adioyning to the towne feild and so keepe it sufficient till may day next in payne 6s 8d

Item that no person doe bedd in the high wayes any turfe or bedding in payne of 5s

Holme

[endorsed] Francis Mathewman/Henry Jackson/Thomas Lockwood/Abraham Horne/

[L]

Fulston

At the Sheriffs turne holden at Burton the xvj[th] day of October 1639

Paynes layd by the swornemen of Fulston William Newton Henry Robucke John Fitton and Godfrey Mathewman.

Inprimis wee doe lay in payne that no person nor persons doe cary greeene wood nor dry without licence of the right owner in payne of euery default 12d

Item that euery person doe keepe the water in the right accustomed Course in paine of euery default 3s 4d

Item wee lay in paine that euery person and persons doe keepe the right accustomed footepathes within the sayd towneshippe in paine of euery default 3s 4d

Item that euery householder doe keepe their swine well ringed in paine of euery default 12d

Item that euery person and persons doe make their out fences adioyning to the Comon well and sufficiently before the xxv[th] day of March next in paine of euery dole vnmade 3s 4d

[signed] Francis Mathewman/Abraham Horne/Henry Jackson/ Humfrey Robucke/

The Jury do present Abraham Morehouse late Cunstable of Holme Frith because he hath not made his accounts the last yeare according to a payne formerly layd in 39s neither paid such ouerplus of money as is in his hands

[signed] Francis Mathewman/Humfrey Robucke/John Kay/ Thomas Lockwood/Thomas Lockwood

Fulston

[M]

Scoles

At the Sheriffs turne holden at Burton the xvj[th] day of October 1639

Paynes layde by the swornemen of Scoole Oliver Roberts and John Brooke

Inprimis wee doe lay in paine that no person nor persons doe cary greene wood nor dry without licence of the right owner in paine of euery default 12d

Item that euery person doe keepe the water in the right accustomed course in payne of euery default 3s 4d

Item wee doe lay in paine that euery person and persons doe keepe the right accustomed hy waies footepathes and bridlestythes within the sayd township in paine of euery default 3s 4d

Item that euery householder doe keepe their swyne well ringed in paine of euery default 12d

[signed] Francis Mathewman/Thomas Lockwood/Thomas Lockwood/Humfrey Robuck

Scoles

[N]

Wooldale

At the Court Leete or Sheriffs turne holden at Burton the xvj[th] day of October 1639

paynes layde by the swornemen of Woodale George Firth, John Brodehead, William Marshall and Christopher Ouldham.

Inprimis wee doe lay in payne that no person nor persons doe cary greene wood nor dry without licence of the right owner in paine of euery default 12d

Item wee lay in paine that euery person doe keepe the water in the right accustomed course in payne of euery default 3s 4d

Item that euery person and persons doe keepe the right accustomed hy wayes footepathes and bridlestythes within the sayd towneship in paine of euery default 3s 4d

Item that euery householder doe keepe their swine well ringed in payne of euery default 12d

Item that no person goe over one close in the occupacion of Godfry Cuttell called Laching without his licence nor throw downe his fence in payne of euery person that maketh default for euery default 3s 4d

Item that no person goe over Oliver Roberts Close called Shaleing without his licence in paine of euery default 3s 4d

Item that euery person doe make their fence of the townefeild before the xxv th day of March next in payne of euery dole vnmade 3s 4d

[signed] Francis Mathewman/Henry Jackson/Thomas Lockwood/
Thomas Lockwood/John Kay/
Wooldale

[O]

Cartworth

At the Court leete or Sheriffs turne holden at Burton the xvj th day of October in the xv th yeare of the raigne of our soueraigne lord Charles by the grace of god king of England etc. Annoque domini 1639.

Paines layd by the swornemen of Cartworth Thomas Charlesworth William Hanson Gilbert Cartwright and Christopher Ouldham.

Inprimis wee doe lay in paine that no person nor persons doe Carry greene wood nor dry without licence of the right owner in paine of euery default 12d

Item that euery person doe keepe the water in the right Course in paine of euery default 3s 4d

Item wee lay in paine that euery person and persons doe keepe the right accustomed hy wayes footepathes and bridlestythes within the sayd towneship in paine of euery default 3s 4d

Item that euery householder doe keepe their swine well ringed in paine of euery default 12d

Item that no person goe over the grounds of James and Jane Charlsworth at Hilhouse with horseloads of Coales or other Caryages without their licence but as a bridlestythe in payne of euery default 3s 4d

Item that John Charlsworth doe scoure the dich betwixt the spoute and ould Coale pitt in the laneside above his house that the water or filth do not annoy the hy way and that he doe it before the first day of November next in paine of 10s

Item that John Hinchliffe James Hinchliffe John Crosland and Humfrey Crosland doe make one brigge well and sufficiently called Cowtlesse brigge before the second day of February next in payne of 5s

[signed] Francis Mathewman/Henry Jackson/Humfrey Robucke/
Thomas Lockwood/Thomas Lockwood/
Cartworth

[P]

Austonley

At the Court leete holden at Burton the 16th day of October 1639

Paynes layde by the swornemen of Austonley Thomas Litlewood and William Charlsworth

Imprimis wee doe lay in payne that no person nor persons doo cary greene wood nor dry without licence of the right owner in payne of euery default 12d

Item wee doe lay in payne that euery person and persons doe keepe the water in the right accustomed course in payne of euery default 3s 4d

Item we lay in payne that euery person and persons doe keepe the right accustomed hy wayes and footepathes within the sayd towneship in payne of euery default 3s 4d

Item we lay in payne that euery householder doe keepe their swyne well ringed in payne of euery default 12d

[signed] Francis Mathewman/Henry Jackson/Humfrey Robucke/
Thomas Lockwood/Thomas Lockwood/Abraham Horne/
Awstonley

[Q]

Hepworth

At the Court leete or Sheriffs turne holden at Burton the 16th day of October in the 15th yeare of the raigne of our Soveraigne lord Charles by the grace of god Kinge of England etc Annoque domini 1639.

Paynes layde by the swornemen of Hepworth,
Edward Bever, Francis Tinker, John Ibottson
and Richard Batty

Inprimis wee doe lay in payne that no person nor persons doe Cary greene woode nor dry without licence of the right owner in payne of every default 12d

Item wee doe lay in paine that euery person doe keepe the water in the right accustomed Course in paine of every default 3s 4d

Item we lay in paine that euery person and persons doe keepe the right accustomed hy waies footepathes and bridlestythes within the sayd towneship in paine of euery default 3s 4d

Item we lay in paine that euery householder doe keepe their swine well ringed in payne of euery default 12d

Item that John Tyas doe keepe his Masty dogge musled in the day time in payne of 20s

Item that no person defyle the townewell in payne of euery default 3s 4d

Item that euery person doe make their fence sufficient and so keepe it betwixt their grounds and George Linlay More-inge before the 25th of march next in paine of euery person that maketh default for euery default 3s 4d

Item that euery person within the said towneship doe make their outfences adioyning to the Comon, and also the in fences betwixt neighbor and neighbor before the sayd xxv[th] of march in paine of every default 3s 4d

[signed] Francis Mathewman/Thomas Lockwood/Abraham Horne/
Hepworth

[R]

Overthonge

At the Court leete or sheriffs turne holden at Burton the xvj[th] day of October 1639

Paynes layde by the swornemen of Overthonge Andrew Swallowe and James Baxter

Inprimis wee doe lay in payne that no person nor persons do cary greene wood nor dry without licence of the right owner in payne of euery default 12d

Item that euery person doe keepe the water in the right accustomed in payne of euery default 3s 4d

Item that euery person do keepe the right accustomed footepathes within the sayd township in payne of euery default 3s 4d

Item that euery householder doe keepe their swyne well ringed in payne of euery default 12d

[signed] Francis Mathewman/Henry Jackson/Homfrey Robucke/
Thomas Lockwood/Thomas Lockwood
Thwonge

[mem 18]

WAKEFIELD VIEW OF FRANKPLEDGE AND COURT LEET WITH TOURN: 11 April 16 Charles [1640]

Inquisition taken for the King on the oath of Robert Killingbecke, John Swifte, William Dunwell, John Scott, John Leake, John Hall, Henry Hutchinson, William Pollard, Robert Rodes, Robert Huit, Robert Spinke, Richard Nettleton and Robert Thompson, who declared

that William Browne, tenant of Leonard Wilson, made a nuisance under the window of John Swifte *12d*

that George Hopkinson *12d* and William Lacylaver *12d* both washed wool in le Newmilnedamme *2s*

that Stephen Jenkinson made affray and drew blood of William Ward *10s*

that Robert Barbour failed to scour his ditch in le Fall lane in Dewisbury *3s 4d*

KIRKGATE: Robert Thomson, constable, and his fellows present that Edmund Sikes failed to repair the pavement before his door and did not mend his watercourse at the end of his croft as previously pained *3s 4d*

that Robert Fawcett *6d*, John Riley *6d*, John Hindle *6d*, Brian Tayler *6d*, Samuel Allen *12d*, Joseph Waterhouse *20d*, Edward Oldroid *6d*, Thomas Firth *6d*, Jarvis Norton *20d*, John Swift *20d*, Isaac Rawnsley *2d*, John Atkinson *2d* and Stephen Oxley *6d* failed to repair and mend the pavement before their several doors *9s 10d*

WESTGATE: Thomas Garnett, constable, and his fellows present that John Ellis did not cleanse (*obfimauit*) his causey in accordance with the statute *3s 4d*

that Laurence Browne did not remove a dunghill lying at the door of William Brownhill *3s 4d*

that William Brownhill put a dunghill before his door *3s 4d*

that Roger Massy of Thornes did not remove a dunghill lying in the street at the door of Peter Hodgson *3s 4d*

that John Ellis *3s 4d*, .. Birkett gen *3s 4d*, Wife Burrowe *3s 4d*, Grace Thompson widow *3s 4d*, Richard Kay gen *3s 4d*, Thomas Royston gen *3s 4d*, Richard Fairbarne *3s 4d*, Wife Moorehouse *3s 4d*, John Stocks *3s 4d*, Thomas Rodes *3s 4d*, Wife Browne *3s 4d*, John Rodes gen *3s 4d*, John Beeston *3s 4d*, Robert Beeston

3s 4d, Laurence Browne *3s 4d*, Robert Walker *3s 4d*, Edward Orrell *3s 4d*, John Snawden *3s 4d* and William Brownhill *3s 4d* did not mend the high street before their several houses *£3 3s 4d*

that the governors of the free school did not mend the high street before the house lately occupied by Thomas Senior *10s*

that Miles Sandisforth did not mend the high street before his own door *3s 4d*

that John Mawde did not mend the pavement before the house lately occupied by Samuel Moore *3s 4d*

that George Brigge gen did not repair the pavement before his own door *3s 4d*

that James Prince *3s 4d*, Barnabas Mawde *3s 4d*, John Holdsworth *3s 4d*, Wife Thompson *3s 4d* and Wife Sym *3s 4d* did not mend severally the pavement before their doors *16s 8d*

that Thomas Wild did not mend the pavement before the door behind his court in Westgate *3s 4d*

NORTHGATE: Thomas Baskervile, constable, and his fellows present

that Peter Robinson *3s 4d*, Robert Smith *3s 4d*, Thomas Lawson *3s 4d*, Jonathan Potter *3s 4d*, George Nayler *3s 4d*, Richard Gryme *3s 4d* and Thomas Ventres *3s 4d* did not severally mend the pavement before their houses *23s 4d*

that Wife Lassy did not mend the pavement by her steps *3s 4d*

that Richard Fairbarne did not mend the street by his court *3s 4d*

that Wife Almon *3s 4d* and John Smith *3s 4d* did not mend the street before their houses *6s 8d*

STANLEY, ALVERTHORPE, THORNES: William Wadisworth, constable, and his fellows present that all is well

SANDALL: Denis Hurst, constable, and his fellows, present

that William Lambert did not make a gate in le Castle Lane at le Broome Closehead *3s 4d*

that the occupier of les sex lands in le Great old feild, lately occupied by . . Briggs gen did not make the ends of the furrows (*selion*') as previously pained *3s 4d*

that Edward Smith did not make sufficiently a fence adjoining the field of Sandall *3s 4d*

that John Morehouse of Agbrigge washed skins treated with quick lime in the stream in Sandall township *12d*

CRIGGLESTON: William Baxter, constable, and his fellows present that all is well.

WALTON: William Pell, constable, and his fellows present that all is well.

BRETTON: William Robinson, constable, and his fellows present that all is well.

HORBURY: Robert Thornes, constable, and his fellows present

that Thomas Townend obstructed and took water from its ancient course *3s 4d*

that the wife of Richard Robert broke a hedge *12d*

OSSETT: John Haigh, constable, and his fellows present

that William Gill *12d*, Joshua Hepworth *12d* and Wife Pease *12d* did not make their several fences at Longland *3s*

that . . Saxton widow *12d*, John Nayler senior *12d*, Joseph Harrison *12d*, Thomas Langfeild *12d* and Thomas Wormall *12d* broke hedges *5s*

that Thomas Hemmingway, Robert Whitacres and Thomas Aikroid did not hang a gate between the lordship of Chickinley and the township of Ossett *6s 8d.*

that Brian Brooke did not take the water from the high street into his grounds *3s 4d*

EMLEY: Richard Clayton, constable, and his fellows present

that Thomas Bedford made affray on Francis Perry *3s 4d*

that John Fish made affray on Richard Clayton *3s 4d*

that Margaret Brodehead made affray on Richard Scammonden *3s 4d*

FLOCKTON: Richard Eastwood, constable, and his fellows present

that Francis Walshawe and John Bilcliffe made affray between themselves *6s 8d*

NORMANTON: William Whyte, constable, and his fellows present

that . . Mallett gen *4d* and John Spinke *4d* did not yoke their pigs *8d*

that John Thimbleby gen did not make the fence at the end of his croft *12d* [mem 18d]

SOYTHILL: Philemon Dixon, deputy of John Tilson, constable, and his fellows present

that John Terry made affray on Robert Goodall *3s 4d*

that Robert Goodall drew blood from John Terry *6s 8d*

ARDISLAWE: John Allerton constable, and his fellows present

that Peter Robinson made affray on Matthew Todd *3s 4d*

DEWISBURY: Michael Whelewright, deputy of James Fearnley, constable, and his fellows present

that John Hall did not make the fence in le Milne feild *3s 4d*

that John Hall took water from its ancient course against a previous pain *3s 4d*

that John Dixon *3s 4d* and Isaac Sunderland *3s 4d* made affray between themselves *6s 8d*

that Nathan Harrison *3s 4d* and Edward Sonyer *3s 4d* made affray between themselves *6s 8d*

that William Ashton *3s 4d* and Thomas Awty junior *3s 4d* made affray between themselves *6s 8d*

ECCLESHILL: Abraham Ogden, constable, and his fellows present that Charles Rigge *4d*, John Reynde *4d*, John Nicholls *2d*, Samuel Nicholls *2d*, John Vickars *2d*, Walter Waterhouse *2d*, Richard Stanhope junior gen *4d* and James Milner did not make their several doles adjoining the lordship of Calverley *20d*

Finally the jurors present that all the above is true.

[A]

Kirkgate: Robert Thompson constable, Robert Howle, John Snawden, George Laycocke and Robert Lee

Westgate: Thomas Garnett constable, *Peter Hodgson* William Rodes, John Hewett, Robert Lister and Edward Bynns.

Northgate: *Robert Speight deputy*, Thomas Baskervile constable, William Shau, Richard Brodebent, Ambrose Couley and Thomas Potter

Stanley Alverthorpe Thornes: William Wadisworth, constable, John Roos, Thomas Banes *3s 4d*, John Sugden and John Clarkson

Sandall: Denis Hirst, constable, Edward Musgrave, Thomas Hill, Brian Longley, Joseph Beatson.

Crigglestou: William Baxter, constable, Thomas Booth, Edward Awdisley, Richard Oxley of Dirt Carr, Richard Oxley of Crigleston

Walton: William Pell, constable, Thomas Arnold and Thomas Wright *William Arnold and Robert Wright*

Bretton: William Robinson, constable, William Arnold and Robert Wright

Horbury: Robert Thornes, constable, John Walker, Richard Roberte and William North and Thomas Dun *pained 10s for not swearing*

Ossett: John Haigh, constable, Roger Pickard, John Forrest, Thomas Audisley and Thomas Bargh.

Emley: Richard Clayton, constable, John Perry, William Haigh', Thomas Blacker and Daniel Dick.

Flocton half: Richard Eastwood, constable, William Mountaine and John Bedford.

Normanton: William White, constable, George Stanidge, Brian Watson, John Pymond and John Bedford.

Soythill: Phelemon Dixon, sworn, John Tilson, constable, Thomas Nettleton, James Speight, Robert Gooddall and Francis Nettleton.

Westardisley: John Allerton, constable, Paul Sharpe, John Wilby, Robert Allerton and Peter Ward.

Dewisbury: Mathew Wheelewright deputy, James Fearnley, constable, Henry Barbour, Robert Barbour, Robert Bedford and Michael Whelewright.

Eccleshill: Abraham Ogden, constable, Abraham Baraclough and William Brookesbancke.

[B]

Wakefeld

Visus Francij pleg' et Curia Let' Domini Regis cum Turno tent' ibidem vndecimo die Aprilis anno Regni Domini nostri Caroli Regis Anglie etc Decimo sexto

Kirkgate

Kirgate Robert Thompson Constable
foure men Robert Howle
John Snawden
George Laycocke jur'
Robert Lee

We doe present Edmond Sikes for his dorestead not paveinge and dressinge nor for mending his flood yate acording to a paine laid at Mighalmas last past 3s 4d

We doe present Robert Faussit and John Riley for not making their pavement before dores and dressing of them 12d

We doe present John Hindle and Brian Taylor for not paiuing and not dressing theire dore 12d

We doe present Samuell Allon for not pauing his dore 12d

We doe present Joseph Watterhouse for not paveing his causey before his houses in Kirkgate 20d

We doe present Edward Ouldroyd and Thomas Foorth his land lord for not pauing and dressing their dore 12d

We doe present Geruis Norton and John Swift or whether it doth conserne for not making their causey at the windend in Kirkgate 3s 4d

We doe present Isack Raunsley and John Atkinsonn for not making their causey before their dores either of them 4d

We doe present Steuen Oxley for not making nor dressing his paiuement before his house 6d

[signed] Robert Killingbecke/John Swift/John Hall

[C]

Wakefeld

Visus Franci pleg' etc 11 April 16 Charles [1640]

Westgate Thomas Garnett Constable
Steuen Walton [added]
fouremen *William Rodes*
John Hewett
Robert Lister
Robert Byns Edward Bynns

Inprimis we present John Ellis for keepeing a Mastiffe dogg vnmusseld 3s 4d

Item we present Lawrence Browne for nor takeinge away a muck-heap lyeinge at William Brownehills dore 3s 4d

Item we present the said William Brownhill for layeinge the said Manure heape att his dore 3s 4d

Item we present Roger Massy of Thornes for not takeinge away a Manure heape lyeinge in the streete att peter Hodgsons door 3s 4d

Item we present John Ellis Mr Birkett Widdow Burrowe Grace Tompson widdowe Mr Richard Kay Mr Thomas Rishton Richard Fayrebarne Widdow Morehouse John Stocks Thomas Roades Widdow Browne *the Governers of free schoole* Mr John Roades John Beeston Robert Beeston Lawrence Browne Robert Walker Edward Orrill John Snawden and William Brownehill for not paveing the high cawsey before theire dores, euery one of them 3s 4d apeice is in all £3 3s 4d

Item we present the Geouerners of the Towne *Free Schoole* for not paueinge the street before a house late in the occupacon of Thomas Senior Carpinter 10s

Item we present Myles Sandiforth for not paueinge the high Cawsey before his dore 3s 4d

Item we present Mr John Mawde for not paueinge the high Cawsey before a house of his late in the occupacon of Sarah Moore late decased (sic) 3s 4d

Item we present Mr George Briggs for not paueinge before his dore 6s 8d

Item we present James Prynce Barnabas Mawde John Holdsworth Widdow Tompson and Widdow Symm for not paueinge and mendinge the pavement before theire dores euery one of them 3s 4d and in all 16s 8d

Item we present Thomas Wylde for not mendinge the pavement before his house upon the backside in westgate 3s 4d

[signed] Robert Killingbecke/Richard Nettleton/Robert Roodes

[D]

Wakefeild

Westgate

Inprimis a payne layde that John Ellis doe keepe his Mastiffe dogg Musseld in payne of —

etc [apparent draft of C, except that Mr John Mawde is omitted in D]

[E]

Wakefeld View for Northgate [11 April]

North Gate Thomas Baskervile Constable

foure men William Shau/
Richard Brodebent/
Ambrose Couley/
Thomas Potter/

Presentments for Northgate

Imprimis wee present

Peeter Robinson for not paveing the street before his house				00:03:4
Robert Smith	,,	,,	,,	00:03:4
Thomas Lowson Gent	,,	,,	,,	00:03:4

Johnathan Potter for lettinge the streete before his house bee vnpaued 00:03:4
George Naylor ,, ,, ,, 00:03:4
Richard Grime for not paueinge the streete before his house 00:03:4
Thomas Ventris for not mending ,, ,, 00:03:4
Widdow Lassee for letinge the streete before her stayers bee vnpaued 00:03:4
Richard Feerbarne for note paveing the streete before the back-house 00:03:4
Widdow Almon for note paueing strete before her house 0:03:4
John Smyth for not mending the strete before his house in Northgate 01:19:00

payens for Northgate

Imprimis wee present Ambrose Couley for not repeareinge the street before his house 00:03:4

Ittem William Shauu for note remoueing the dung at his house side being in the Kings high way 00:03:4

Item Richard Clarkeson for leueinge his block and Stall in the streete in the night 00:03:4

Item Thomas Norfolke for not remoueing his stall 00:03:4

Item Robart Senior ,, ,, 00:03:4

Item Gawan Neuill Gent for not mending the streete before his gates 00:03:4

[signed] Thomas Baskervile, constable

Ambrose Couley
Richard Brodbent
William Shauu [mark]
Thomas Potter [P]

[signed] Robert Killingbecke/Richard Nettleton/John Swift/[F]

[Stanley Aluerthorpe Thornes]

Item wee lay in pane William Liuarsage or his tenans of the greate Hoyle inge doth scour his dich that the watar may haue fre passage betwene and Midsomar nexte in pane of 30s

Item wee lay in pane that George Leightefoute do make his fence aganste Brounshay grene betwene and Midsomar next and so vphould the same from tyme to tyme 3s 4d

Item wee lay in payne that Thomas Walkar and George Leightefoute the occoupyars of wat grene doth make thare hedge as agansce the hey wayes there agoyning betwene and Midsomar next and so vphowld the same from tyme to tyme in payne of 3s 4d

Item wee lay in payne that Mr John Story and John Rodes do Repayre the foute Brige leading from walkefeild to allarthorpe betwixt thare seaueurall groundes at the Brodfore betwene and Lamis day nexte in pane off not sodoing 10s

Item wee lay in pane that John Fleminge Richard Kente and the

Ockupyars of the seuerall landes in the hauroyd feld there in Joyninge of the wattar course leading from Stanlay lane and Coldar before and Midsomar next in pane of not so doing of euerone 3s 4d

Item wee lay in pane that no parson nor parsones whatsoever do driue any goodes whatsoeuare ouer the *haywafe* Horykefeld betwixt Oute wood and Stanlay in payne of so doinge 10s

John Rose [mark]	William Wadsworth [mark]
Thomas Baynes	Constable of Stanley
John Sugding [mark]	John Clarkson

[G[1]]

Paynes layd by the Constuble and foure men of Sandall at the Sereturne houldn at Wakefeld the 11 of April 1640 in maner and forme Following

Inprimis that euerie man make their yates and Hedges about the Hardcorne and Warecorne feilds betweene this and Thursday at night next in paine of euerie yate not made 3s 4d euerie side Hedge 3s 4d and euerie landend 12d

Item that euerie one yoke and ringe their Swine and so keepe them at all times betwixt this and Thursday at night next in payne of not doinge 4d

Item that no man put any infected Horses vnto the Common nor that no man put any goods to the Common but such as Pay layes and Assessments liueinge within the Towneshippe of Sandall

Item that euerie one scoure their ditches well and sufficiently betweene the Townewell of Sandall and the Brooke in paine of not soe doinge euerie close 3s 4d

Item that euerie one that hath any land on the Kilnehill scoure their land ends to take the water out of the highwaies betweene this and whitsunday next in paine of euerie land end not done 4d

and also that euerie man scoure their land ends betwixt the Round Ingge and Greene ditch and scoure their ditches in paine of euerie close not done 3s 4d

Item that Mr Wray scoure the ditch at the Milne Leyes betweene this and Whitsuntide next in paine of not so doinge 3s 4d

and also Brice Norton for scouringe the Parke closes ditch in paine of not doinge 3s 4d

Dynis Hirst, Constable
Edward Musgraue
Joseph Beatson
Thomas Hill
Bryan Longley
} foure men

Sandall

[G[2]]

Sandall presentments

Inprimis we doe present William Lamberte for not making a yate in the Castle lane at the Brome Close head 3s 4d

Item we present the occupiers of 6 lands in the great ouldfeeld late in the occupacon of Mr Brig' for not making his land ends according to a payne layd 3s 4d

Item we present that Edward Smyth gent fer a side hedge aioying to Sandall Feld not being well made 3s 4d

Item we present John Morehouse of Agbrig the yonger for washing lymed Skines in the runing Streame within the Townshipp of Sandall 12d

[signed] Robert Killingbecke/John Swift/John Hall/Robert Roodes/
Dynis Hirst Constable

Edward Musgraue
Joseph Beatsonn
Thomas Hill
Bryan Longley } four men

Sandall

[H]

11 Aprilis 1640 Crigleston

William Baxter Constable

Thomas Boothe
Edward Awdesley } old presenters

Richard Oxley of Dirtcarr
Richard Oxley of Crigleston } new presenters

Inprimis wee lay in payne that euery person and persons doe make vp their yates and hedges about the harde Corne and ware Corne Feilds of Criglestone betwixt this and St Marke day next and so vphold the same in payne of euery one not so doeing to forfeite for euery yate 3s 4d and euery side hedge 3s and euery gapp or land end 12d

Item that euery person and persons doe yoke and ring their swine betwixt this and the Sixteenth day of Aprill instant, vpon payne of euery person makeinge defalt therein to forfeict for euery swyne 4d

Item that euery person and persons doe scoure their ditches and switch their hedges betwixt Dirtcarr greene and Milne Brooke betwixt this and the Firste day of May next in payne of euery one to forfeict for euery said hedge 6s 8d and euery land end 12d

Item that George Worrell doe take the water out of the highway at Deynesike into his Close adioyning to the same, betwixt this and May day next in payne of not so doeing to forfeict 5s

Item that Thomas Brigg' doe keepe the Dyke contynually scoured at Houdall yate vpon payne of euery defaulte 3s 4d

Item that euery person and persons that have any ground betwixt Greneshawe Closehead and Milnebrookes doe scoure their ditches against their seuerall grounds betwixt this and May day next vpon payne of euery person makeinge defalte therein to forfeict 10s

Item that Roger Thornton doe take the water out of the land above his house and adioyninge vpon his groundes betwixt this and May day next in payne of 3s 4d

Item that noe person or persons doe tent any Cattell in the Common lans belonging to Crigleston in payne of euery one makeinge defalte therein to forfeict 10s

Item that noe person or persons doe putt any infected horses or Cattells into the Comons or lans belonging to Crigleston vpon payne of euery one making default therein to forfeict 13s 4d

[dorse]

Item that noe person or persons doe putt into the Commons belonging to Crigleston any goods or Cattells but their owne, in payne of euery one makeinge defalte therein to forfeict 13s 4d

Item that euery Alehouse keeper doe brew good and wholesome drink and Bake good breade in payne of not so doeing to forfeict 10s

Item that noe Alehouse keeper doe keepe any mans servants drinkeing in their houses after Eight of the Clock in the night, in payne of euery one 3s 4d

[signed] William Baxter [mark] Thomas Boothe [T] Edward Audsley Richard Oxley Richard Oxley of Crigleston [mark]

[I]

The Bill of Walton cum Bretton

Omne Bene

[signed] Robert Killingbecke/Richard Nettleton/

[J[1]]

A presentment made by the cunstable and four men of Horburye the 11 of Aprell

Inprimis we present Thomas Twonand for deming the hie way and taking the water out of the right cource 3s 4d

Item wee present Robert Jadger for a fray 3s 4d

Item wee present Richard Roberd wife of norgate for heege breking 12d

Item wee present Ann dich 12d

[signed] William North/Robert Thornes [T]/Richard Robert [R]/ John Walker/

Horbury

[J[2]]

paynes laide by the cunstable and four men of Horburye the xj day of Aprell 1640

Item wee lay in paine that all the watter courses in and about the twoune be well and sufficintly scourred and soe kept that the watter may be kept in the right cource in paine of 10s

Item we lay in paine that no man com ouer our cowpaster with carte or carige except of our oune twne in paine of euerye defolte 20s

Item wee lay in paine that no man put nor tent no sheepe before the warcorne feeld be reed on the storke hil vpon euerye defolte 10s

Horbury

[endorsed] Robert Killingbecke/John Swift/John Scott/

[K[1]] Ossett Paines

Paines layed at the Sherriffe turne hovlden at Waiekfeild the 11th day of Aprill Anno domnie 1640 by the Constable and swornemen as followeth

Imprimis we lay in paine that all the yeats and fences about out ware cornefeild be made sufficient betwixt this and Wendensday next and soe kept from tyme to tyme in paine of every defalt fovnd in any yeate 3s and every other fence fovnd not sufficient 12d

[the next eight items are paraphrases of the Ossett pains for October 1639, marked ●]

Item we lay in paine that William Gill doe take the water into the brear ynge which of right he ought to doe betwixt this and the first day of May next in paine of not soe doinge 3s

Item we lay in paine that Thomas Langfeild and William Gill doe scowre there diches in the bottome of Healey laine and all along the washynge side betwixt this and the first day of may next in paine of either of them offendinge herein 3s 4d

Item we lay in paine that Mr Cockin Tonge doe scowre his ditche alonge his longlands close side and alsoe over the nether end of the same close betwixt this and the first day of May next in paine 3s 4d

Item we lay in pain that all the inhabitants of Gawthorp that hath any land adioyneinge to the Kings higheway within the township of Ossett doe scowre theire ditches and switche theire hedges where any neede is betwixt this and the first day of May next in paine of 3s 4d

Item we lay in paine that Thomas Awdsley doe take the water out of the Riewod laine and alsoe switch his hedge betwixt this and the last of May next in paine of 3s

Ossett

[K[2]]

Item wee lay in paine that George Allame doe set two sufficient steels in the close vnenste his howse where they formerlie have bene betwixt this and the first day of May next in paine of 5s

Item we lay in paine that all those that have any land adioyneinge on either side of the Ickar laine and John Preckleton for the nether end of the same laine do take the water out of yt and alsoe switch theire hedges there betwixt this and whitsuntide next in paine of every one offendinge therin 5s

Item we lay in paine that Christopher Broke do scowre his ditch in Oxley laine alonge his crofte and bringe the water ouer the back-laine end to the brigstone betwixt this and Midsomerday next in paine of 3s 4d

Item we lay on paine that Thomas Akeroyde Thomas Hemingway and Roberte Whitakers doe make the laine sufficient betwixt pilldars laine and Chickingley which is our Churchway for carieyinge our corpes betwixt this and the twentie fourth of June next comeinge in paine of every one of them refusinge so to doe 10s

Item we lay in paine that Widdow Peace doe scowre her ditches in haygate laine and covey the water of the same laine betwixt this and Midsomer day next in paine of 5s

Item we lay in paine the occapiers of Pilldars closes doe scowre theire ditches sufficiently on both sides the pilldars laine betwixt this and Midsomer day next in paine of every one offendinge therein 10s

Item we lay in paine that Edward Langfeild doe scoure his diche along his backside betwixt this and may daye in paine 3s

Item we lay in paine that Robart Bradforth doe take the water out of white dikes, as of right he ought to doe betwixt and may day in paine of 3s

John Hage Constabell [mark]

Thomas Barghe [mark]/Roger Pickard/Thomas Audslay/John Forrest [I]

Ossett

[K 3]

Osset presentments

Item we present William Gill for defalt in his Fence att longlands ende 1s

Jousua Hepworth for his fense 1s

Vxor Pease for her fense att longlands end 1s

Vxor Saxton for hege breakeing 1s

John Nayler elder for the like 1s

Jossif Harrison „ 1s

Thomas Langfeild „ 1s

Thomas Wormald „ 1s

Thomas Hemingway, Robart Whitecares and Thomas Aycroide for nott hanging one yatte betwixt the lordeship of Chickingley and the towneshipp of Ossett 6s 8d

Item Brian Brouke for not takeing the water oute of the hie streete into his groundes as of right he ought to doe 3s 4d

John Hage Constabell [mark]

Thomas Barghe [mark]/Roger Pickard/Thomas Audslay/John Forrest [I]

Ossett

[endorsed] Robert Killingbecke/Richard Nettleton/John Swift/

[L]

The Constabl of Emley Richard Clayton
and foure sworne men
Presentments made by them: We Present
Im Primus Thomas Bedforth for a fray made of Francis Perry
Item A fray made of Richard Clayton by John Fish
Item we present Margret Brodhead for a fray made of Ane Scamandun
William Hage [mark]/John Perry [mark]/Thomas Blacker [B]/ Daniel Dicke [mark]/
[signed] Robert Killingbecke/John Swift/
Emley

[M]

Constable of Flokton
Richard Eastwood
William Mountane sworne man
John Bedforth sworne man
Presentments made by them
A fray made betwixt Francis Walshey and John Billklife younger ather of them 3s 4d a pese
[signed] Robert Killingbecke/John Hall/Robert Roodes/John Swift/
Flockton

[N]

Presentments: Normanton: made by the Constable and fowre men
Inprimis we present Mr Mallet for one swine being vnringed 4d
Item we present John Spink for one swine vnringed 4d
Item we present Mr John Thimelby for his Croft end being vnmaide to our corne field 12d
By vs William White Constable
Robert Breuster/Robert Simpson/Bryan Watson/George Stanige/
Normanton
[endorsed] Robert Killingworth/John Hall/John Scott/John Swift/

[O]

A bill for the constable of Souttell as foloweth
we presente John Terrie for afraye made vpon Roberte Goodale
Item we presente Roberte Goodale for bloude made vpon Johe Terrie
James Speighte [I]/Thomas Nettellton/Robert Goodale [mark]/ Francis Netleton/
[signed] Robert Killingbecke/Richard Nettleton/John Hall/Robart Roodes/
Soothill

[P]

Presentments made by the Constable and Sworne men of Ardislaw West the xjth day of Aprill Anno Domini 1640

Imprimis we present thowners and occupiers of William Lindley lande att Dumingley for not doinge five Common day workes with a draught this yeare last past *20s* 6s 8d

Item we present James Roydes for not doing his Common day workes with a man the last yeare for five dayes *6s* 2s

Item we present the saide James Roydes for not scowringe of his ditches in the Orpitts Layne also Almeshowse Layne, all alonge two Closes there called the Almeshowse Closes *3s 4d* 2s

Item we present Mr Thornehill of Fixby for not scowring of his ditche in one Layne called Spinkewell layne all along one Close called Spinkewell Close, and for not doinge of the same in the Neather streete all alonge the lower end of the saide Close 10s

Item we present James Baxter for keepinge of sheepe vpon the Common of other mens which dwelles not within our Towneshippe 6s 8d

Item we lay in paine that no manner of person or persons dwelling or Inhabiting within the saide towneshippe shall hereafter keepe any sheepe or other Cattell vpon the saide Common, which are not their owne proper goods: vpon paine to forfeits for euery suche default the somme of 39s 11d

Item we lay in paine Mathew Todde, Raphe Speight and John Batley that neyther they nor any of them doe put forth or turne any of their sheepe or Cattell to the Commons belonging to the saide Towne nor do suffer their saide sheepe or Cattell or any of them to remaine or depasture vpon the saide Commons vpon paine to forfeith for euery suche default the somme of 6s 8d

Item we lay in paine Cary Morris and Nicholas Booth that neither they nor either of them doe put forth or turne any of their goodes or Cattells vpon the saide Commons or any parte thereof, nor doe suffer them to remaine or depasture vpon the said Commons or any parte thereof vpon paine to forfeict for euery such default the somme of 13s 4d

Item we present Peter Robinson younger for an affray made vpon the body of Mathew Todd 3s 4d

John Allerton [mark] Constable   Paul Sharpe [mark], John Wilby [mark] } sworne men

[signed] Robert Killingbecke/John Swift/John Scott/John Hall/ Ardislawe

[Q]
Ouchethorpe infra
Maner' de Wakefeild

Item we laie in paine that Thomas Medcalfe of Stanley shall sett his hedge straighte between Wainewright Wicte' and him as auncіently hearetofore it hathe beene accustomed to be sett and stande betweene this daie the xj[th] of Aprill and mydsomerdaie next comminge And so heareafter keepe the same vppon paine to forfeite to the Lorde of this mannour the somme of 30s

[signed] Robert Killingbecke/John Swift/John Hall/John Scott/

Ouchthorpe

[R]

Presentments made by the Cunstable of Dewsburie and foure men

Imprimis we present John Haull for not makeing his fence in the milnefeld 3s 4d

Item we present John Haull for takeing the water out of the right course according to the paine laide 3s 4d

Item we present John Dixon and Isake Sunderland for a fray vne vpon the other 6s 8d

Item we present Nathan Harison and Edward Sunyer for making afray one vpon other 6s 8d

Item we present William Ashton and Thomas Autye Junior for making afray one vpon the other 6s 8d

James Feanlay Constable

Robert Bedforth/Henry Barbar/Michaell Whelewright [mark]/ Robert Barber/

[signed] Robert Killingbecke/Richard Nettleton/John Swift/

Dewesbury

[S]

Eckleshill

The Constable Abraham Ogden

Presenters { Abraham Barracloughe
William Brookesbancke

Inprimis wee laye in payne that all the inhabitants of Eckleshill aforesaid shall make and maynteine all theyr seuerall Ringhedges or outfence and all theyr doles yates and fences which are in Byredole in sufficient repayre vntill the next Courte in payne of euery three days default 12d

Item we laye in payne that none of the inhabitants of Eckleshill shall grave any Turffes or sodds in that parcell of Common which lyeth betwene Corbriggdikes and Stonehall in payne of 3s 4d

Item wee laye in payne that euerye of the inhabitants aforesayde shall kepe theyr swyne yoked and ringed vntill the next Courte in payne of euerye three dayes default 4d

Item wee present Charles Rigg and John Reyner for that they have not made theyr dole called the becke dole adioyninge to the Lordshippe of Caluerley Accordinge to a payne layde the last Court 4d

Item wee present John Nichalls and Samuell Nichells for the like 4d

,, ,, John Vickars and Walter Waterhowse ,, 4d

,, ,, Richard Stanhopp gent yonger ,, 4d

Item wee present James Milner for the like 4d

Item wee appoynt Richard Stanhopp gent and George Fletcher ouerseers for Repayre of the hyewayes this yeare

examined by the bailiff of Wakefield

[signed] Robert Killingbecke Abraham Ogden [U]
John Swift Abraham Barracloughe [mark]
Richard Nettleton William Brookesbancke

Eckleshill

[T]

Pinder bill for Wakefeild

Henary Pikes for makin a Resku vpon the pinder 3s 4d

Willyam Hill for not yokin and Ringin his swine 3s

Item of the inhabetant of Allathorp for not makin on yat called Kurkum yat 3s

[signed] Robert Killingbecke/John Swift

the pinder bill

[U]

Within the Constablery of Soothill

We present Richard Dowson for arectting a in matt Contrary to the Stattisse *one shilling*

[signed] Robert Killingbecke/John Hall/Richard Nettleton/

[V]

Panel for 11 April 1640

Robert Killingbecke 4:4:4 [Richard Birkhead deleted]

[W]

November the 20 1639

I do acknowlege that I have Wronged mr Raiton of Okenshawe in speaking the woords in the declaracon menconed for which hee sued mee which I desire the said Mr Raiton to remitt

John Mosley [mark]

Witnes

[signed] E. Wooderofe/Jo. Couper/John Barker/

This to be read next Court Leete for the mannor of Wakefeild in the Court

[mem 18 d]

HALIFAX: VIEW OF FRANKPLEDGE AND COURT LEET WITH TOURN: 13 April 16 Charles [1640]

Inquisition taken for the King on the oath of Jonathan Crowther, John Crosland, Michael Gill, Abraham Grenewood, Elias Hanson, Thomas Oldfeild, Edward Wainhouse, John Hoile, Henry Wilson, William Farrer, Christopher Thomas, Luke Horsfall and Henry Cockcrofte, who declared

that Richard Lawson of Norland and Mary his wife made affray and drew blood of Michael Byns of the same *10s*

that William Cowper and his wife made affray and drew blood of Jane Harrison *10s*

Abraham Wilkinson of Sowerby	,,	,,	Edward Brearley of Warley	*10s*
Grace wife of John Cotes	,,	,,	Susan wife of Thomas Appleyard	*10s*
Jonas Boardall of Skircote	,,	,,	Samuel Mitchell [of Halifax]	*10s*
Thomas Radcliffe gen [of Halifax]	,,	,,	John Crosland gen	,,
John Bairstow of Ovenden	,,	,,	John Crosland	,,
Mary wife of Christopher Robinson	,,	,,	Susan Ridinge	,,
Thomas Gill	,,	,,	Richard Gibson	,,
Michael Firth of Ovenden	,,	,,	John Ingham [of the same]	,,
the said John Ingham	,,	,,	the said Michael Firth	,,
Richard Lawson	,,	,,	Nathaniel Chadwicke	,,
William Deane of Ovenden	,,	,,	Ezekiel Cooke	,,
Henry Wadesworth	,,	,,	Ezekiel Cooke	,,
William Deane	,,	,,	Samuel Starky	,,
Daniel Mitchell	,,	,,	Hugh Smith	,,
Isaac Sladen	,,	,,	Katherine Stott of Midgley	,,
Thomas War	,,	,,	Richard Horsfall	,,
Richard Horsfall	,,	,,	Thomas Warr	,,
Simeon Hellewell	,,	,,	Jonah Holgate	,,

HALIFAX: Christopher Robinson and John Smith constables and their fellows present

that James Sharples *10s* and Hugh Worrall *10s* made affray and drew blood between themselves *20s*

that Michael Haworth made affray and drew blood of Thomas Lee *10s*

that Laurence Thackwray made affray on William Bothomley *3s 4d*

that Robert Bradford *3s 4d* and Michael Butterworth *3s 4d* made affray between themselves *6s 8d*

that the wife of Mark Turner *3s 4d*, the wife of Anthony Rocherrn *3s 4d*, the wife of William Farrer *3s 4d* and the wife of Samson Aikroid *3s 4d* contaminated the water *13s 4d*
SKIRCOTE: Richard Waterhouse, constable, and his fellows declare that all is well
SOWERBY: Josiah Stansfeild, deputy of Richard Bentley, constable, and his fellows declare that all is well
WARLEY: Simeon Otes, deputy of Thomas Oldfeild, constable, and his fellows declare that all is well
OVENDEN: Edward Ridinge, constable, and his fellows —
WADISWORTH: John Pighells, constable, and his fellows declare
that the inhabitants of Midgley failed to repair and mend the highway leading between le Brodefould and Holmehousebridge in Midgley according to the previous pain *£4 3s 4d*
that the inhabitants of Warley did not pave and mend a highway in Warley between Holmehousebridge and Bankhouselanehead according to the previous pain *£4 3s 4d*
MIDGLEY: John Hellewell, constable, and his fellows present
that Richard Midgley and Samuel Midgley did not mend sufficiently the highway called Bradfordlane in Midgley behind their land according to the previous pain *£3 6s 8d*
that Brian Crowther of Warley did not sufficiently mend the highway behind his holding, nor remove from the highway muck (*ruder*) and stones from the wall of his land according to the previous pain *20s*
that Richard Midgley and Samuel Midgley did not mend the highway between Holmehouse and Brodefoulde in Midgley according to the previous pain *20s*
RISHWORTH: John Barrowe, deputy of Abraham Batchler, constable, and his fellows declare that all is well
STANSFEILD: John Stansfield, constable, and his fellows present
that William Bingley *3s 4d* and Abraham Roberteshawe *3s 4d* made affray between themselves *6s 8d*
that Thomas Cockcrofte of Grenewoodlee *20s*, John Feilden *20s*, John Stansfeild *20s* and Michael Eastwood *20s* did not mend the highway in Stansfeild to the back of their ground *£4*
HEPTONSTALL: Thomas Grenewood, constable, and his fellows present
that Isaac Briggs made affray and drew blood of John Bentley *10s*
John Bentley made affray on Isaac Briggs *3s 4d*
William Parkinson ,, John Wilkinson *3s 4d*
the said John Wilkinson made affray on the said William Parkinson *3s 4d*
LANGFEILD: Jeremy Ingham, constable, and his fellows, declare that all is well

AIRINGDEN: Daniel Halstead, deputy of Samuel Hanson, constable, and his fellows declare that all is well

Finally they present that all the above is true

Sowerby (*130*) Testimony by James Oldfeild, lord's tenant, that Richard Viccars of Tonge, co. Lancs. blacksmith, son and heir of Richard Viccars late of the same, blacksmith, deceased, surrendered the immediate reversion on the death of Anne Viccars, widow, lately wife of the said deceased Richard Viccars, of 3 roods of land with buildings thereon previously taken by William Viccars deceased from the lord's waste [with 3 other roods of land from the lord's waste] called Overmeasure in the graveship of Sowerby and then occupied by John Oldefeild or his assigns at a lord's rent of 6d and certain fine: to the use of Thomas Oldfeild of Newland in Warley, co. York, yeoman, on condition that if Richard Viccars the son, his heirs etc should pay the said Thomas Oldfeild, his attorney etc £21 12s on 21 November 1639 (sic) in the mansion of the said Thomas Oldfeild at Newland the surrender would be void. Entry fine of 9d. [mem 19]

Sowerby (*131*) Nathan Carter of Sowerby yeoman and Mary now his wife, she agreeing separately, by Isaac Nayler, lord's tenant and sworn, surrendered that messuage commonly called Upperfeildhouse and all land etc associated with it in Sowerby now occupied by the said Nathan Carter or his assigns, also another messuage commonly called Littlefeildhouse, a barn, a garden and two closes of land estimated at one acre associated in Sowerby, now occupied by a Samuel Carter or his assigns, also a cottage in Sowerby now occupied by a George Byns or his assigns, all at a lord's rent of 6s 7d and certain fine (saving those three closes of land, meadow and pasture commonly called les Royds estimated at $5\frac{1}{2}$ acres, previous associated with Upperfeildhouse and now occupied by one Michael Earnshawe or his assigns): to the use of John Mitchell of Sowerby, clothier. Agreed: entry fine of 19s 9d. *Compounded for by Nathan Carter*

Sowerby (*132*) Michael Wadisworth of Sowerby, clothier, by John Fournes, lord's tenant and sworn, surrendered that parcel of land estimated at half a day's ploughwork and now bounded on the south by a close called le ynge, being the inheritance of the said Michael Wadisworth, in Sowerby, now occupied by one George Mitchell or his assigns at a lord's rent of one penny and certain fine: to the use of Henry Wadisworth of Ovenden. Agreed: entry fine of 3d. *Compounded for by Henry Wadisworth*

Sowerby (*133*) Henry Wadisworth of Ovenden, yeoman, by John Fournes, lord's tenant and sworn, surrendered the right to use and manage, clean and scour the course of a spring rising in a close called le Highest-hey in Sowerby of the inheritance of the said Henry Wadisworth and now occupied by one George Mitchell or his assigns from its source and as far as its ancient channel belonging to the messuage or mansion inhabited by Michael Wadisworth, and a similar right in another spring called le Litlewell, rising on Sowerby Common from whence it runs by the west end of a close called le Crofte, of the inheritance of the said Henry Wadisworth, and by the west angle of the close called le Highest-hey until it comes to a close of the inheritance of Michael Wadisworth called le ynge, at a lord's rent of one penny and certain fine: to the use of the said Michael Wadisworth. Agreed: entry fine of 3d. *Compounded for by John Fournes*

Sowerby (134) Christopher Shackleton of Goodgreave in Wadisworth, yeoman, by Paul Grenewood, lord's tenant and sworn, surrendered half a messuage and two and a half acres in Sowerby now occupied by George Crabtree or his assigns, and a rood in Sowerby between the highway and Hollingbanke, which halves render a lord's rent of 5¾d and certain fine to the following uses: (1) of Mary, now wife of the said Christopher for the next 14 years on payment during the first seven years to Jonas Pighells of Stanbury, co. York, yeoman, of a rent of 40s at the feast of the Nativity of St. John Baptist [24 June] and Christmas, payable within 20 days at the mansion of Michael Pighells junior at Stanbury, as part of an annual rent of £6, provided that if an indenture dated 12 December 1639 between the said Jonas Pighells and Christopher Shackleton should be void before the end of these seven years this sum of 40s remain in the hands of Mary and be not paid after the avoidance: (2) that Mary 'bringe up' James Shackleton and William Shackleton, sons of the said Christopher, and after the end of the said 14 years the half estate will remain with William Shackleton, son of Christopher and his heirs, provided that if Christopher Shackleton pay Paul Grenewood and Edward Banister, either of them or their assigns the sum of 12d at any future time to void this surrender, and declare his intention before two, three or more honest witnesses, the present surrender would become void. Mary fined 8½d and a half farthing, and William Shackleton fined the same.

Sowerby (135) Richard Fournes of Sowerby, yeoman, by John Sutcliffe, lord's tenant and sworn, surrendered all that messuage commonly called Woodlane and all houses, structures, barns, gardens, closes etc estimated at 9 acres 3 roods in the graveship of Sowerby lately occupied by one Thomas Fournes deceased or his assigns and now by the said Richard [m. 19d] Fournes and his assigns, also 3 cottages beside the said messuage called Woodlane in the graveship of Sowerby now severally occupied by a Daniel Culpon, Stephen Hoile and Widow Fletcher or their assigns at a lord's rent of 3s 4½d and certain fine: to the use of Isaac Nayler of Woodlane in Sowerby, yeoman, his wife and children from 24 February and until the completion of 21 years after 1 May next, paying annually to Richard Fournes £11 at Whitsun and Martinmas with the right to re-enter if the rent is in arrears for twenty days. Agreed: entry fine of 5s. *Compounded for by George Fournes*

Sowerby (*136*) Richard Fournes of Sowerby, yeoman, by Richard Tattersall, lord's tenant and sworn, surrendered that messuage commonly called Boothhouse and 9 acres associated in Blackwood in the graveship of Sowerby now occupied by one Isabel Dobson widow or her assigns, also 3½ acres in Blackwood in the graveship of Sowerby now occupied by the said Isabel Dobson or her assigns with all other lands now in the possession of the same at a lord's rent of 4s 2d and certain fine: to the use of the said Isabel Dobson from the date of the surrender for 21 years should she live so long and for as long as she live, at an annual rent of £17 at Whitsun and Martinmas. Should payment fall into 20 days' arrears Richard Fournes, his heirs etc may enter and distrain. Agreed: entry fine of 6s 3d.

Sowerby (*137*) Whereas at the great court baron of Sir Gervais Clifton of the manor of Wakefeld on 29 April 12 Charles [1636] Michael Bothomley then of Cockcrofte in Rishworth, yeoman, by Thomas Crosley, tenant of the manor of Wakefeld and sworn, surrendered that house called Litlehouse in Sowerby and a barn, a garden and a parcel of land and meadow estimated at a rood, then and now occupied by one John Sugden of Sowerby, clothier, or his assigns at a lord's rent of a penny and certain fine: to the use of the said John Sugden in accordance with a little indenture of 16 May 11 Charles [1635] between the same Michael Bothomley and John Sugden, his executors etc subject to reserved rents for this and other lands as more fully appears in the copy of the court roll: this present surrender is to the effect that John Sugden by Michael Bentley, lord's tenant and sworn, surrendered the said house called Littlehouse, the barn, garden and parcel of land and meadow to the use of Mary now wife of the said John Sugden, and her assigns for that part of the term remaining after the death of the said John Sugden should she still be living and in her widowhood, but if she predecease or re-marry before the end of the term the use to remain with her, her executors etc until 25 March next ensuing and for a full year, and then to the use of John Sugden, son of the said John Sugden senior, for the rest of the term, provided that if John Sugden senior still survive by 10 August 1640 this surrender is void. Agreed: entry fine by Mary of 1½d.

Sowerby (*138*) Richard Fournes of Sowerby, yeoman, by John Sutcliffe of Turvyn, lord's tenant and sworn, surrendered that messuage commonly called Boothhouse and 9 acres associated in Blackwood in the graveship of Sowerby now occupied by Isabel Dobson widow or her assigns and 3½ acres in Blackwood in the graveship of Sowerby and now and lately in the occupation of the said Isabel Dobson or her assigns, also 3 acres 1 rood of land, meadow and pasture with the buildings thereon in the graveship of Sowerby previously occupied by John Lomme and Margaret Lomme or their assigns and now occupied by John Wilson or his assigns, and a cottage in Blackwood now occupied by John Wilson or his assigns, and a cottage in Blackwood now occupied by James Crowther or his assigns, all at a lord's rent of 5s 3d and certain fine: also a messuage commonly called Westfeild, a barn, a garden, a croft, and 4 closes of land, meadow and pasture and 3 acres of land, meadow and pasture commonly called Thorngreaves and a close [m 20] called Overthwarts estimated at one acre in Warley in the graveship of Sowerby now occupied by Thomas Carre or his assigns, also a house or cottage and 4 other closes of land, meadow and pasture in Warley in the graveship of Sowerby now and lately occupied by Peter Moore or his assigns and a parcel of land as now enclosed being 6 yards long and 14 yards wide with all buildings thereon, which parcel previously lay in the lower part of the close of Thomas Oldfeild of Newland on the north of Harroodwell in Warley in the graveship of Sowerby and now is occupied by one Samuel Denton or his assigns, all of which are in Warley, at a lord's rent of 3s 3d and certain fine: and a parcel of land used as a path on the west of the said close called Overthwarts at a lord's rent of ½d and certain fine, also 2 messuages commonly called Hollings and all houses buildings, barns, gardens, lands, holdings, closes, meadow, pasture, ways, waters, watercourses, commons and hereditaments associated, estimated at 20 acres 1 rood in Blackwood in the graveship of Sowerby now occupied by Richard Wadisworth, John Hopkinson, Joseph Meller and the said Isabel Dobson at a lord's rent of 6s 9d and certain fine: and a messuage and 9 acres 3 roods associated in Blackwood in the graveship of Sowerby previously occupied by Richard Brookesbanke deceased and now by Isaac Crowther or his assigns at a lord's rent of 3s 9d and certain fine: also another messuage commonly called Woodlane and all houses, buildings, barns, gardens, closes, lands, holdings and hereditaments associated, estimated at 9 acres 3 roods in the graveship of Sowerby lately occupied by Thomas Fournes deceased and 2 cottages beside the said messuage called Woodlane in the graveship of Sowerby now and lately held severally by Daniel Culpon and Stephen Hoile or their assigns at a lord's rent of 3s 4½d and certain fine: and 6 closes of land, meadow, and pasture in the graveship of Sowerby now in 7 closes and all houses and buildings thereon, estimated at 3 acres 1 rood now or lately occupied by James Fawcett or his assigns at a lord's rent of 13d and certain fine: and a fourth part of three half-acres of meadow with buildings between the land lately of William Oldefeild deceased on the east and the land now and lately of John Crowther on the west and north, now in 2 closes called les yngs in the graveship of Sowerby and now or lately also occupied by Isabel Dobson or her assigns at a lord's rent of 3$\frac{1}{2}$d and certain fine: to the use of Henry Bentley of Turvyn in Sowerby yeoman, his executors etc from 24 June 1643 for the following year and thereafter to the use of Susan Bentley, daughter of the said Henry Bentley for 9 months, and then to the use of Grace the other daughter of the said Henry Bentley for 3 months, and then to the use of John Tilson of Wike, co. York, chapman, Sara Wright of the same, widow, and Mary wife of Nicholas Peele of . . , co. York, chapman, they being the grandchildren of the said Richard Fournes, for two years, and then to the use of Jane Tayler of Clackeheaton in the same county, widow, daughter of the said Richard Fournes for another two years: providing that the present surrender be void if Richard Fournes his attorney etc pay £300 in the great south porch of Halifax church as follows, to Henry Bentley his executors etc £60 on 24 June 1643, to Susan Bentley her executors etc £30 within 10 months of the same date, and to Grace, daughter of the said Henry Bentley her executors etc £10 on 24 June 1644, and to John Tilson, Sara Wright and Mary Peele, their executors etc £100, viz £50 on 24 June 1645 and £50 on 24 June 1646, and to Jane Tayler, her executors etc £100 remaining of the £300, viz. £50 on 24 June 1647 and £50 on 24 June 1648. Agreed: Henry Bentley fined for entry of his term 35s 8$\frac{1}{4}$d, Susan Bentley fined 35s 8$\frac{1}{4}$d, Grace Bentley fined 35s 8$\frac{1}{4}$d, John Tilson, Sara Wright and Mary Peele fined 35s 8$\frac{1}{4}$d, and Jane Tayler fined 35s 8$\frac{1}{4}$d.

Sowerby (139) Michael Haldisworth of le Royd in Soyland in the township of Sowerby yeoman by Samuel Gawkroger, lord's tenant and sworn, surrendered three parts (divided equally into four) of a messuage commonly called les Birks in Soyland with all houses and buildings and 5 closes of land, meadow and pasture commonly called and known as les yokeyngs, le vpperbanke, le Lowerbanke, le upp and downe and le upperholme estimated at 6 acres and now occupied by the said Michael Haldisworth or his assigns at a lord's rent of 18d: also a watercourse through a close called Leeynge Carre leading to the same, and the right to scour at all times as necessary, also a parcel of land called le Lane as now divided, estimated at a rood, at a lord's rent of 1d, all in the graveship of Sowerby and now or lately in the occupation of the said Michael Haldisworth or his assigns: to the use of John Hitchon, a son of Joseph Hitchon late of Sowerby, deceased, until the end of the term leased to the said Michael Haldisworth or his assigns in the copy of the court roll dated 22 April 1 Charles [1625]. Agreed: entry fine of 2s 4$\frac{1}{2}$d.

Sowerby (140) Henry Wilson of Soyland in the graveship of Sowerby, clothier, by James Dobson, lord's tenant and sworn, surrendered a house or cottage in Soyland in the graveship of Sowerby lately

occupied by Judith Rawnsley and now by Henry Wilson or his assigns at a lord's rent of 1d and certain fine: to the use of Simon Sharrocke of Soyland for life at a rent to Henry Wilson of a penny at Christmas. Sharrocke will repair or build the cottage at his own expense and make it habitable. [m. 20d] If the rent falls into arrears of twenty days the surrender will be void. Agreed: entry fine of 1½d.
Sowerby (*141*) Jeremy Grenewood of Warley, clothier, by John Murgatroid, lord's tenant and sworn, surrendered those 2 acres 1 rood called Newclose and Heathbankehead with all buildings thereon in Warley in the graveship of Sowerby and now occupied by the said Jeremy Grenewood or his assigns at a lord's rent of 15d: to the use of Henry Murgatroid of Midgley yeoman, his heirs etc, provided that if Jeremy Grenewood, his heirs etc indemnify in the future Henry Murgatroid, his heirs etc as to an obligation dated as this surrender by which Henry Murgatroid, at the request of the said Jeremy and for his own debt, stands obliged with Jeremy to a Luke Crowther senior of Ovenden in the sum of £30 for the true payment of £16 2s 4d on 26 January next coming and all expenses, actions, suits etc arising therefrom, then the surrender will be void. Agreed: entry fine – [22½d cancelled in draft, as rent not covered by a composition]

[In the draft, surrender (130) is followed by the list of 'sworn men' and then by surrenders (131) to (141)]
[A¹]
Halifax: Christopher Robinson and John Smith of Hallend, constables, Richard Lightollers, John Gunson, John Wilkinson, [Samuel] Farrer, Samuel Hartley, Richard Denton, John Briscoe and Thomas Haughton, sworn
Skircote: Richard Waterhouse, constable, Henry Whitacres, Henry Gill, Jonas Bordall and Edmond Hoyle, sworn
Sowerby: Josias Stansfeild deputy, Richard Bentley, constable, Samuel Gawkroger, James Dobson, John Sutcliffe, *Simeon D......*, John Crosley, sworn
Warley: Simeon Otes deputy, Thomas Oldfeild of Cliffehill, constable, Jonathan Gawkroger, *Thomas Deane*, Henry Walker, Bryan Royde and William Grenewood, sworn
Overden: Edward Ridinge, constable, Samuel Aykroid, Richard Longbothome, Edward Doughty and John Fournes of Ovendenwood, sworn
Wadisworth: John Pighells, constable, Luke Widdopp, John Grenewood, Henry Parker and Joseph Shackleton, sworn
[A²]
Midgley: John Hellewell, constable, William Deane, John Shawe, Francis Midgley and John Middlebrough, sworn

Rishworth: John Barrow deputy, Abraham Batcheler, constable, George Holdroid, Henry Ramsden, John Waterhouse, Isaac Waterhouse, sworn
Stansfeild: John Stansfeild, constable, Thomas Grenewood, John Whitwham, Michael Bentley and George Buckley, sworn
Heptonstall: Thomas Grenewood, constable, Joshua Bentley, John Austen, Samuel Hudson and John Ingham, sworn
Langfeild: Jeremy Ingham, constable, Richard Nayler, John Lord, Abraham Horne and John Crosley, sworn
Ayringden: Daniel Helsted sworn, Samuel Hanson, constable, John Ingham, Richard Cockcroft, John Illingworth and Thomas Clay, sworn

[B]

Panel of Leet jurors, undifferentiated

[C]

Panel of Halifax leet jurors, 13 April 1640

Jonathan Crowther 4:4:3:1

[Edward Wainhouse 'of Crosselane end in Norland']

[D[1]]

Richard Lowson of Norland for makeing afray and draweing bloode vpon Nathaniell Chadwicke of Warley

William Deane of Ovenden for makeing afray and draweing blood vpon Ezekill Cooke

Henry Wadisworth for the like vpon the said Cooke

William Deane for makeinge afray and draweing bloode vpon Samuell Starkie

Item we present Daniell Mitchell for makinge an affray and drawinge blood vpon Hugh Smith

Michael Bynns [mark] sworn	[signed]	Jonathan Crowther
John Millnes } sworn		Edward Wainhouse
William Thomas [T] } sworn		Luke Horsfall
Henry Riley [R]		

[dorse]

Richard Lowson and Mary his wife of Norland for makeing afray and drawing blood of Michael Binnes de eadem

William Cowper [and] his wife for the like of Jane Harison both of Halifax

Abraham Wilkinson of Sowerby for makeing afray and draweing blood vpon Edward Brearley of Warley [etc as in engrossed roll]

[D[2]] [*ditto* Isacke Sladen ...

[D[3]] [*ditto* Thomas Warr to end]

[signed] Abraham Mitchell

[E]

Hallifax paines and Presentments Laid Aprill 13th 1640
per vs whose names are subscribed

Imprimis wee paine Thomas Wilkinson of the Brakenbed for not mending the high Streete at the Shambles and as far as belongeth to him in 10s

Item wee paine John Hargreuues for not Mending the high Streete at the Shambles end in 10s

[Three items cancelled and illegible]

Item wee *present* paine George Fowernsse of Deane Cloughe for not mending the walle at his owne house side John Gunson haueing a Beast Spoyled theire and allso in danger to doe greate hurt, if hee doe not sufficiently amend the same before Midsomer next in 20s

Aprill 11th: 1640 Item wee present James Sharples and Hugh Weorall for Makeing a fray and drawing of bloode the one vppon the other

Apill 6 Item wee present Michaell Haworth otherwayes Called Cocke Haworth for Makeing a fray and draweing blood vppon the Bodye of Thomas Lee

November 16: 1639 Item wee present Lawrence Thackray for makeing a fray vppon the body of Will. Bothumlay

December 19: 1639 Item wee present Robert Bradforth and Michaell Butterworth for Makeing a fray the one vppon the other

Item we present euery man betwixt the Smiddye stayke and the Shambles all those that lacketh mendinge in 20s if they be not done the last of Julye

John Smith [IS]	Samuell Farror	presenters
Christopher Robinson	John Wilkinson [I]	

Halifax

[in margin]

Amersie Georg Denton in 5s for anoying the hie way with his dunghill and pain him in 3s 4d for eury month it Continues.

[dorse] Item we present George Denton for lying a dunghill in the highway beinge a common annoyance in *10s* 5s

And wee lay in payne that he shall remove it before the 13th day of May next in 20s

Also we lay in payne that all the owners or occupyers of the houses and wooll shopps betwixt a place called Smithystake and the Flesh shambles shall repaire the streete sufficiently euery man against his owne houseinge shopp or shopps before the first day of August next in payne of every man 10s

[signed] Richard Lightoulers

John Smith — John Gunsonn

Christopher Robinson — Samuell Farrer

John Wilkinson [I]

[signed] Jonathan Crowther/Edward Wainhouse/Luke Horsfall/

[F]

Thoms Hoult presentment

Imprimis I present Marke Turner for his wife defileing the water 3s 4d†

Item I present Anthony Rotherrn for his wife doeing the same 3s 4d†

Item I present uxor Wills. Farrar for his *wife* for doeing the same 3s 4d†

Item I present uxor Samson Aikeroyde for doeing the same 3s 4d†

[G] Halifax [†diff. ink]

13 Aprell 1640

Skircoate The Constable together with the presenters heere vnder written doe subscribe

vizt. The stockes the whipp stockes the Buttes and the Pinfold and all other things in good repayre

for all other Misdemeanours wee fynd Onmia bene

[signed] Richard Waterhous/Henry Ghill/Edmund Hoyle [EH]/
Henre Whitaker/James Bardall

Skircote

[endorsed] Michaell Gill/Henry Cockcrofte/

[H]

Aprill 13th 1640 A Bill of such presentments as is within the Constablery for Sowerby

Wee find all thinges in good order and repaire accordinge to our knowledge and accordinge to the charge formerly giuen, saueinge these thinges subscribed and certainely specified.

Inprimis wee lay a paine vppon John Banister for two watercoarses betwixt a yate neare his owne house and the Hall Banck topp, beinge in the highway leadinge betwixt Sowerby and Heptonstall, in Ten shillings, if it bee nott repaired before the 24th of June next.

Item wee lay in paine James Butterworth and George Ratcliffe for stoppinge of diuerse ordinarye watercourses beinge in the high way afforesaid betwixt Sowerby and Croselane ends if it bee nott amended before the first of June next, twentye shillinges, either of them tenn shillinges.

Item wee lay in paine Jephery Jacksonn Tenn groates for one watercourse beinge in the high way lyeinge betwixt Rachdale and Elland, if it bee nott amended before the first of June next.

Item Michael Carter Twentye shillinges for neglectinge to keepe open his watercourse beinge in the high way beforesaid betwixt Rachdale and Eland, if it bee not repayred before the 14th of June next.

Item wee payne Richord Michell for one other watercourse, beinge in the same high way affore said, in fiue shillinges, if it bee not opened and amended before the 24th of June next.

Item wee payne John Mitchell, in fiue shillinges, for neglectinge to

open another watercourse lyeinge and beinge in the high way afforesaid, if it bee not opened and amended before the 24th of June next.
[signed] Josias Stansfeld Constable
Samuell Gawkrodger/John Sutliffe/John Crosley/James Dobsone/
Sowerby
[endorsed] Michaell Gill/Henry Cockcrofte
[I]

13° Aprell 1640 Warley

The Constable together with the presenters heere vnderwritten doe subscribe,

Travers' infer' wee payne a way betwixte widow Gregson and Luke Marsdens house in 6s 8d to be repaird by the 4 of August

Travers' infer' Also Wee *present* payne a way called stocke-Lane betwixt Warelay Towne and Harrard well in 39s to be repard betwixt this and next court Leete Holden at Hallifax

Travers' infer' These wayes are to be repared by the towne of Warley — Item we payne a Lane twixt Hoylehouse and Daniell Hoyles in Warelay in the somme of 6s 8d to be repayred at or before the next Court Leete att Hallifax.

And as for the stockes whipp-stockes and Buttes and Pinfold and all other thinges in good repayre Other Misdemeanours wee know none but Omnia bene

Thomas Oldfeild Constable [signed] Thomas Oldfeild/William Greenwood
[mark] Brian Boyd [B]/Jonathan Gawkroger
Henery Walker
Warley
[endorsed] Michaell Gill/Henry Cockcrofte/
[J]

Constable *amerced 10s for not attending Presentments*

13° April 1640 Samuell Aykroid Richard Longbottom presenters for Ovenden for the halfe yeare by past
Edward Doughtie and John Fournes presenters for the next halfe yeare

The payne layde vpon the high way leading from Denham and the watercourse in Bradshawe Lane are both amended within the time limited.

There is not any misdemenar concerneing our office within our libertie founde presentable or worthy to be layd in payne att this presente tyme.

Edward Riding [ER] Constable
Samuel Akrode [S]/Richard Longbothom [R]
Ovenden

[endorsed] Michaell Gill/Henry Cockcrofte/
[K]

Wadsworth
Bill The Court leete Houlden att Hallifax the 13th day of Aprill 1640

Inprimis: Whereas there was a payne layed at the Last Sherifturne of a Hyghway between a place called Blackden Bridge and Widdopp heade, theise are to Certiffie vnto you that itt is nowe sufficiently amended.

Item: whereas there was another payne layed of the Inhabitants of Wadsworth att the Last Sherifturne *of Heptonbridge* for Repayreing of a parte of Heptonbridge theise are to Certiffie vnto you that itt is nowe well and sufficiently Amended.

Item: whereas there was a payne layed att the Last Sherifturne of a hygh way in Midgley betweene the Broadfoulde and Houlmhouse Bridge belongeinge to *Richard Midsgley and Samuell Midsgley* the Inhabitants of Midsgley which is not yet amended therefore we Amercy them in 20s and likewise in 3s 4d for euery weeke since the Last day of Neuember Last past *in toto £4 3s 4d*

Item there was a payne layde att the Last Sherifturne of a hyghway in Wareley between the Houlmhouse Bridge and Banckehouse Lane heade belongeinge to *John Briggs, James Murgateroyd and Briane Crowther* the Inhabitants of Wareley which is not yet amended therefore we amercy them in 20s and likewise in 3s 4d for euery weeke since the Last day of Nouember Last past.

Item: We lay a payne of 30s of the Inhabitants of Heptonstall if they doe not sufficiently Amende the West end of Hepton Bridge before Midsomer day next in 30s

Item Wee lay a payne of 20s of Paule Grenewood of Stonesheyyate in Heptonstall if hee doe not sufficientely amende the high way betweene the Stones-hey-yate and a place called the Litle-hey before Midsomer day next and Likewyse that hee drawe the water forth of the hygh way into the slares, to make drie the sayde way, in 20s

Item we lay a paine of Thomas Satcliffe if he doe not hang a yat in not Clough and mend his fence before last of May in 5s

John Pyghelles [I]/Luke Widdopp [mark]/Henry Parker [H]/Joseph Shackleton [mark]/John Grenewoode
Wadisworth

[endorsed] John Hoyle Jonathan Crowther
Edward Wainhouse/John Crosland [IC]/Michaell Gill/ Abraham Grenwood [A]/Elias Hansonn [mark]/Thomas Ouldfeld [O]/Henry Wilson/John Hoyle/William Farrer/ Christopher Thomas [CT]/Luke Horsfall/Henry Cockcrofte/

[L[1]]

Midgley

Imprimis we lay in paine *£4 10s* that Richard Midgley and Samuell Midgley shall sufficiently amend the Highway Called Bradford lane in Midgley aforesaid all alonge their lands there before the last day of November next in paine of 30s and shall from thenceforth for euer keepe the same in good repaire in paine of every weeke wherein it is not so kept 3s 4d

we doe amercie the parties in this payne accordinge to their default [*inserted*]

Item that the said Samuell Midgley shall amend the highway in Midgley all alonge his land there from Holmforth bridgend the lower end of Bradfordlane before the first day of December next in paine of 20s and shall from thenceforth keepe the same in good repaire in paine of euery weeke wherein the same is not so kept 2s *this payne is traversed*

Item that James Oldfeild of Warley shall sufficiently amend the highway all alonge his lands in Wareley aforesaid from Holmehouse-bridge-end to the lower end of the land called Banckhouse lane before the first December next in paine of 10s and shall from thenceforth for euer keepe the same sufficiently repaired in paine of euery month wherein it is vnrepaired 3s 4d *this pane is traversed*

Item that Brian Crowther of Warley aforesaid shall sufficiently amend the highway alonge the land in his tenure in Warley by removeinge the stones and rubbish of the walls of his said land out of the said highway wherein now they ly before the 15th day of November next in paine of 20s

We doe Amercie Brian Crowther Acording to this payne [added] [endorsed] Jonathan Crowther/Luke Horsfall/Henry Cockcrofte/

[L[2]]

Midgley

13 Aprill 1640 At the Court Leete Holden at Halifax

Paines

Wee lay in paine that thinhabitants of Warley shall sufficiently amend the highway betweene Luddingden and Brecktop before Penticost next in payne of 20s and thenceforth for euer keepe and maintaine the same in good repayre in payne of euery monthe wherein it is not so mainteyned 5s

wee lay in paine that John Shaw of Shawbooth in Warley aforesaid shall remoue the stones Fallen downe into the highway from of his walls adioyning thereto from the lane head nere to the Peelehouse vp to the Brecktop, forth of the said highway, and lay them ouer his said walls before Penticost next in payne of 13s 4d

Wee amercy Richard Midgley and Samuell Midgley of Midgley for not amending the highway betweene the Holmehouse and Broad-

fold in Midgley abovesaid according to a paine formerly laid, 20s
Richard Midgley Constable
William Deane [mark]/John Shaw [mark]/Francis Midgley [mark]/ John Midlebrough [I]/
Midgley
[endorsed] Michaell Gill/Henry Cockcrofte/
[M]
April 13: Rishworth cum Norland
For our butes and stockes we have them in repaire sufficient and for our other presentements or any other misdaymaniors we have not any
[signed] George Howellroyd/Henrie Ramsden/Isacke Watterhous/ John Watterhowse/
[endorsed] Michaell Gill/Henry Cockcrofte/
[N]
Stansfeild
13 April 1640
Paines laid at the Court Leet holden att Halifax
Wee lay in paine that Thomas Cockcroft of Greenewoodlee, John Feilden, Edward Mitchell, James Stansfeild, John Stansfeild, James Shepheard, and John Crosley all of Stansfeild, and James Sugar of the parish of Burnley in the County of Lancaster and Michaell Eastwood of Clitiger and Adam Holden of Rosendale in the said County yeomen shall sufficiently amend the highway betweene Stiperden and Ibartley-clough all along their respective grounds in Stansfeild aforesaid before the 24th of June next in paine of euery one of them fayling in amending the said way adioyning to his grounds 39s and shall from thenceforth for euer maintayne the same in payne of euery month wherein it is so done, euery month fayling of 10s.
Wee present William Bingley of Stansfeild and Abraham Robertshaw of the same for makeing an affray either vpon other 6s 8d
John Widdopp Constable
Thomas Greenewood
Michaell Bentley [mark] } presenters
John Whitwham [I]
George Buckley [G]
Wee present Thomas Cockcroft of Greenewoodlee, John Feilden, John Stansfeild, and Michaell Eastwood of Stansfeild for not amending the highway in Stansfeild aforesaid adioyning to their respective grounds there euery one *13s* 20s
[signed] John Widdopp/Michaell Bentley [mark]/Thomas Greenewod/George Buckley [G]/John Whitwhame/
Stansfeild
[endorsed] Michaell Gill/Henry Cockcrofte/Luke Horsfall/

[O]

Att the Sheriffes turne houlden att Hallifax the 13 th of Aprill 1640

Heptonstall Thomas Grenewood Constable

Josua Bentley
John Asten
Samuell Hudsone
John Ingham } Presenters

Wee present Isacke Briges for making affray and draweing of blode of John Bentley, Allso wee present John Bentley for makeing affray of Isacke Briges with out bloud 3s 4d

Wee present William Perkinson for makeing affray of John Wilkinsone and likewise John Wilkingson for makeing afray of William Perkinson

Wee lay a payne of 13s 4d vpon the occupiers of the groundes aioying to the hie way betwene the edgend grene and Horsfall Brige if they doe not suffiently amend the same before the 24 th day of June next.

Thomas Grenewood

John Ingham [I]/Samuell Hudsum [H]/Josua Bentley [I]/John Austen [I]/

Heptonstall

[endorsed] Michaell Gill/Henry Cockcrofte/

[P]

The Constable of Langfeild with his foure menn
for buttes and stockes we haue in reasonable good repayre

We do payne William Crosley of the same towne in 6s 8d If he do not open and Clouse a ditch in Langfeld Holmes betwixt the said William Crosley and John Crosley, betwixt this and last of may next to the great Annoyance of divorse other neighbours.

And for Other misdemainors wee do knowe none

Jeremy Ingham Constable

Richard Nayler/Abraham Horne/John Crosley [mark]/John Lord/

Langfeild

[endorsed] Michaell Gill/Henry Cockcrofte/

[Q]

13 o Aprill 1640 Samuell Hanson Constable of Erinden

Richard Cockcrofte
John Ingham } presenters for the last halfe yeare

the high wayes and all other things belonging to our office was viewed by vs the last weeke and nothing founde presentable

John Illingworth
Thomas Clay } new presenters

Samuell Hanson [mark]/John Ingham [I]/Richard Cockcrofte [R]

Ayringden

[endorsed] Michaell Gill/Henry Cockcrofte/

[mem 20 d]

BRIGHOUSE: VIEW OF FRANKPLEDGE AND COURT LEET WITH TOURN: 14 April 16 Charles [1640]

Inquisition taken for the King on the oath of Richard Ramsden, Arthur Hanson, Samuel Bothomley, Isaac Brodeley, Daniel Hoile, John Nutter, John Roper, Nathan Crowther, Edmund Moorehouse, Thomas Dyson, James Fournes, Thomas Whitwham, Samuel Preistley and John Firth

HIPPERHOLME:	township jury said that all is well			
RASTRICKE:	,,	,,	,,	
FEKISBY:	,,	,,	,,	
NORTHOWROME:	,,	,,	,,	
SHELFFE:	,,	,,	,,	
QUARMBY:	,,	that John Lockwood made affray and drew blood of George Shaw		*10s*
		Francis Wood made affray on George Shawe		*3s 4d*
		James Moore made affray and drew blood of Thomas Firth		*10s*
		Thomas Moore made affray on Miles Hirst		*3s 4d*
		Mathew Crosland made affray and drew blood of Edward Thornton		*10s*

James Smith	made affray	and drew blood of	Henry Hudson	*10s*
Joseph Walker	,,	,,	John Smith	*10s*
George Walker	,,	on	John Smith	*3s 4d*
Mathew Crosland	,,		William Kay	*3s 4d*
John Kay and his wife	made affray	and drew blood of	William Kay	*10s*
John Taylor	,,	,,	William Hirst	*10s*
George Parkin	,,	,,	John Tayler	*10s*
Thomas Warre	,,	,,	,,	,,
James Baxter	,,	,,	,,	,,
John Mallinson	,,	,,	,,	,,
John Hellewell	,,	,,	,,	,,
Ed. Hellewell	made affray	on	John Tayler	*3s 4d*
James Thorpe	,,	and drew blood of	John Wainewright	*10s*
James Kirshawe	,,	,,	George Clay	,,
George Clay	,,	,,	James Kirshawe	,,
James Sykes	,,	,,	Edward Dawson	,,
James Sykes	,,	,,	William Denton	,,
John Mallinson	,,	,,	John Tayler	,,

DALTON: township jury said that all is well

HARTSHEAD: township jury said that all is well

CLIFTON: township jury said that John Soothill did not ring nor yoke his pig *12d* that Edward Ashton broke hedges and 'sleated' (*effugavit*) his sheep over the common *2s*

that Michael Shepley of Liversedge made affray on Nathan Gleidhill of Brighouse *3s 4d*

STAINLAND: township jury said that John Townend dug in the highway by Sowood *3s 4d*

that Jonathan Walton dug at Hellewell Grene *3s 4d*

that the said Jonathan Walton made affray and drew blood of John Sheaphead *10s*

John Sheapheard was chosen pinder this year and was sworn.

BARKISLAND: township jury said that all is well

Finally the jurors present that all the above is true.

Hipperholme (*142*) Thomas Rawson of Wadsworth, co. York, yeoman, Robert Rawson and William Rawson of the same, sons of the said Thomas [*and Dorothy now wife of the said Robert*] by Arthur Hanson, lord's tenant and sworn, surrendered the half part held by them of 6 closes of meadow and pasture in Lightcliffe in the township of Hipperholme in the manor of Wakefeld now occupied by Robert Hargreaves or his assigns, three of which are called or commonly known as Wharles and the other three as Allonroyds, for which a certain fine is due: to the use of Thomas Sugden of Lightcliffe in Hipperholme, yeoman, his heirs etc for ever. Agreed: entry fine of 4s 1½d.

Hipperholme (*143*) Thomas Rawson of Wadsworth, co. York, yeoman, Robert Rawson and William Rawson of the same, sons of the said Thomas [*and Dorothy now wife of the said Robert, she agreeing separately*] by Arthur Hanson, lord's tenant and sworn, surrendered their half of 2 messuages, one called Cliffhill and the other Westheadley, now occupied by Robert Hargreaves of Lightcliffe in the same, yeoman, or his assigns, and all lands, holdings, closes etc associated in Lightcliffe in the township of Hipperholme now held by the same, for which there is no certain fine, and also their customary land in Lightcliffe in Hipperholme and their half of an annuity of 20s from 8 acres in Sowerby where there is a certain fine (this agreement exluding the three closes called Wharles and the three called Allonroid): to the use of Robert Hargreaves for ever. Agreed: entry fine of – for the uncertain lands, and of 20d for the certain annuity of 20s. [mem 21]

Hipperholme (*144*) Susan Feild of Northowrome widow by Robert Nicholls, lord's tenant and sworn, surrendered that close of land, meadow and pasture commonly called le Leyclose *alias* Backfeild, with all buildings thereon, also the upper end of another close of land, meadow and pasture commonly called le Wellynge as divided from the lower part in Northowrome in the graveship of Hipperholme now occupied by the said Susan Feild or her assigns at a lord's rent of 4d and certain fine: to the use of Mathew Sowden of Cockan in the township of Clayton in Bradforddale, yeoman, his heirs etc for ever. Agreed: entry fine of 12d *Compounded for by Thomas Longbothome*

Sowerby (*145*) Testimony by Arthur Hanson of Brighouse, lord's tenant, that Richard Hanson of Lepton on 18 April 11 Charles [1635] surrendered 1 acre 3 roods of land and all buildings thereon in Soyland in the graveship of Sowerby then occupied by John Hoile of Shawe in Sowerby or his assigns, of which one parcel lies at les Maidenstones, estimated at a half acre, not enclosed nor with certain fine, and for the rest at a lord's rent of 5d and certain fine: to the use of the said John Hoile and John Hoile his son, and to their wives and children or their assigns as from 2 February last past for 18 years, subject to such reserved rents as are borne by these and other lands under an indenture of lease of the same date as this surrender between the said Richard Hanson and the said John and John Hoile. Agreed: entry fine of – for the uncertain land, and of 7½d for the certain land.

Sowerby (*146*) Robert Hargreaves of Lightcliffe in the township of Hipperholme [*and Mary his wife*], and George Elvish of Wadisworth, co. York, by Arthur Hanson of Brighouse, lord's tenant and sworn, surrendered and quitclaimed an annuity of 20s arising from 8 acres of land, meadow and pasture in Sowerby in the manor of Wakefeld now of the customed heredity of George Riley of le Clough in Sowerby at a certain fine, also their interest in the same land from which the annuity is derived: to the use of the said George Riley for ever. Agreed: fine for quitclaim, 6d.

Rastricke (*147*) John Fox of Boothroid in Rastricke and Mary now his wife, she agreeing separately, by Edward Hanson of Netherwoodhouse, lord's tenant and sworn, surrendered the reversion after the death of the said John Fox of a messuage with appurtenances at le Boothroid in the graveship of Rastricke lately held by Grace Firth widow or her assigns and now by John Firth her son or his assigns, consisting of a kitchen [*culina*] now made into a house with a chamber above, a stable adjoining the barn, a parcel of land on the north of the building or 'houseinge' of 6½ yards length by 5 yards breadth as now bounded, and the appropriate fold and 3 closes of land, meadow and pasture in Rastricke now in 4 closes called or commonly known as le Overbackside de les Stones, le Netherbackside de les Stones and le Houghfeild, estimated at 6 acres, at a lord's rent of 2s: also a parcel of land estimated at 68 yards in length and 7 yards in breadth to the north and as much to the east of a close called Tentercrofte extending between the fold at Boothroid and the close called Backsidestones, also all that parcel of a barn called an Eelinge or Outshutt now held by the said John Firth or his assigns at le Boothroyd and all paths, water, easements etc at a lord's rent of 1d and for certain fine: to the use of Edward Fox and William Fox of Totehill, brothers of the said John, and their heirs and assigns for ever. Agreed: entry fine of 3s $1\frac{1}{2}$d.

[In the draft surrender (142) is followed by the constablery juries, and then by surrenders (143) to (147)]

[A[1]]

Hipperholme: William Walker, constable, William Hirde, Samuel Hoyle, John Mitchell and Abraham Lomme, sworn

Rastricke: Thomas Flather, constable, Edmund Fox, Edward Fox, Edward Hanson and Henry Brooke, sworn

Fekisby: Joseph Lockwood, constable, Joshua Lockwood and William Dyson, sworn

Northowrome: George Longbothome, constable, Hugh Berry, James Mitchell, Robert Nicholls, Joseph Waterhouse, sworn

Shelffe: Robert Birkhead, constable, John Ben, Thomas Mellin and James Hogge, sworn

Quarmby: Michael Haigh, constable, Edward Hanson, Nicholas Hirst, George Walker and Henry Savile, sworn

Dalton: John Horsfall, constable, Richard Brooke, deputy, John Spivey and William Brookesbancke, sworn

[A[2]]

Clifton: Robert Drake, cardmaker, constable, Henry Rawnsley and John Rayner, sworn

Harteshead: Miles Clayton, constable, Alvered Gibson and Edward Hepworth, sworn

Stainland: Thomas Cordingley, constable, Bernard Denton, Thomas Pickles, George Gleidhill and Isaac Whitley, sworn

Barkisland: James Cordley, constable, James Grene, John Townend, Edward Marsden and John Gleidhill, sworn

[B]

Brighouse panel for 14 April
Richard Ramsden 4:4:5

[C]

Aprill the 14th anno dom. 1640	Paines laide at the sheareturne at Brighous by the Constable and the foure men whose names are heare vnder written

Hipperholme

William Walker Constable
William Hird
Samuel Hoyle
John Michaell
Abraham Lome

Inprimis we lay in paine all person or persons that put any scabed horse to the Commonn in euery default so ofendinge 3s 4d

Item we lay in paine any person or persons that putteth any swine to the Commonn vnringed or vnyocked in euery default so ofendinge 2s 6d

Item we lay in paine Robart Hargreues Andrew Gill Gorge Willsonn Gorge Hargreues William Modely William Willsonn to mend the way betwixt Gorge Hargreues and the Hellewell sike before midsummer next in paine of 20s

Item we lay in paine Michaell Emsall to scoure his dich at the pound at Scud lane end betwixt this and midsummer next in paine of 10s

Item we lay in paine Abraham Willsonn John Hargreues Widow Brighous William Medely Richard Gill to mend the lane called Northige Lane betwixt Abraham Willsonn stele and William Northend yate betwixt this and Midsummer next in paine of 10s

Item we lay in paine Josua Roydes to scoure the wattercourse from the welles betwixt Christofer Steeuensones and Simond Smithes betwixt this and Whisonday next in paine of 5s

Item we lay in paine John Baraclough Thomas Pollard John Michaell Edward Baraclough James Wilkinsonn to make the yattes betwixt Norwoodgrene and the Rooydeshalbrooke in paine of euery default 5s

Item we lay in paine the occopires of one Cloase Called Jack Croft to make up theire fence betwixt it and brige Inge betwixt this and Mayday next in paine of 3s 4d

Item we lay in paine any personn or persones that maketh any way outherwise thenn the highway ouer to Bround Cloases that lieth at the Northside of John Apellyeard house at the Winteredge in euery default so ofendinge and now in the Occapationn of John Parsley 1s

Item we lay in paine Robart Briges to make his fence betwix Edward Baraclough and himselfe betwixt this and Mayday next in pane of 3s 4d

Item we lay in paine any person or persones that maketh any foout way Contrarie to the high way ouer one Close called Round Graue now in the Occopationn of widow hoole in lighliffe in euery default so doinge 3s 4d

Item we lay in paine any person or persons that maketh any foout way ouer one Close of Isackes Broadleys called Wood Cloase in euery default so doinge 1s

Ouerseares for the high way
Samuell Hoole/Robart Baraclough/Anthonie Flather/
Michaell Northend/

[signed] Richard Ramsden Isaak Brodley James Fourniss
Daniell Hoile/Edmond Morehouse
Hipperholme

[D]

The Constable of Rastricke Thomas Flather
the Foure men Edward Fox/Edmond Fox/
Edward Hanson/Henrie Brooke

We apoynte overseares for Comondayes Worke
Arthur Hirste and John Fox of Botheroyde
Omne bene

[signed] Richard Ramsden/Arthur Hanson/Daniel Hoile/James Fourniss/

Rastricke

[E]

The Constable of Fekisby his bill

As for presentments we haue none omney beney

Joseph Lockwode/Joshua Lockwood/William Dison/

[signed] Richard Ramsden/Daniel Hoile/Thomas Whitwham/ Edmond Morehouse/James Fourniss/

Fekisby omnia bene

[F]

The paines laid vpon the township of Northouram

Imprimis we paine the owners and ocupiers of shibden millen to repair and mend betwixt the killen door of shibden and the ouper end of the dam betwixt this day and midsumer the next in paine of *thirtie* ten shillings

Item we paine vpon widow hobkinson to repair and mend the highway anent hir ground vp to the simcar and to switch hir hedgis betwixt this and midsomer in paine of twentie shillings

Item we paine Michael Bentlay to mend the way anent one cloys befor midsomer in paine of ten grotes.

Item we paine John Bairstow and Robert Bairstow or the ocupiers of the limed hous ground that they repaire and mend the horsway and make it sufficient betwixt this and midsomerday in paine of euery ocupier thirtie shillings

Item we paine Georg Whitlay Richerd Bentlay Thomas Flather John Smith Georg Romsden and vxor Thomas Smith to mend and mak suficient one horsway betwixt barhead delfe and grene loynend euery man against his owen ground betwixt or bevor midsumerday next in euer one of them ten *fortie* shillings

Item we paine vxor Hughe Romsdon Edward Northing of the knightroyd and his mother, Georg whitlay Marmaduck Baull to mak a suficient horsway euery one against their owne ground beffor midsomer next in paine of euery one of then ten shillings

Item we paine Richard Lacok Georg whitlay Mathew Jager John Wallis to mak a soficient horsway anent his owen Ground betwixt the lower end of dicon field and longeshawe betwixt this and midsomer nex in paine of euery of them 5s

Item we paine William Pollerd to mend and make a suficient horsway and foutway against his ground of the longeshawe befor midsomer nex in paine of twentie shillings

Item we paine Thomas Royds Jonas Vicars and John Sunderland that they mak a suficient horsway euery one against his owen ground betwix this and midsumer nex in paine of Euery of them 5s

Item we paine Adam Romsden and vxor Thomas Smith to mak a suficient horsway against thir owen ground in paine of either of them 5s shillings

Item we paine the oweners and ocupiers of lined hous ground and stout to mak a suficient foot brigge, Well railed on either sid at the lower end of the gude inge betwixt this and midsumer day nex in paine of whom it belongeth to mend in paine of Thirtie shillings

Item we paine Huge Bery that he mak a suficient fout way against his owen ground betwixt the puleslack and Royd stiell betixt this and midsomer the next in paine of 5s

Item we paine Richard Murgitroy that he musile his doge acordinge to the statut impane of so often as he ofendeth in that kind in paine of euery time ten grautes

Item we paine John Wadsworth that he amend the way anent his owen close betwixt this and midsoner in paine of 5s

Item we paine John wadsworth and Henry moor that they mak a suficient horsway the loyne betwix northouram and ouenden betwixt this and midsomer in paine of ten shillings

Item we paine Robert Rishwor that he fill vp his delf which he opened at the bothom of Huge bery field bothom betwixt this and midsomer in paine of ten shillings

Item we paine Henry Crabtrie and the ocupiers of the land anent him betwix the millen and Jonias Holdsworth that they make a suficient horsway betwixt this and midsomer in paine of twentie shillings.

Northowrome

[dorse]

Item we paine such persones as shall goe ouer tow inges liing betwix Jerimie bairstow hous and Robert nichols of Northouran in paine of euery person at euery time goinge ouer it 3s 4d

Item we paine such persons as shall goe ouer one close betwixt John Baitmans and Jonas Priestlayes in paine of euery person so often going that way ten shillinges

Item we paine the owners and ocupiers of the land betwixt the bothom of godlay loyn and the vper end one either sid that they switch their hedges betwixt this and mayday in paine of Thirtie shillings

Oursiers for the highway

Nathan Bentlay/Nicholas Smith/Gilles Tenand/Samuell Smith/

[signed] Huge Bery [mark]/Jacob Michell [M]/Robert Nicholls/ Joseph Waterhous [I]/

[signed] Richard Ramsden/Arthur Hanson/Daniell Hoile/Edmond Morehouse/James Fourniss/John Firth/Nathan Crowther/ Thomas Dyson/John Roper/John Nuttar/

[G]

Item wee paine John Lister of ouenden to mend the foot way of the este of his intacke Called wind Milne hill before this and midsumar next in paine of 10s

Item wee paine Francis Jackson to fill his pit holes in the same laine betwixt this and midsumar next in paine of 10s

Item wee paine James Wallis and Francis Jackson to mend the way betwixt hakes Clough and saw laine end betwixte this and midsumer next in paine of 5s

Item wee paine Abraham Sunderland to mend his way of the north side of his house Joynige to his intacke betwixt this and midsumar next in paine of 5s

Item wee paine Edmond woode to mend his way at east side of his intacke leadinge vp to William Benn house betwixt this and midsumar in paine of 5s

Item wee paine Richard Best John Phillipe Robart Birkhead and Richard Butlar to mend the way betwixt Blackshawe Brocke and Robart Birkhead intack end betwixt this and midsumar next in paine of 10s

Item wee paine John Benn to mend a Cawsei end leadinge vp to his owne house betwixt this and midsumer next in paine of 10s

Item wee paine Thomas Mellin to mend his way at Stanindgefild nucke betwixt this and midsumar next in paine of 5s

Item we paine widdow Hogg to mend the way ageenst hir intack betwixt this and midsumar next in paine of 5s

Constable of Shelfe with these 3 presentars

John Benn [B]

Thomas Mellin [signed] Richard Ramsden Isaak Brodley

James Hog Daniell Hoile James Fourniss

Shelffe

[H]

Quarmby Bill

The foure presenters, Edward Hanson Nicholas Hirste Henery Savill George Walker

Item present vpon the oath of George Shawe John Lockwoode for makeing a fraye and drawinge of Bloode vpon the saide George Shawe

Item present vpon the oath of George Shawe Henery Savill for makeing a fray and Draweinge of Bloode vpon the saide George Shawe

on the oath of

,,	George Shawe, Francis Wood	for makeing a fray on		George Shawe
,,	John Dyson, James Moore	,,	and blood on	Thomas Firth
,,	John Dyson, Thomas Moore	,,	—	Myles Hirst
,,	Edwarde Thorneton, Mathewe Crosland	,,	and blood on	Edwarde Thornton
,,	Henery Hudson, James Smythes	,,	,,	Henery Hudson
,,	Henery Hudson, Joseph Walker	,,	,,	John Smythe
,,	Henery Hudson, George Walker	,,	—	John Smyth

on the oath of William Kaye,

	Mathew Crosland	for makeing a fray on		William Kaye
,,	William Kaye, John Kaye and his wife	,,	and blood on	William Kaye
,,	William Kaye, John Talor	,,	,,	William Hirst
,,	John Talour, George Parkin	,,	,,	John Talor

[dorse]

John Talor, Thomas Warre	,,	,,	,,
,, James Backester	,,	,,	,,
,, John Mallingson yonger	,,	,,	,,
,, John Heallewell	,,	,,	,,
,, Edmond Heallewel	,,	—	,,
,, James Thorppe	,,	and blood on	John Waynewright
Edwarde Meller, James Kirshawe	,,	,,	George Claye
,, George Claye	,,	,,	James Kirshawe
Edwarde Dawson, James Syckes	,,	,,	Edward Dawson
,, James Syckes	,,	,,	William Denton
John Talour, John Mallingson	,,	,,	John Talour

Item wee lay in paine that John Haighe doe make the fence in the vsuall place in a close called the nether Inge before the next Courte in payne of 30s

Traversed Item wee mercy Roger Armitaige for takeinge the water from the weste wells which doth belonge vnto the walcrofte into a newe Intacke called west wel hill as by a payne formerly layde 20s

This is traversed negative

[inside folded sheet]

[signed] Richard Ramsden Isaak Bradley Samuell Bothomley [S] James Fourniss/Daniell Hoile/Thomas Whitwham/Edmond Morehouse/John Firth/Nathan Crowther/Thomas Dyson/John Roper/John Nuttar/Samuell Prestley [S]/ Arthur Hanson/

Quarmby

[I]

The Constable of Dalton John Horsfall Constable

sworne John Spivie/William Brooksbanck

Omne bene

[signed] Richard Ramsden/Arthur Hanson/James Fourniss

Dalton

[J]

Hartshead cum Clifton

First we present John Soothill for a swyne goinge vnyocked and vnringed contrary to the law one shillinge

We present Edward Ashton for Hedges breakinge and sleatinge sheepe vpon the Common for ether default twelve pence

We lay in payne that all the fences within the Tounshipp Joyinge to thc Common or high wayes be well and sufficiently made before the first day of may in payne of euery offender herein 6s 8d

We lay in payne that the high way betwixt belly bridge and birkby-lane head be well and sufficiently repaired by them that accustom-ablely haue made the same, before the tenth of June in payne of euery offender 39s

We lay in payne that the high way betwixt Thornhillbridge and Stone bridge be well and sufficiently repaired by the accustomed people before the last of May in paine of euer offender 5s

We lay in paine that none shall keepe their swyne vnyocked or vnringed in payne of euery offender herein 3s 4d

We lay in paine that Thomas Child Scour his ditch in the Oul-field and make his stile sufficiently which is noysome to passingers before the first of may in payne of 3s 4d

We lay in payne that none shall sleat any Cattell vpon the Common in payne of euery offender herein twelve pence

We present Michaell Shepley of Liuersedge for makinge a fray vpon the body of Nathan Gledhill of Brighouse.

[signed] Richard Ramsden Isaak Bradley
Daniell Hoile
James Fourniss

Hartshead cum Clifton

[K[1]]

Stainland Bill

Thomas Cordley Constable

New presenters Barnard Denton Thomas Pighells

Imprimis we present John Townend for digginge a delfe in the highway neare Sowood in 3s 4d. And that he shall fill it vp before the tenth day of May next in payne of 20s

Item we present Jonathan Walton for digginge a delfe in the high-way at Hellewell greene in 3s 4d. And that he shall fill it vp before the tenth day of May next in payne of 10s

Item wee present the foresaid Jonathan Walton for makeinge an affray and draweinge blood vpon John Shepheard 10s

Barnerd denton [mark] Isaak Whitley
Thomas Pighills [mark] Georg Gleidhill
[signed] Richard Ramsden/Daniell Hoile/James Fourniss/

Stainland

[K[2]]

Constable of Stenland

Swhorn men Barnerd Denton and Thomas pickels Georg Gledhill Isack Whitley for jury

Thomas Whitwham

Johannes Shepheard elect' est in officio imparcator' pro Stainland et Jur'

[L[1]]

We lay in payne against Richard Firth of Hoight and Elizabeth Firth of Bykybothome that they the said Richard Firth and Elizabeth Firth theire Children and seuerall servants and families and all other persons whatsoeuer shall not come ouer or make any way through one close called Byky bothome field neare Riponden betwixt the second day of February and the Eleuenth day of Nouember yearely vpon payne of 13s 4d for euery default

Barkisland

[L[2]]

Sworne men for Barkesland

James Grene John Townend Edward Marsden John Gledhill

We lay in paine if any make any foote way betwixt Grenlane end through Edward Marsden brick and firthous Corne Milne 3s 4d a time

James Cordley Constable of Barkisland

[signed] Richard Ramsden/Daniell Hoile/James Fourniss/Thomas Whitwham/

Barkisland

[mem 21]

KIRKBURTON: VIEW OF FRANKPLEDGE AND COURT LEET WITH TOURN: 15 April 16 Charles [1640]

Inquisition taken for the King on the oath of John Hirst, Joshua Earnshawe, Christopher Micklethwaite, Edward Wortley, James Hinchcliffe, John Tincker, John Charlesworth, Thomas Robucke, Godfrey Mathewman, Richard Nicholls, John Grene, Richard Firth, Abraham Fitton and George Firth, who testified that (*148*) Thomas Earnshawe late of Holme, deceased, who lately held by charter two closes of land, meadow and pasture called Corneclose and Cowclose estimated at 5 acres in Holme in the graveship of Holme now or lately occupied by James Earnshawe or his assigns, also those 6 acres of land, meadow and pasture in Holme now or lately occupied by the said James Earnshawe or his assigns, lately of the lands of Robert, late earl of Leicester, died seised thereof: James Earnshawe is son and next heir of the same, and owes relief of 3s 8d at 4d an acre *Relief for lands lately of earl of Leicester 3s 4d* [*sic*]

HOLME [rectius BURTON]: township jury says all is well

SHELLEY: township jury says Edward Sonier made affray and drew blood of Edward Wood *10s*

SHEPLEY: township jury says all is well

CUMBERWORTH HALF: township jury says all is well

THURSTONLAND: ,, ,, ,, ,, ,,

HOLME: ,, ,, ,, ,, ,,

FULSTON: ,, ,, ,, ,, ,,

SCOLES: ,, ,, ,, ,, ,,

WOLDALL: ,, ,, ,, ,, ,,

CARTSWORTH: ,, ,, John Batty and John Feter made affray between selves *3s 4d*

AUSTONLEY: ,, ,, all is well

HEPWORTH: ,, ,, Mathew Marsh made affray on John Marsden *3s 4d*

THWONGE: ,, ,, all is well

Finally the jurors present that all the above is true.

Holme (*148*) James Earnshaw son and next heir of Thomas Earnshawe late of Holme deceased appeared before the steward and fined for leave to heriot for a rood of land on the east of a close called Intacke and another rood on the west of a close called Cowclose

estimated at a half acre at a lord's rent of 2d and no certain fine. Agreed. *Fine for heriot not compounded* [mem 21 d]
Holme (*149*) Thomas Roberts son and next heir of John Roberts lately of Wolddale appeared before the steward and paid 2s 7½d for licence to heriot for three parts (out of four) of all those houses, structures, 'backsides' etc now occupied by James Roberts, with half of the gardens, folds, doles, paths, watercourses etc associated, with all reserved rents thereon in Woldale and Fulston in the graveship of Holme at a lord's rent of 10½d and certain fine (apart from the two closes called les Heyes). Agreed.
Holme (*150*) Joshua Castell of Cartworth and Elizabeth his wife, she agreeing separately, by Francis Mathewman, lord's tenant and sworn, surrendered a parcel of land in Cartworth at Copthirst with a house called 'a sheepecoate' thereon, with all easements, common, common pasture etc in Cartworth in the graveship of Holme now occupied by the said Joshua Castell and Thomas Charlesworth or their assigns at a lord's rent of 14d and certain fine: to the use of John Nicholls, Agnes his wife and Mary Cartwright their executors etc from 27 April 1637 for a hundred years should they live so long, paying during the natural life of Joshua Castell, his heirs and assigns an annual rent of 12d at Whitsun and Martinmas if asked. Agreed: entry fine of 21d. *Compounded for by Godfrey Castell*
Holme (*151*) Testimony by John Hirst, lord's tenant, that Richard Hirst and Humfrey Hirst on 6 January 15 Charles, 1639, surrendered a third of a messuage and 14 acres of land and meadow in Austonley in the graveship of Holme and now or lately occupied by Charles Hinchcliffe or his assigns at a lord's rent of 18¾d and certain fine: to the use of John Hinchcliffe son of Charles Hinchcliffe after the decease of Charles Hinchcliffe and Dorothy his wife for 21 years following at an annual rent to Richard Hirst his heirs etc of 40s at Whitsun and Martinmas. Agreed: entry fine of 2s 4¾d.
Holme (*152*) Testimony by John Hirst, lord's tenant, that John Littlewood and Mary his wife, she agreeing separately, on 6 March 15 Charles, 1639, surrendered a third of a messuage and 32½ acres of land and meadow (a close called dobroyd bothome excepted) in Austonley in the graveship of Holme and now or lately occupied by John Litlewood junior or his assigns at a lord's rent of 4s and certain fine: to the use of Richard Littlewood and Anne now his wife from 2 February last past for their natural lives and the longer liver by payment to John Littlewood senior of £6 10s a year at Whitsun and Martinmas. Agreed: entry fine of 6s.
Holme (*153*) Testimony by Edward Batty, lord's tenant, that John Hirst, John Littlewood and Richard Armitage on 6 April 16 Charles [1640] surrendered those three parts (of five) of a messuage called Ewtrees lately of Henry Charlesworth deceased and rents reversions

etc in all three parts of the houses, lands, holdings, meadows, pastures etc or appurtenant to the other two parts (except for two closes called Midledowneshutts and Litledowneshutts) in Austonley in the graveship of Holme and now occupied by Thomas Waterhouse or his assigns at a lord's rent of 18¾d and certain fine: to the use of the said Thomas Waterhouse, his executors etc from the date of the surrender for as long as John Hirst, John Litlewood and Richard Armitage have term in the same (*expendere habeant*) by virtue of a surrender to their use made by John Shawe, deceased, and entered on the Wakefeld court roll by Humfrey Hirst at the court held on 22 February 14 Charles [1639]. Agreed: entry fine of 2s 4¾d.

Holme (*154*) William Brodeheade by Edward Batty, lord's tenant and sworn, surrendered a house called Newhouse in Cartworth and a close called Lathecrofte with the buildings thereon now occupied by John Thewlis at a lord's rent of 3½d and certain fine: to the use of George Dixon for 7 years, paying the said William Brodehead, his executors etc a rent of 53s 4d at Whitsun and Martinmas in equal parts. Agreed: entry fine of 5¼d.

Holme (*155*) John Grene junior and Sara his wife, she agreeing separately, by John Hirst, lord's tenant and sworn, surrendered and quitclaimed to John Shawe of Ewtrees his heirs etc all title, dower etc in two closes of land and pasture called Middledowneshutts and Littledownshutts at Ewtrees in the graveship of Holme and now occupied by one John Shawe or his assigns at a lord's rent of 8d and certain fine. Agreed: John Shawe fines for enrolment of quitclaim 6d.

Holme (*156*) Edward Bever of Hepworth-feildhead by Christopher Micklethwaite, lord's tenant and sworn, surrendered a close of land called Anningley ynge estimated at 3 roods in Hepworth in the graveship of Holme and now occupied by Richard Murgatroid or his assigns at a lord's rent of 3d and certain fine, which closes lately belonged to William Bever of Hayslack, father of the said Edward Bever, and were surrendered by him to the use of the said Edward Bever and his assigns for ever: to the use of the said William Bever and his heirs for ever. Agreed: entry fine of 9d.

Holme (*157*) William Bever of Hayslacke by Christopher Micklethwaite, lord's tenant and sworn, surrendered 3 acres at Hayslack lately taken from the lord's waste in Hepworth in the graveship of Holme now occupied by the said William Bever or his assigns at a lord's rent of 12d and certain fine: to the use of John Moorehouse of Birkehouse, his executors etc from 7 March last past for the life of the said William Bever and Jennett his wife and the longer liver [mem. 22] with an additional 6 years, on the terms expressed in a pair of indentures between William Bever and John Moorehouse dated 7 March 1639/40. Agreed: entry of 18d.

Holme (*158*) Testimony on oath of Godfrey Littlewood, lord's tenant, that Anthony Grene on 10 April 16 Charles [1640] surrendered a mansion at Austonley lately occupied by John Littlewood and Humfrey Littlewood, part of 'a threshinge bay' in a barn, part of a fold adjoining the house, a garden, a close called Overstuble Crofte, a close called Netherhighfeild, a close called Netherlongroid, another little close adjoining called Longroid and a meadow with all easements associated in Austonley in the graveship of Holme and lately occupied by the said John and Humfrey Littlewood or their assigns at a lord's rent of 13½d and certain fine: to the use of Anthony Hinchcliffe and Elizabeth his wife, their executors etc from 2 February last past for 10 years, paying Anthony Grene, his heirs etc a rent of £3 11s 8d a year at Whitsun and Martinmas, also a fat capon at Whitsun and a fat capon or hen at Christmas. Agreed: entry fine of 20¼d.

[In the draft, surrenders (149) to (158) are preceded by surrender (148) and the juries]

[A[1]]

Burton: Robert Senior deputy, *on King's service*, Edward Haigh constable, John Robucke, John Wood, Christopher Sykes and John Armitage *1d paid*

Shelley: Mathew Nicholls constable, Edward Wood, William Tincker, Joseph Hepworth and John Hutchinson *1d paid*

Shepley: John Rowley constable, *on King's service*, Robert Hepworth, Edward Morehous, John Archer and Edward Firth *1d paid*

Cumberworth: John Moorehouse constable, Thomas Coldwell and Mathew Oxley *1d paid*

Thurstonland: Thomas Archer constable, Godfrey Barnsley, Robert Pitts, Edward Hinchcliffe and William Lockwood *1d paid*

Holme: James Genne constable, Francis Hinchcliffe and Oliver Hatfeild *1d paid*

Fulston: Humfrey Robucke, Humfrey Kay, George Cocken and Richard Kay *1d paid*

[A[2]]

Scoles: John Yellott and Mathew Bray *1d paid*

Wooldale: Henry Roberte, Ed. Moorehouse, John Elleson and Thomas Rowbothome *1d paid*

Cartworth: Abraham Moorehouse, Abraham Grene, Francis Vessy and John Moorehouse *1d paid*

Austonley: Christopher Wilson and Anthony Hinchcliffe *1d paid*

Hepworth: Hugh Tayler, John Linley, John Crosland and Abraham Jagger *1d paid*

Twonge: William Gooddard and *James Batty* Abraham Berry *1d paid*

[B]

Paines laide att the kings majesties Courte houlden att Burton the xv[th] day of Aprill 1640 by the Constable and Sworne men of Burton as Followeth

Inprimis wee lay in paine that all the househoulders within this Townshipe shall make theire Fences betwixt neighbor and neighbor att or before the First day of May in paine of 10s

Item wee lay in paine that noe maner of person shall put any scabed or infectious horse or meare to any the Commons belonginge to Burton in paine of euery default *30s* 10s

Item wee lay in paine that noe maner of person or persons Cast any Filth or Carrion into any hie way or into any water either standinge or runinge beinge a hurte to any one in paine of 10s

Item wee lay in paine that all the househoulders within this Township shall yoake and Ringe theire Swine att or before the first day of may and soe keepe them yoaked and Ringed vntill the next Court day in paine of euery default 4d

Item wee lay in paine that william Smith shall scoure his dich all alonge his paddacke side, according as it hath formerly done, aioyninge to the hie way att or before may day in paine of 3s 4d

Item wee lay in paine that John Kaye thelder shall scoure his dich and brush the hedge att the little Slacke aioyninge to the hie way att or before the First day of May in paine of 5s

Item wee lay in paine that all those which doe belonge to make the Birchinhill loyne yate, gallowes yate towards Thorncliffe, and more yate that they make them sufficient att or before the First day of may in paine of euery default 10s

Item wee lay in paine that Thomas Meller shall scoure his dich and brush vp his hedge about the wheate Croft att or before the First day of May in paine of *10s* 12d

Item wee lay in paine that noe maner of person or persons shall goe ouer other mens ground where there is noe vsuall way in paine of euery default 12d

Item wee lay in paine that noe maner of person or persons shall goe ouer the Deane Closes which doe belonge to Edward Scorer Farmald betwixt hie burton and Ryley in paine of euery default *10s* 12d

[signed] John Hirst John Greene
Edward Wortley Joshua Earnshaw
Burton

[C]

Paynes laid at our Kings Majesties Court Holden at Kirkburtton by the Constable and sworne men of Shelley the 15th day of Aprill Anno domini 1640: as Followeth

Imprimis we lay in payne that noe manner of person or persons whatsoever shall neither Cutt nor Cary away either greene wood or drye out of other mens grounds without Lycence of the owner thereof in payne of euery tyme soe seene knowne or taken *3s* 12d

Item we lay in payne that noe manner of person or persons whatsoever shall putt any scabbed or infectious horse or meare to any of the Comons belonging to the said towne in payne of euery tyme so seene knowne or taken 10s

Item we lay in payne that all the householders within the said towne shall ringe and yoke their swine and soe keep them vntill the next Court in payne of euery default 12d

Item we lay in payne that noe manner of person or persons whatsoever shall cast or putt any Carryon into any water belonginge to the said towne whereby it may be hurtfull to the said towne in payne of euery tyme soe seene knowne or taken 10s

Item we lay in payne that noe manner of person or persons whatsoever shall make any vsuall way ouer any mans grounds where noe way is in payne of euery tyme so seene knowne or taken 12d

Item we lay in paine that noe manner of person or persons shall goe ouer one little Croft of Richard Nicholls in paine of euery tyme so seene known or taken 12d

Ittem we doe present Edward Sonyer for a bloud and afray which he made of Edward Wood Aprill the 7th 1640

Ittem we lay in paine that John Lee of Roid house shall make his fence adioyneinge to the hie way sufficient before the first day of May in paine of default 20s

Shelley

[endorsed] John Hirst/Joshua Earnshaw/Edward Wortley/
John Greene

[D]

Paines laid att our kings majesties Courte houlden att Burton the 15th day of Aprill 1640 by the Constable and Sworne men of Sheapley as Followeth:

Inprimis wee lay in paine that noe maner of person take or Carrie either greene or drie wood out of other mens ground without licence of the owner in paine of euery default 3s 4d

Item wee lay in paine that all the househoulders within this Towneshipe shall make theire Fences att or before the First day of may in paine of 10s

Item wee lay in paine that all the househoulders within this Towneshipe of Sheapley shall not put any scabed or infectious horse or meare to any Common within this towneshipe in paine of euery default *30s* 10s

Item wee lay in paine that all the househoulders within this Townshipe shall yoake and Ringe theire Swine att or before the First day of May in paine of euery default 4d

Item wee lay in paine that noe maner of person goe ouer other mens ground where there is noe vsuall way in paine of euery default 12d

[signed] John Hirst/Joshua Earnshaw/Edward Wortley/John Greene

Shepley

[E]

Paynes layd at our Kings Majesties Court Holden at Kirkburton by the Constable and sworne men of Comberworth halfe the 15th day of Aprill Anno domini 1640 as Followeth

Imprimis we lay in paine that noe manner of person or persons whatsoever shall neither Cut nor Cary away either greene wood or drie out of other mens grounds without Lycence of the owner thereof in paine of euery tyme soe seene knowne or taken 12d

Ittem we lay in paine that noe manner of person or persons whatsoever shall put any scabbed or infectious horse or meare to any of the Comons of Comberworth halfe in paine of euery tyme soe seene known or taken 10s

Ittem we lay in paine that all the househoulders within the said towne shall yoke and ringe there swine and soe keepe them vntill the next Court day in paine of euery tyme soe seene knowne or takene *12d* 4d

Ittem we lay in paine that noe manner of person or persons whatsoever shall make any vsuall way ouer other mens ground where noe way is in paine of euery tyme so seene knowne or taken 12d

Ittem we lay in paine that noe manner of person or persons shall ride ouer one Close of Mathew Oxleys Comonly Called the Loyne Hackings in paine of euery tyme soe seene knowne or taken *10s* 3s 4d

Cumberworth

[endorsed] John Hirst/Joshua Earnshaw/ Edward Wortley/John Greene

[F]

Thursteland

Paines laid att our kings majesties Courte houlden att Burton the 15th day of Aprill 1640 by the Constable and Sworne men of Thurstonland as Followeth

Inprimis wee lay in paine that noe maner of person take or Carrie either greene or drie wood out of other mens ground without licence of the owner in paine of euery default 3s 4d

Item wee lay in paine that all the househoulders within this Township shall make theire Fences att or before the First day of May in paine of 10s

Item wee lay in paine that noe maner of person goe ouer other mens ground where there is noe vsuall way in paine of euery default 12d

Item wee lay in paine that all the househoulders within this township of Thurstonland shall yoake and Ringe theire Swine and soe keepe them yoaked and Ringed vntill the next Courte Day in paine of euery default 4d

Item wee lay in paine that noe maner of person putt any scabed or infectious horse or meare to any the Commons belonginge to Thurstonland in paine of euery default *30s* 10s

[signed] John Hirst/Joshua Earnshaw/Edward Wortley/John Greene

Thurstonland

[G]

Holme

At the Court holden at Burton the 15th day of Aprill 1640 paynes layd by the swornemen of Holme, Francis Hinchcliffe and Oliver Hadfeild

Inprimis we doe lay in paine that no person nor persons doe cary greene wood nor dry without licence of the right owner in paine of every default 12d

Item that euery househoulder doe keepe their swine well ringed in payne of euery default 12d

Item that euery person and persons doe keepe the right accustomed hy wayes and footepathes within the sayd towneship in payne of euery default 3s 4d

Item we doe lay in payne that euery person doe keepe the water in the right accustomed course within the sayd towneship in payne of euery default 3s 4d

Item that no person nor persons doe sleate other mens sheepe or Cattell of the Comon in paine of euery default 3s 4d

Item wee lay in payne that the Towneshipp of Holme shall mend the waye Called shawegate betwixt Holme towne and bankebothome before the feast of Penticost next in payne of 20s

Item we lay in payne that euery householder do come or send a suffitient labourer to the mending of the high wayes and turfgates vpon indifferent warning in payne of 3s 4d

Holme

[endorsed] John Hirst/Joshua Earnshaw/Edward Wortley/John Greene

[H]

Pains laide by the sworne men of Folstone Humfrie Robucke George Cocker Richard Kay and Humfrie Kay

Imprimis we ley in peine that no persons shall carie ether dreye woode or greene ore breke anie hedge in paine of 3s 4d

We ley in peine that no person or persons shall goe ovt of the acostomed paths in paine of 3s 4d

We lay in paine that no porson ore persons shall keepe anie swine vnyoked or ringed in paine of 3s 4d

We lay in peine that all pursons shall make there out fence within folston before the first day of May in paine of 5s and so kepe it

We ley in paine that the inhabetans of sheapley shal repaire the hie way betwixt knacklee yatt and stocke wood dicke before asention-day next in paine of 10s *39s*

Fulston

[endorsed] John Hirst/Joshua Earnshaw/Edward Wortley/John Greene

[I]

Paynes layd by the sworne men of Scooles at the Court holden at Kirkeburton the 15th day of Aprill, Anno domini 1640 to Witt Mathew Bray and John Yeallott

In primis We Lay in payne that no person or persons Cary away ether greene wood or dry without lycence of the Right owner in payne of euery burden seene or taken 12d

Item we lay in payne that no person or persons vse any foote pathes within the Townshipp of Scooles otherwise then accustomed in payne of every default therein 12d

Item we Lay in payne that every man shall make his out fence sufficient in any ground belonging to Scooles before Assention Day next and so keepe them vntill All Saints Day in payne of everye default therein 3s 4d

[signed] Mathew Bray [mark]/John Yeallott/John Hirst/Joshua Earnshaw/Edward Wortley/John Greene

Scoles

[J]

Wooldale

At the Court holden at Burton the 15th day of Aprill, 1640

paynes layd by the swornemen of Wooldale Henry Robert' Thomas Robothom John Ellisson and Edmund Morehouse

Inprimis we doe lay in paine that no person nor persons doe cary greene wood nor dry without licence of the right owner in paine of euery default 12d

Item that euery householder doe keepe their swine well ringed in paine of euery default 12d

Item that euery person and persons doe keepe the right acustomed hy wayes footepathes and bridlestythes within the sayd towneship in paine of euery default 3s 4d

Item we doe lay in paine that euery person doe keepe the water in the right accustomed course within the sayd towneship in paine of euery default 3s 4d

Item that no person nor persons doe sleate other mens sheepe or cattell of the Comon in paine of euery default 3s 4d

Item that Godfray Armitage doe fill one waterpitte that he hath lately digged in the hy way in one lane called litle lane before the first day of May next in payne of *10s* 12d

Item that no person nor persons goe out of the acustomed way betwixt Mythom and thong' brigge in the litle new wood or Hurley banke in paine of euery default 3s 4d

[signed] John Hirst/Joshua Earnshaw/Edward Wortley/John Greene

Wooldale

[K]

Cartworth

At the court holden at Burton the 15th day of Aprill 1640: paines layd by the swornemen of Cartworth Abraham Morehouse, Abraham Greene, John Morehouse and Francis Vessy.

Inprimis we doe lay in paine that no person nor persons doe Cary greene wood nor dry without licence of the right owner in paine of euery default 12d

Item that euery householder do keepe their swine well ringed in paine of euery default 12d

Item that euery person and persons doe keepe the right acustomed hy waies and footepathes within the sayd towneship in paine of euery default 3s 4d

Item we doe lay in paine that euery person doe keepe the water in the right acustomed course within the sayd towneship in paine of euery default 3s 4d

Item that no person nor persons doe sleate other mens sheepe or Cattell of the Comon in paine of euery default 3s 4d

Item wee present John Batty and John Booth for makinge an affray thone vpon thother eyther of them 1s 8d

Item that euery person within the towneship of Cartworth doe send a sufficient worke man to the mending of the hiway betwixt strat-landhead and Damhouse at such times as there shal bee warning giuen by the Collector in payne of euery default 3s 4d

[signed] John Hirst/Joshua Earnshaw/Edward Wortley/John Greene

Cartworth

[L]

Austonley

At the Court holden at Burton the 15th day of Aprill 1640. Paines layd by the swornemen of Austonley Christopher Wilson and Anthony Hinchcliffe.

Inprimis we doe lay in paine that no person nor persons doe cary greene wood nor dry without licence of the right owner in paine of every default 12d

Item that euery householder doe keepe their swine well ringed in paine of euery default 12d

Item that euery person and persons do keepe the right acustomed hy wayes and footepathes within the said towneship in paine of euery default 3s 4d

Item we doe lay in paine that euery person do keepe the water in the right accustomed course within the said towneship in paine of euery default 3s 4d

Item that no person nor persons doe sleate other mens sheepe or Cattell of the Comon in paine of euery default 3s 4d

Item that no person nor persons doe vse any way in the townefeild at Austonley in the tenure of Anthony Greene save one that is appointed and sett forth in paine of euery person that maketh defalt for euery defalt 39s

[signed] John Hirst/Joshua Earnshaw/Edward Wortley/John Greene

Austonley

[M]

Hepworth

At the Court holden at Burton the 15th day of Aprill 1640: paynes layd by the swornemen of Hepworth Hugh Taylier, John Linley, John Crosland and Abraham Jagger.

Inprimis we doe lay in payne that no person nor persons doe Cary greene wood nor dry without licence of the right owner in paine of euery default 12d

Item that euery householder do keepe their swine well ringed in paine of euery default 12d

Item that euery person and persons doe keepe the right accustomed hy waies and footepathes within the sayd towneship in paine of euery default 3s 4d

Item we doe lay in paine that euery person doe keepe the water in the right accustomed Course within the sayd towneship in paine of every default 3s 4d

Item that no person nor persons doe sleate other mens shepe or Cattell of the Comon in paine of every default 3s 4d

Item that no person nor persons goe over one Close of John Linley called Meaneing without his licence in paine of euery default 3s 4d

Item that John Tinker Francis Tinker Abraham Binnes and Thomas Bever amend the hy way in the nab lane well and sufficiently before the penticost next and so keepe it in payne of 10s

Item that William Haighe and Mathew Marsh do fill two stone pitts in hepworth townegate where they have digged stones, that there may be a sufficient way for cart and Caryage before the feast day of ascention next in payne of 10s

Item that William Bever doe remove John Shirt forth of his house before the end of one month next in payne of euery month after that he doth harbor him 39s

Item that no person doe digge or grave any turves or sodes within 4 yards of the hy way within the sayd towneship in payne of euery default 3s 4d

Item that John Kaye make the way sufficient in the Heslacke before ascention day next as it was before he spoyled the same in paine of 10s

Item we do present Mathew Marsh for makeinge a fray of John Marsden

Hepworth

[endorsed] John Hirst/Joshua Earnshaw/Edward Wortley/John Greene

[N]

Thounge

At the Court houlden at Burton the 15th day of Aprill 1640: Paines layd by the sworne men of the Overthounge William Goddard Abraham Berrie.

Inprimis we doe lay in paine that noe personne nor personis doe Cutt nor Carry away neither greene wood nor dry without licence of the Right owner in paine of every defaulte 12d

Item wee doe lay in paine that every Houshoulder within the said Tounshipp doe keepe theire Swine well Ringed in paine of every defaulte 12d

Item we doe lay in paine that every persoun and persouns doe keepe the water in the Right accustomed Course within the said Tounshipp that itt doe not annoy the hie way, in paine of everie defaulte 3s 4d

Item we doe lay in paine that everie Houshoulder within our Towne doe send a sufficient workman to mend the peat way in paine of defaulte 3s 4d

Item we doe lay in paine that every houshoulder doe send a sufficient workeman to mend the hie way when the[y] haue a day apponted in paine of everie defaulte 3s 4d

[signed] John Hirst/Joshua Earnshaw/Edward Wortley/John Greene

Overthwonge

[O]

At the Court leete or Shellefe turne houlden at Burton the 15th of Aprill Anno Domini 1640

The Jurie doe present and find as followeth

Robert Broadehead doe present Godfray Robert' for making a fray and drawing of Blood of the said Robert 10s

Robert Broadehead doe present Thomas Berrie for making a fray of Susane Roydes 3s 4d

Homfray Booth	,,	John Firth	,,	and drawing of blood of the said Homphray	10s
	,,	William Wimpenie	,,	,, John Ellistones	10s
Thomas Robucke	,,	Edward Sonier	,,	,, Thomas Robucke	10s

Homfray Hopkin for making a fray and drawing of blood of John Robucke 10s

we present John Hinchlife for not remoueing one James Haighe according to a Payne laide formerly in payne of 6s 8d

The Jurie doe laye in paine that the Towneshipp of Thursteland shall make the hie way Betwixt Stockes more and Symonroyde yate before Penticost next in payne of 20s

Item wee laye in payne that Inhabitants of Holme doe make the Shaw gate betwixt Holme towne and banke bottom before *Penticost* midsomer next in payne of 20s

Item wee lay in paine that the Inhabitants of Awstonley doe mend the hye waye betwixt Hinchlifmiln and burndlee brook before midsomer next in paine of 20s

Item we lay in payne that the Inhabitants of Thoung doe make the waye sufficient betwixt burndlee and Ouerbridge before the last of Maye next in payne of 20s

[signed] John Hirst/Joshua Earnshaw/Edward Wortley/John Greene

[P]

Pannell' pro Domino Rege .xv. die Aprilis 1640 apud Holme (*sic*)

John Hirst of Caldwell
Joshua Earnshaw of Holme
William Morehouse of Sheplay
Christopher Micklethwaite jur'
Edward Wortley of Sheplay
James Hinchliffe of Aranden
John Tinker of Shelley
John Charlsworth of Nab jur'
Thomas Robucke of Roydehouse
Godfray Mathewman of *Scooles* Aucefelesden
Richard Nicholls
John Greene of Holme
Richard Firth of Boothowse
Edward wood of Shellay jur'
Abraham Fitton
George Firth de had'

INDEX OF PERSONS

The index of persons aims to be comprehensive. Surnames are given in the form nearest approximating to the modern spelling, with major variations indicated in brackets. Bold type indicates page references to members of the leet juries.

H

I

J

Y

INDEX OF PLACES

Place-names are given in their modern form. Only a selection has been given of the small holdings, whose numbers made it impossible to verify modern spelling or reduce them to manageable proportions. Bold type indicates page references to bills of the respective townships. Names of graveships are printed in small capitals.

Y